INFORMATION DASHBOARD DESIGN

INFORMATION DASHBOARD DESIGN

Displaying data for at-a-glance monitoring

SECOND EDITION

STEPHEN FEW

Analytics Press

BURLINGAME, CALIFORNIA

Analytics Press

PO Box 1545
Burlingame, CA 94011
SAN 253-5602
www.analyticspress.com
Email: info@analyticspress.com

© 2013 by Stephen C. Few

PUBLISHER: Jonathan G. Koomey

COPY EDITOR: Nan Wishner
COMPOSITION: Bryan Pierce
COVER DESIGN: Alberto Cairo and Stephen Few
PRINTER AND BINDER: C&C Offset Printing Company

ISBN: 978-1-938377-00-6

This book was printed on acid-free paper in China.

10 9 8 7 6 5 4 3

In loving memory of my buddy,
Atticus Finch

CONTENTS

PREFACE TO THE SECOND EDITION

When I finished writing the first edition of this book in early 2006, I could not find a single example of a well-designed dashboard to illustrate the principles and practices that I advocate. Prior to this book, no specific guidelines for dashboard design existed. Not only did no good examples exist at the time, but no software could easily produce them. For example, in early 2006 no products supported data visualization expert Edward Tufte's sparklines, which often work ideally on dashboards to provide an abbreviated view of history. No products supported bullet graphs either; shortly before this book was first published, I had introduced the bullet graph as a better alternative to typical dashboard gauges. I took a risk by writing a book that urged people to do what exceeded the capabilities of existing technology at the time. The risk paid off in that dashboard software has come a long way since then (although it still has a long way to go). However, had I worked within the boundaries of existing products at the time, the book would have not been worthwhile.

One complaint that I received about the first edition of this book was that it didn't include enough examples of well-designed dashboards. Given the technological limitations that I've just described, I had to create, using Adobe Illustrator, the few good examples that appeared in the final chapter of the first edition. One of the main reasons that I've now written this second edition is to respond to this legitimate but unavoidable complaint by adding several more good examples, most of which were created by others.

In the years since 2006, another minor gap has developed between the book that I initially wrote and this second edition: the dashboard examples are somewhat dated. What's surprising, however, is the fact that most of the dashboards that people create today using the latest technology are no better than their early predecessors. Almost every software vendor that claims to support dashboards features a hall of shameful examples on its website. I had a wealth of poorly designed dashboards to choose from vendor websites; I've included those examples throughout this new edition to illustrate bad but typical design practices.

ACKNOWLEDGEMENTS

Without a doubt I owe the greatest debt of gratitude to the many software vendors who have done so much to make this book necessary by failing to address or even contemplate the visual design requirements of dashboards. Their kind disregard for visual design has given me focus, ignited my passion, and guaranteed my livelihood for years to come.

INTRODUCTION

Few phenomena characterize our time more uniquely and powerfully than the rapid rise and influence of information technologies. These technologies have unleashed a tsunami of information that rolls over and flattens us. Controlling this tidal wave has become a primary goal of the information industry. One tool that has emerged from this effort in recent years is the *information dashboard*. This single-screen display of the most important information people need to do a job, presented in a way that allows them to monitor what's going on in an instant, is a powerful new medium of communication. At least it can be, but only when properly designed.

Most information dashboards that are used in organizations today fall far short of their potential. The root of the problem is not technology—at least not primarily—but poor visual design. To serve their purpose and fulfill their potential, dashboards must display a dense array of information in a small amount of space and in a manner that communicates clearly and immediately. This requires design that taps into and leverages the power of visual perception, which enables us to sense and process large chunks of information rapidly. This power can only be utilized when the visual design of dashboards is central to the development process and is informed by a solid understanding of visual perception—what works, what doesn't, and why.

No technology can do this for us. We must bring this expertise to the process. Don't be dismayed. The visual design skills that are needed to develop effective dashboards can be learned, and helping you learn them is the sole purpose of this book.

If the information is important, it deserves to be communicated well.

Above all else, this is a book about communication. It focuses exclusively on a particular means of communication called a *dashboard*. Dashboards present information on a computer screen to help us monitor what's going on. Dashboards are among the latest new information technology (IT) waves to hit the shore in the last 10 years. Like many new technologies, dashboards have unique, exciting possibilities if we build them based on a stable bedrock of good design principles and practices. Like all methods of communicating data graphically, they can obscure, fail to communicate, and even misrepresent information if used without awareness of those principles and practices.

Today, it seems that everybody wants a dashboard. Like many newcomers to the technology scene, dashboards are sexy. Software vendors work hard to make their dashboards shimmy with sex appeal. They taunt, "You don't want to be the only company in your neighborhood without one, do you?" They warn, "You can no longer live without one." They whisper sweetly, "Still haven't achieved the expected return on investment from your expensive data ware-house? Just stick a dashboard in front of it and watch the money pour in." Be still, my heart.

The gauges, meters, and traffic lights on a dashboard are so damn flashy! Literally. We can imagine that we're sitting behind the wheel of a German sports car, feeling the wind whip through our hair as we tear around curves on the Autobahn at high speed, all without leaving our desks.

However, despite the hype surrounding dashboards, they work much like other long-familiar strategies and technologies for delivering information and can only do their job if they are designed with effective communication as the top priority. It's time to cut through the hype and learn the practical skills that can help us transform dashboards from yet another fad with more flash than substance into an effective means to enlighten.

Beyond the hype and sizzle, dashboards offer a unique, effective way to meet a very real need for information. The dashboard that can do this is the dash-board that deserves to live on our screens.

All That Glitters Is Not Gold

Most dashboards fail to communicate efficiently and effectively, not because of inadequate technology (at least not primarily), but because of poorly designed information displays. No matter how great the technology, a dashboard's success as a medium of communication is a product of design. Dashboards can be designed to tap into the tremendous power of visual perception to communicate rapidly and effectively, but only if we understand visual perception and apply design principles and practices that are aligned with the way people see and think. Software won't do this for us. In fact, most dashboard products nudge us in the opposite direction. It's up to us to develop the necessary skills to design them well.

Unfortunately, most vendors that provide dashboard software have done nothing to encourage its effective use. Vendors focus their marketing efforts on dazzle that subverts the goal of clear communication. They fight to win our interest by maximizing sizzle, highlighting eye-catching gauges and other charts that appeal to our desire for entertainment. Once implemented, however, these cute displays lose their sparkle in a matter of days and become just plain annoying. An effective dashboard is the product not of cute gauges like the example below, but of informed design: more science than art, more simplicity than sizzle. An effective dashboard is, above all else, about communication.

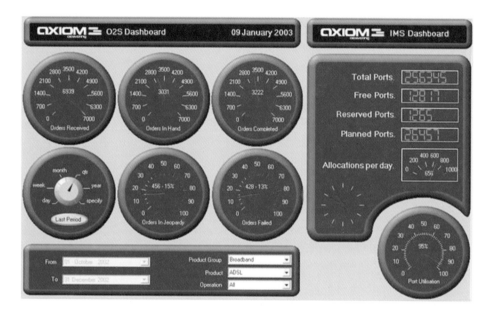

FIGURE 1.1. A typical flashy dashboard; can't you just feel the engine revving?

Software vendors' failure to focus on what we actually need is hardly unique to dashboards. Most software suffers from the same shortcomings and, despite all the hype about user-friendliness, is difficult to use. This sad state is so common, and has been this way for so long, we've grown accustomed to the pain. In the moments when this ugly truth penetrates the surface of our consciousness, we usually blame the problem on ourselves rather than the software, framing it in terms of "computer illiteracy." If we could only adapt more to the computer and how it works, there wouldn't be a problem, or so we reason. In his insightful book entitled *The Inmates Are Running the Asylum*, master designer Alan Cooper writes:

> *The sad thing about dancing bearware* [Cooper's term for poorly designed software that is difficult to use] *is that most people are quite satisfied with the lumbering beast. Only when they see some real dancing do they begin to suspect that there is a world beyond ursine shuffling. So few software-based products have exhibited any real dancing ability that most people are honestly unaware that things could be better—a lot better.*

Alan Cooper (1999). *The Inmates Are Running the Asylum*. SAMS Publishing, page 59.

Cooper argues that poorly designed, difficult-to-use products result from an approach to software development that simply doesn't work. In a genuine attempt to please their customers, software engineers focus on trying to include every requested feature. This approach creates lumbering beasts. Customers are expert in knowing what they need to accomplish, but not in knowing how software ought to be designed to support their needs. Allowing customers to design software through feature requests is the worst form of disaster by committee.

Software vendors should bring design vision and expertise to the development process. They ought to know the difference between superficial glitz and what really works. But they're so exhausted from working ungodly hours trying to squeeze more features into the next release that they're left with no time to do the research needed to discover what actually works, or to step back and observe how their products are actually being used (or failing).

The realm of information technology that focuses on reporting and analysis has for many years gone by the name *business intelligence* (BI). To date, BI vendors have concentrated on developing the underlying technologies that are used to gather data from source systems, transform data into a usable form, store data in high-performance databases, access data for use, and present data in the form of production reports. Tremendous progress has been made in these areas, resulting in robust technologies that can handle huge repositories of data. However, although we have managed to warehouse a lot of data, we have made little progress in deriving real value from information. Relatively little effort has been dedicated to engaging human intelligence, which is what BI, by definition, is supposed to be about.

A glossary on the Gartner Group's website defines "business intelligence" as "An interactive process for exploring and analyzing structured, domain-specific information… to discern business trends or patterns, thereby deriving insights and drawing conclusions." To progress in this worthwhile venture, the BI industry must shift its focus to an engaging interaction with human perception and intelligence. Vendors must base their efforts on a firm understanding of how people perceive and think, building interfaces, visual displays, and methods of interaction that seamlessly fit human ability.

Even Dashboards Have a History

In many respects, "dashboard" is simply a new name for the *Executive Information Systems* (EISs) that were first developed in the 1980s. These systems remained exclusively in the offices of executives and never numbered more than a few, so it is unlikely that you've ever actually seen one. I sat through a few vendor demos when these systems first came out but never saw an actual system in use. The usual purpose of an EIS was to display a handful of key financial measures through a simple interface that "even an executive could understand." Though limited in scope, the goal was visionary and worthwhile but ahead of its time. Back then, before data warehousing and BI had evolved the necessary methodologies and technologies to handle large amounts of data, the vision simply wasn't practical; it couldn't be realized because the information needed to support the visual interface was incomplete, unreliable, and spread among disparate sources. Thus, in the same decade that the EIS arose, it also went into hibernation, waiting until the time was ripe for its vision to be realized...that is, until now.

During the 1990s, data warehousing, *online analytical processing* (OLAP), and, eventually, BI worked as partners to tame the wild avalanche of data generated by the so-called information age. The emphasis during those years was on collecting, correcting, integrating, storing, and accessing information in accurate, timely, and useful ways. Since the early days of data warehousing in the 1980s, the effort has largely focused on the technologies, and to a lesser degree the methodologies, needed to make data available and useful. The direct beneficiaries so far have mostly been folks who are highly proficient in the use of computers and able to use the available but cumbersome tools to navigate through large, often complex databases.

What also emerged during the early 1990s but didn't become popular until late in that decade was a new approach to management that involved the identification and use of *key performance indicators* (KPIs). This method, introduced by Robert S. Kaplan and David P. Norton, is known as the Balanced Scorecard. The advances in data warehousing and related technologies set the stage for the interest in management through the use of metrics—not just financial metrics—that dominates the business landscape today. *Business Performance Management* (BPM) became an international preoccupation. The infrastructure built by data warehousing and the interest of BPM in metrics that can be easily monitored together tilled and fertilized the soil in which the hibernating seeds of EIS-type displays were once again able to grow.

What really turned attention toward dashboards, however, was the Enron scandal in 2001. That financial debacle put new pressure on corporate managers to closely monitor what was going on in their midst and thereby assure shareholders that they were in control. This increased pressure for corporate accountability, combined with the economic downturn at the time, sent Chief Information Officers (CIOs) on a mission to find anything that could help managers at all levels easily and efficiently keep an eye on performance. Most BI vendors that hadn't already started offering dashboard products began to do so, sometimes by opportunistically changing the name of an existing product, sometimes by quickly purchasing the rights to a product from a smaller vendor, and sometimes by cobbling together pieces of products that already existed. The marketplace soon offered a vast array of dashboard software.

At roughly the same time that dashboards and their predecessors were emerging, computer-based displays for manufacturing control operators—known as distributed control system (DCS) software—was developing along a separate track. This software attempted to consolidate the many displays that had previously been built into large control panels that covered entire walls. Similar in purpose to dashboards, DCS displays were developed by software vendors that specialized in manufacturing systems. What's striking when we look at these displays is that, just like dashboards, they were also largely developed by software engineers with no training in human-computer interface design. Just as dashboards have taken the metaphor of the automobile dashboard too literally, developers of industrial monitoring systems tried to reproduce the shop floor using visual representations of machinery that obscured the data, as we can see in the following example.

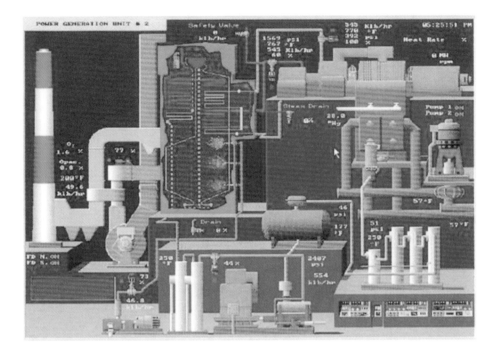

FIGURE 1.2. A typical distributed control system display

Bill Hollifield, Dana Oliver, Ian Nimmo, and Eddie Habibi (2008). *The High Performance HMI Handbook: A Comprehensive Guide to Designing, Implementing and Maintaining Effective HMIs for Industrial Plant Operations.* PAS, page 15.

Neither dashboards on the desktops of business managers nor DCS displays in the control rooms of operators were designed by people who were trained in human-focused fields of study such as cognitive psychology or human factors.

> *DCS vendors have now provided the capability of creating HMIs [human machine interfaces] with extremely high sophistication, power, and usefulness. Unfortunately, this capability is usually unused, misused, or abused. The basic principles of effective displays are often not known or followed. Large amounts of process data are provided on graphics, but little information. Information is "data in context made useful." In many cases, the DCS buyer will proceed to design and implement graphics based on the flashy examples created to sell the systems—unaware that from a usability and effectiveness point of view, they are terrible.*

Ibid., page 13.

Sound familiar?

Dispelling the Confusion

Like many products that hit the high-tech scene with a splash, dashboards are extravagantly wrapped in marketing hype. Virtually every BI vendor claims to sell dashboard software, but few clarify what dashboards actually are. I'm reminded of the early years of data warehousing, when, eager to learn about this new approach to data management, I asked my IBM account manager how IBM defined the term. His response was classic and refreshingly candid: "By data warehousing, we at IBM mean whatever the customer thinks it means." I realize that this wasn't IBM's official definition, which I'm sure existed somewhere in their literature, but it was my blue-suited friend's way of saying that, for him as a salesperson, it was useful to leave the term vague and flexible. As long as a product or service remains undefined or loosely defined, it is easy to claim that your company provides it.

Those software vendors that have taken the time to define the term in their marketing literature start with the specific features of their own products as the core of the definition, rather than using a generic description. As a result, vendor definitions tend to be self-validating lists of features. For example, Dr. Gregory L. Hovis, Director of Product Deployment for Snippets Software, Inc., asserts:

> Able to universally connect to any XML or HTML data source, robust dashboard products intelligently gather and display data, providing business intelligence without interrupting work flow…An enterprise dashboard is characterized by a collection of intelligent agents (or gauges), each performing frequent bidirectional communication with data sources. Like a virtual staff of 24x7 analysts, each agent in the dashboard intelligently gathers, processes and presents data, generating alerts and revising actions as conditions change.

Gregory L. Hovis (February 2002). "Stop Searching for Information—Monitor it with Dashboard Technology," *DM Direct*.

An article in the June 16, 2003 edition of *ComputerWorld* cites a study done by AMR Research, Inc., which found that "more than half of the 135 companies… recently surveyed are implementing dashboards." Unfortunately, the author never tells us what dashboards are. He teases us with hints, stating that dashboards and scorecards are BI tools that "have found a new home in the cubicles," having moved from where they once resided—exclusively in executive suites under the name Executive Information Systems. He gives examples of how dashboards are being used and speaks of their benefits but leaves it to us to piece together a sense of what they are. The closest he comes to a definition is this rather general quote from John Hagerty of AMR Research, Inc.: "Dashboards and scorecards are about measuring."

Mark Leon (June 16, 2003). "Dashboard Democracy," *ComputerWorld*.

While conducting an extensive literature review in 2003 in search of a good working definition of a dashboard, I visited DataWarehousingOnline.com and clicked on the link to "Executive Dashboard" articles. In response, I received the same 18 web pages of links that I found when I separately clicked on links for "Balanced Scorecard," "Data Quality and Integration," and "Data Mining." Either the links weren't working properly, or this web portal for the data warehousing industry believed that these terms all meant the same thing.

I finally decided to devise a working definition of my own. I began by examining every example of a dashboard I could find on the web, in search of their common characteristics. You might find it interesting to take a similar journey. In the next few pages, we'll see screenshots of an assortment of dashboards. I collected the first few back in 2003 while working on my own definition for the term, and, to show that little has changed since, I've added several more that I found while writing the second edition of this book in 2012. Most were found on the websites of vendors that sell dashboard software, but there are a few examples of real dashboards have actually been used as well. Take the time now to browse through these examples and see whether you can discern common threads that might be woven into a useful definition.

By including these examples from the websites of software vendors and a few other sources, I am not positively or negatively endorsing any of these dashboards or the software products that were used to create them. That is, I am not presenting them as examples of extraordinarily good or poor design. To varying degrees, they all exhibit visual design problems that I'll address in later chapters.

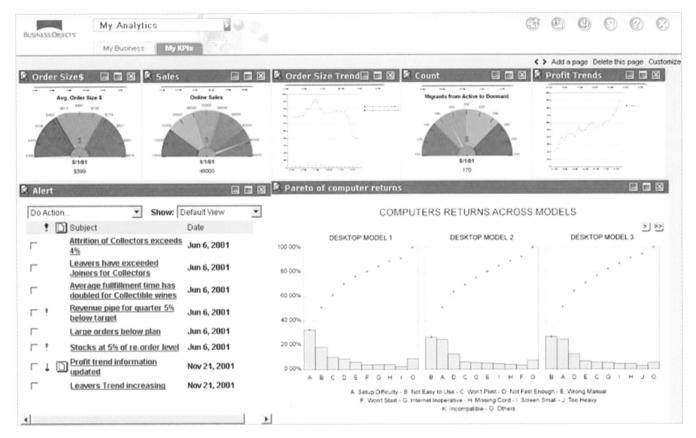

FIGURE 1.3.

This dashboard from SAP Business Objects relies primarily on graphical means to display a series of performance measures along with a list of alerts. Notice that the title of this dashboard is "My KPIs." Key performance indicators and dashboards appear to be synonymous in the minds of most vendors. Notice the gauges as well; we'll see quite a few of them in other examples.

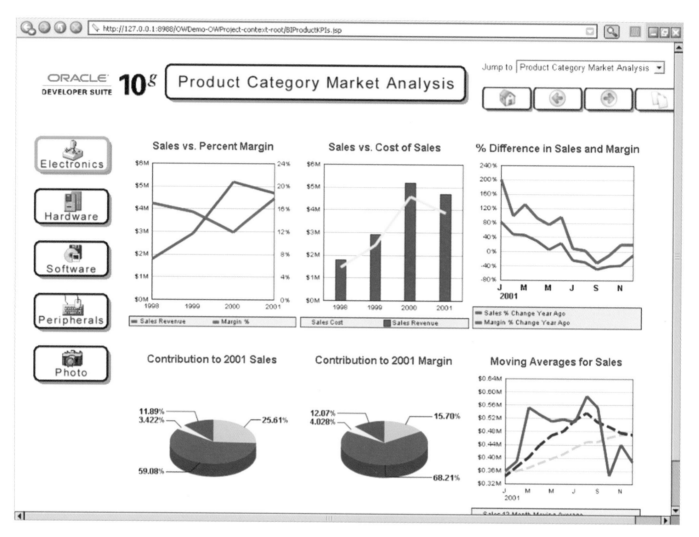

FIGURE 1.4.

This dashboard from Oracle Corporation displays a collection of sales measures for analyzing product performance by category. All of the measures are displayed graphically. We'll find that this emphasis on graphical display media is fairly common.

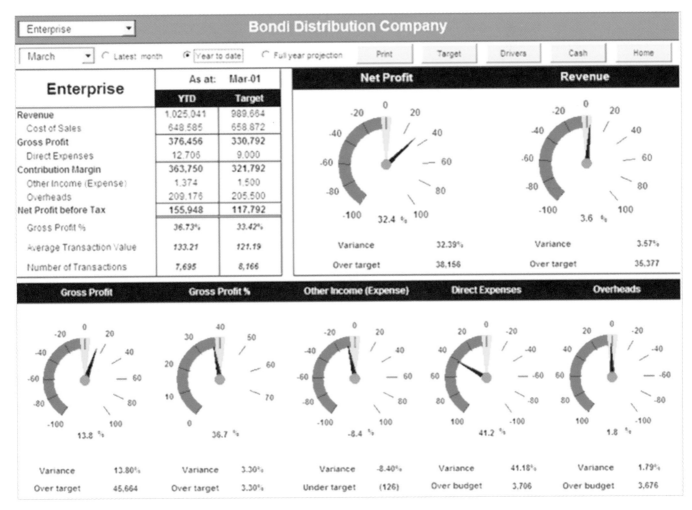

FIGURE 1.5.

This dashboard from Principa provides an overview of a company's financial performance compared to targets for the month of March, both in tabular form and as a series of gauges. The information can be tailored by selecting different months and periods of history. Once again, we see a strong expression of the dashboard metaphor, this time in the form of graphical devices that were designed to look like fuel gauges or speedometers.

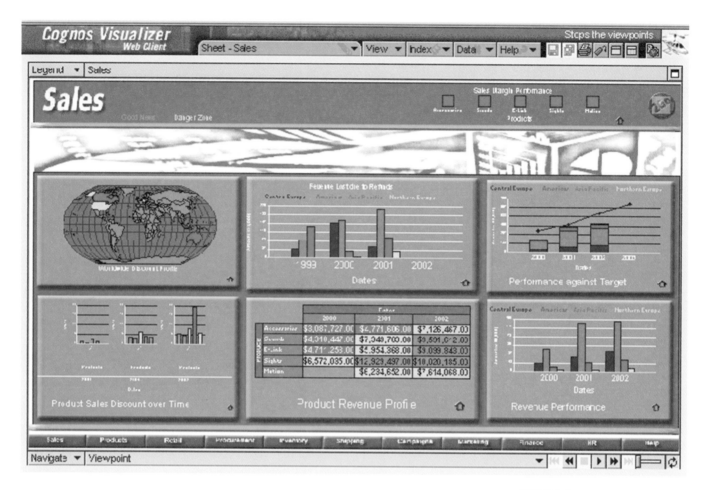

FIGURE 1.6.

This dashboard from Cognos, Inc. displays a table and five graphs—one in the form of a world map—to communicate sales information. Despite the one table, there's a continued emphasis on graphical media. Notice that a theme is emerging in these dashboards. They're all visual in nature, and the designers intend for them to be visually appealing to their users. This is especially apparent from the inclusion of the decorative band of abstract shapes beneath the title.

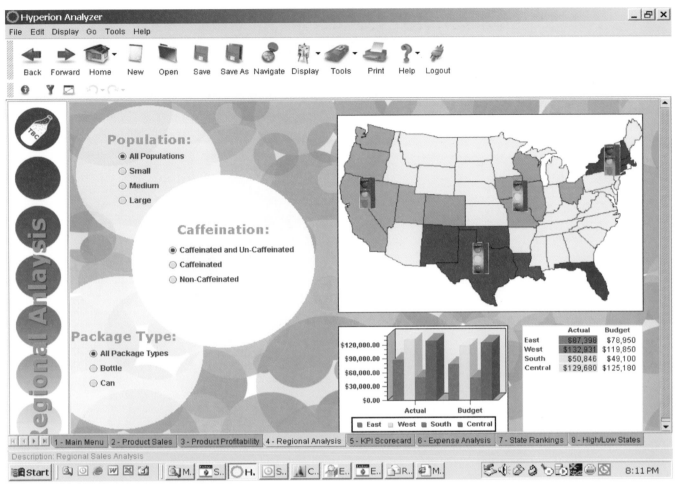

FIGURE 1.7.

This dashboard from Hyperion Solutions Corporation displays regional sales revenue in three forms: on a map, in a bar graph, and in a table. Data can be filtered by means of three sets of radio buttons on the left. These filtering controls build lookup functionality into this dashboard. The wallpaper-like pattern in the background reinforces our observation that dashboards intentionally strive for visual appeal. Like many dashboards, this example displays very little actual information.

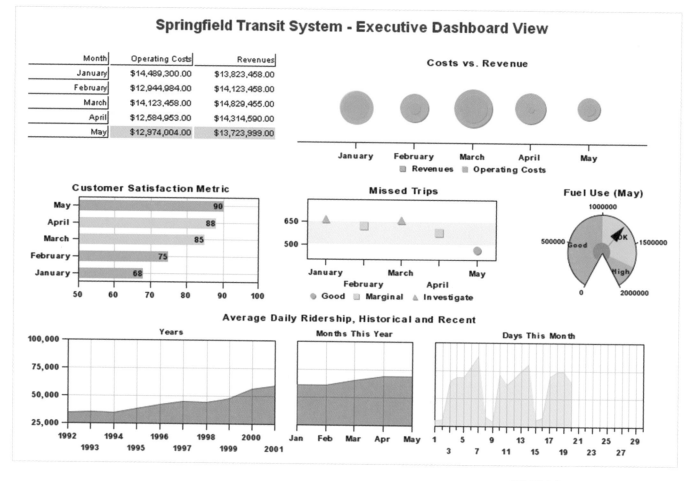

FIGURE 1.8.

This dashboard from Visual Mining, Inc. displays various measures of a city's transit system to give administrators a quick overview of the system's current and historical performance. (Actually, only the graph on the bottom right displays data for the current month of June.) Use of the colors green, yellow, and red to indicate good, satisfactory, and bad performance, as on the three graphical displays arranged horizontally across the middle here, is common in dashboards.

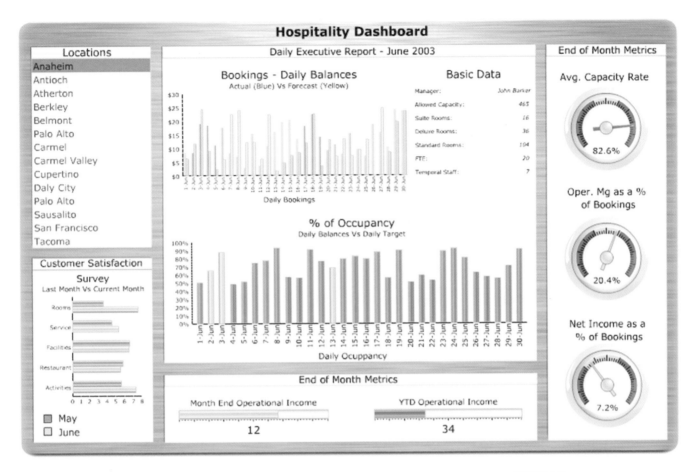

FIGURE 1.9.

This dashboard from Infommersion (now the product named SAP Business Objects Dashboards, but for years named Crystal Xcelsius) gives executives of a hotel chain the means to view multiple measures of performance, one hotel at a time. It is not unusual for dashboards to divide a full set of data into individual views, as this one does by using the listbox in the upper left corner to enable viewers to select an individual hotel by location. Many vendors exhibit the care that we see in this example to realistically reproduce elements of the dashboard metaphor, down to the sheen of polished metal.

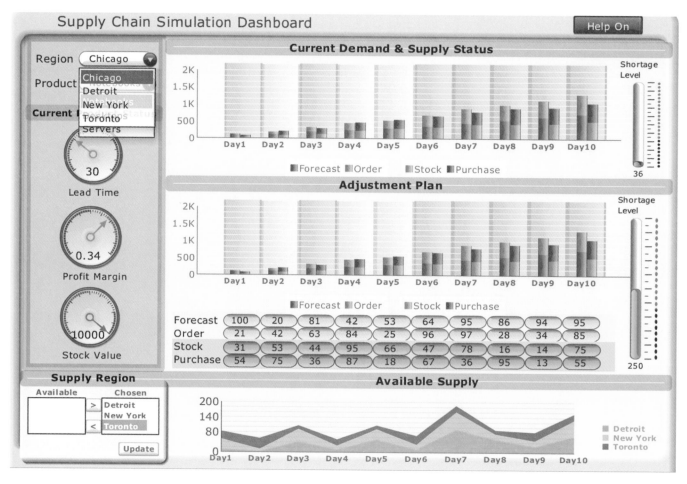

FIGURE 1.10.

This dashboard won first prize in Crystal Xcelsius competition, for which its creator was awarded $10,000. The criteria that were used for selecting the winner clearly preferred dashboards that featured the capabilities of the tool rather than those that displayed data effectively.

Close Window

☐ ▣ ⊠

GE Business Digital Cockpit

GE Stock: **38.7** ▲+1.0 at 16:02 ET Jan 22, 2002

Welcome, Jeffrey

⊡ **E-mail this Page** | 🖨 **Print this page**

| Tools | Total | Sub-business | Sub-business | Sub-business | Sub-business |

Message Center (2)

Cockpit Map

Cockpit Pop-up

Download to PDA

View Charts

Total Performance Summary

Last Update 1/21/02 7:59:16am

Sell

Metric	Alerts ▽	Result ▽	Alert Spec ▽	Last Update ▽
QTD Sales ($MM)	2	● $ 153.0	$ 166.0	1/21/02
QTD Average Daily Order Rate (ADOR) ($MM)	1	◉ $ 16.1	$ 11.9	1/21/02
Previous Day's Orders ($MM)	0	◉ $ 26.2	$ 11.9	1/21/02
QTD % e-Orders	3	● 53.0%	59.0%	1/21/02
Current Qtr Price vs Target ($/lb)	6	◉ $ 1.27	$ 1.20	1/21/02

Make

Metric	Alerts ▽	Result ▽	Alert Spec ▽	Last Update ▽
Span in Days	2	◉ 5	6	1/18/02
Finished Good Inventory	0	◉ NA	NA	1/17/02
% Make To Inventory (MTI) of Total Inventory	0	◉ NA	NA	1/17/02
QTD Digitization Savings ($MM)	7	● $ 13.2	$ 20.3	1/21/02

Buy

Metric	Alerts ▽	Result ▽	Alert Spec ▽	Last Update ▽
YTD Indirect Conversion Cost % Change	1	● -14%	-15%	1/17/02
YTD Indirect Short Term Cost % Change	2	◉ -22%	-15%	1/17/02
Realized Direct e-Auction Savings YTD ($MM)	2	◉ $ 5.4	$ 1.3	1/21/02
Closed Direct e-Auctions YTD ($MM)	4	◉ $ 142.0	$ 55.0	1/21/02

FIGURE 1.11.

This dashboard from General Electric, called a "digital cockpit," provides a tabular summary of performance, complemented by a color-coded indicator light for each measure's status. Rather than a dashboard designed by a software vendor to exhibit its product, this is an actual working dashboard that was designed by a company to serve its own business needs. In this example, no effort was made to literally represent the dashboard (or cockpit) metaphor. Nothing is graphical except for the use of the colors green, yellow, and red to indicate performance levels.

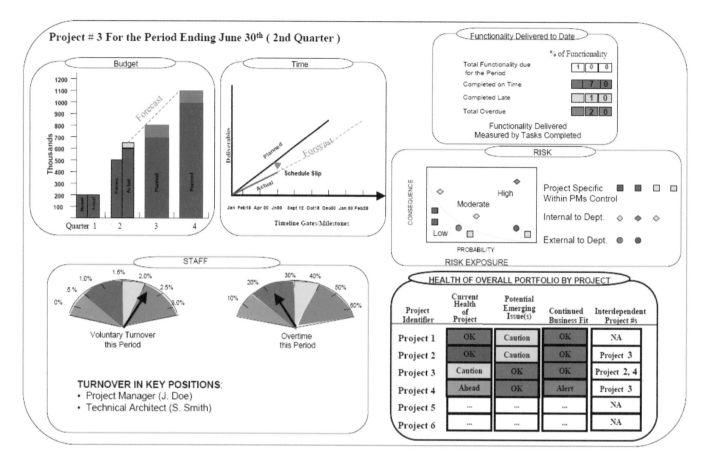

FIGURE 1.12.

This dashboard was used by the Treasury Board of Canada to monitor the performance of a project. Once again we have a dashboard that was designed by an organization for its own use. This time, the dashboard metaphor makes a token appearance in the form of gauges. The traffic-light colors green, yellow, and red—here with the addition of blue for the exceptionally good status of "ahead of schedule"—are also used. Unlike some of the examples that we've seen, which displayed relatively little information, this one attempts to provide a comprehensive overview that would be needed to effectively monitor progress and performance.

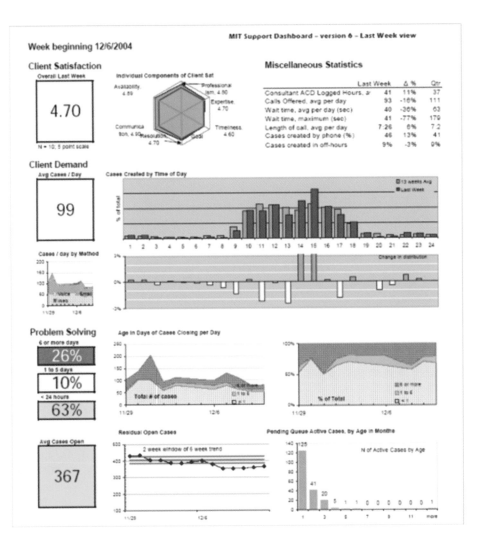

FIGURE 1.13.

This is another dashboard that was designed for actual use. The IT department at the Massachusetts Institute of Technology (MIT) used it at one time to monitor the performance of its systems and support services. As a weekly publication designed for print, however, it raises the question: "How are dashboards different from other types of reports?"

The examples that follow were collected since the original edition of this book was published in 2006. Compared to the earlier examples, many of these dashboards exhibit improvements in the ability to render graphics clearly because of better graphics engines and higher-resolution screens. This doesn't necessarily translate, however, into more informative displays.

FIGURE 1.14.

This dashboard from Business Gauges illustrates two emerging trends: 1) the tendency to treat graphical information displays as art, and 2) the approach some software vendors take to supply a library of display widgets that can be arranged however you wish.

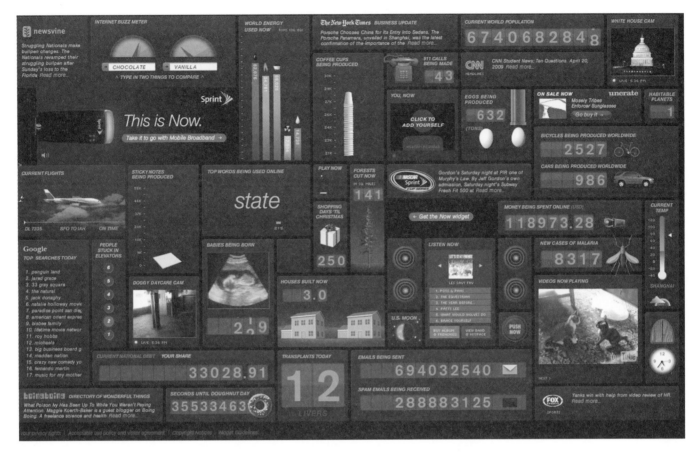

FIGURE 1.15.

This example from Sprint, called the Plug Into Now Dashboard, extends the tendency to merge information and art into a form that is usually called an interactive infographic.

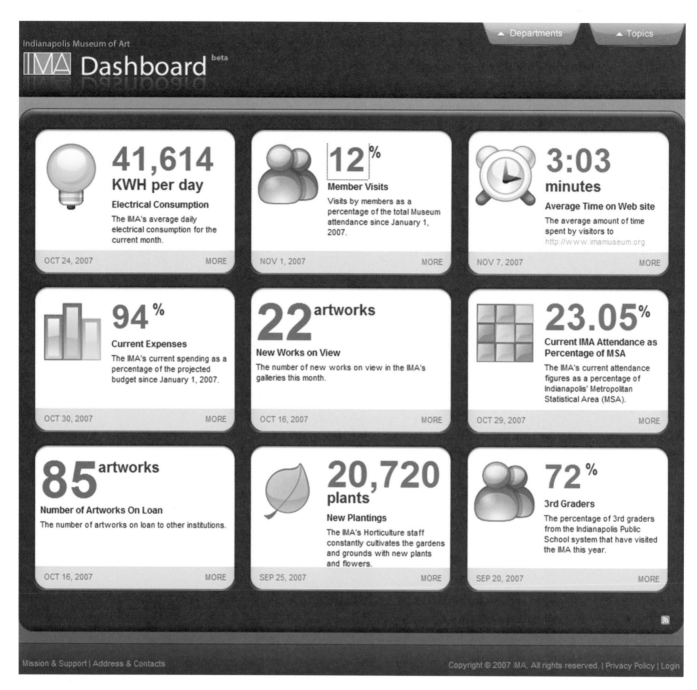

FIGURE 1.16.

In this example, the Indianapolis Museum of Art combines several facts about the organization on a single public web page that functions as a portal to additional information.

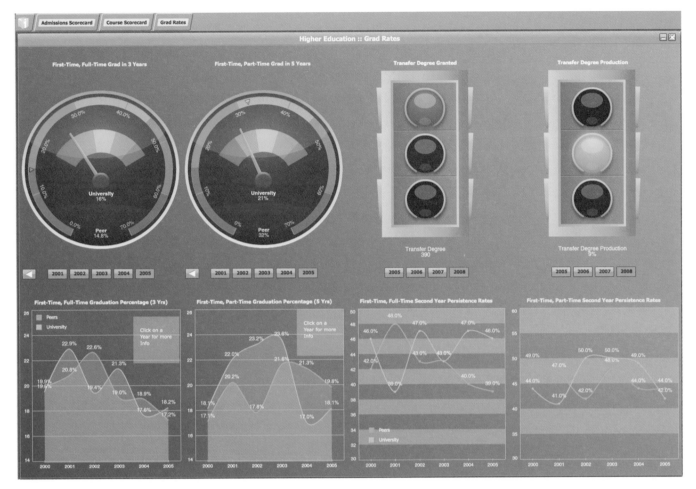

FIGURE 1.17.

This example from iDashboards illustrates a continuing preoccupation with gauge-like displays but little regard for the data that they display. Hasn't the automobile dashboard metaphor been beaten to death yet?

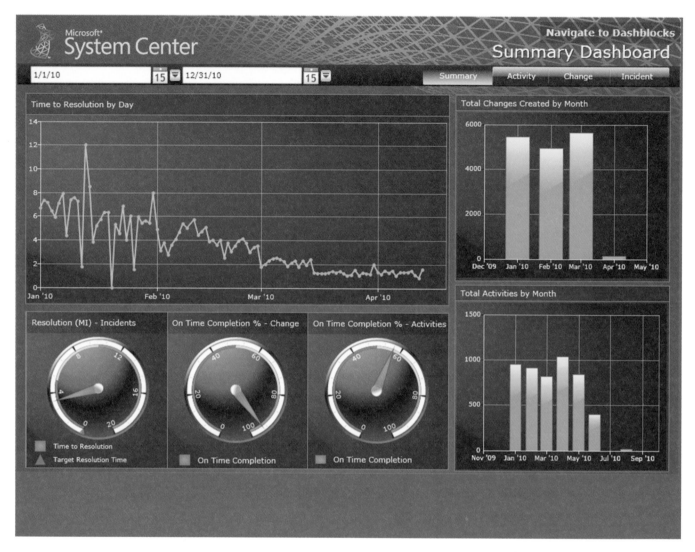

FIGURE 1.18.

This example from Dundas illustrates a new style of display that has become popular on mobile devices, such as smartphones and tablets, which features a dark background and charts with graphical effects of light and shadow.

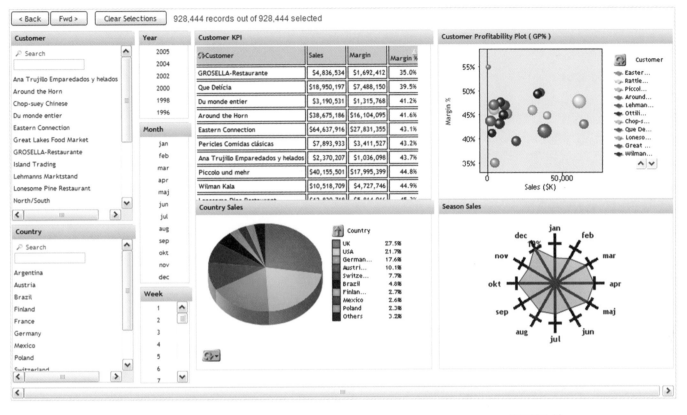

FIGURE 1.19.

This example from QlikTech illustrates a continuing tendency to blur the boundaries between online reports that are used for looking up particular facts (notice the selection controls on the left) and displays that bear the name dashboard. Looking at this example once again prompts us to ask, "What uniquely qualifies a display as a dashboard?"

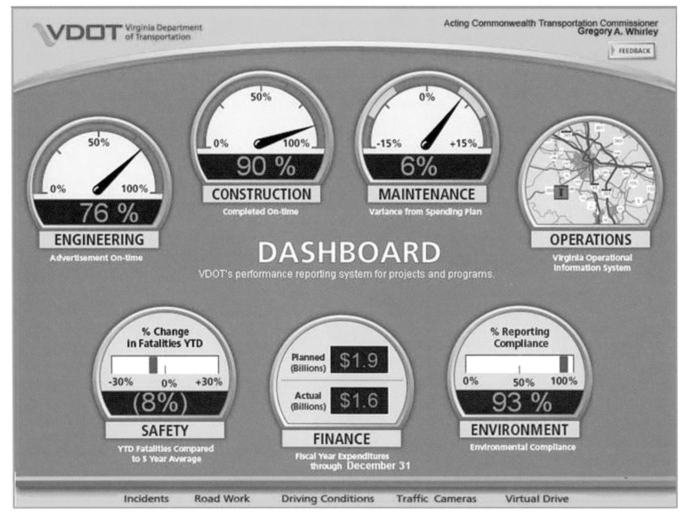

FIGURE 1.20.

This example from the Virginia Department of Transportation illustrates the growing use of dashboard-like displays by government agencies to provide information to the general public. Here again the automobile dashboard metaphor is featured to excess, but at least it's somewhat fitting for displaying information about transportation.

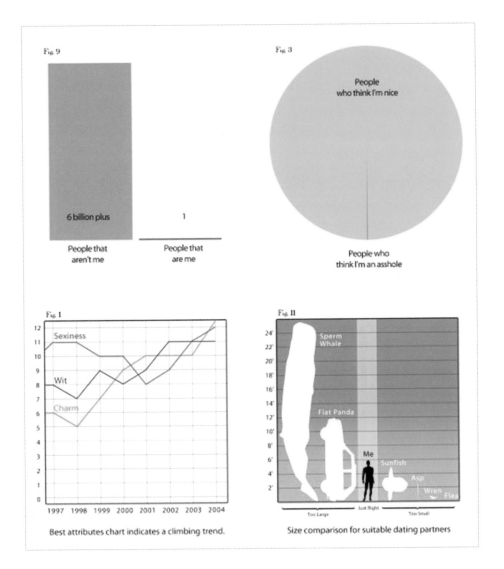

FIGURE 1.21.

This final example is perhaps the most unusual of the lot, and definitely the most entertaining. It was posted as a personal ad on craigslist by a fellow promoting his potential as a dating companion. Dashboards have now entered the realm of popular culture.

What Is a Dashboard?

As demonstrated in the previous examples, there's a fair degree of diversity among information displays that go by the name "dashboard." One of the few characteristics that most vendors seem to agree on is that for something to be called a dashboard it must contain multiple charts, and it often includes traffic lights and a variety of gauges and meters, many similar to the fuel gauges and speedometers found in automobiles. This clearly associates BI dashboards with the familiar versions found in cars, thereby leveraging a useful metaphor, but the metaphor alone doesn't provide an adequate definition. About the only other thread that is common to these dashboard examples is that they often attempt to provide an overview of something that's currently going on in the organization.

After a great deal of research and thought, I composed a definition of my own that captures the essence of what I believe a dashboard is, which is clearly biased toward the characteristics of this medium that I find most useful and unique. To serve us well, this definition must clearly differentiate dashboards from other forms of data presentation, and it must emphasize the characteristics that effectively support the goal of communication. Here's my definition, which originally appeared in *Intelligent Enterprise* magazine:

> *A dashboard is a visual display of the most important information needed to achieve one or more objectives, consolidated and arranged on a single screen so the information can be monitored at a glance.*

Stephen Few (March 20, 2004). "Dashboard Confusion." *Intelligent Enterprise.*

Just as the dashboard of a car provides critical information that one must monitor at a glance to operate the vehicle, an information dashboard serves a similar purpose, whether the client is using it to make strategic decisions for a huge corporation, run the daily operations of a team, or perform tasks that involve no one but himself. The means is a single-screen display, and the purpose is to efficiently monitor what's going on.

A dashboard is a visual display

of

the most important information needed to achieve one or more objectives

that has been

consolidated on a single computer screen

so it can be

monitored at a glance

Let's examine each part of the definition.

Dashboards are visual displays.

The information on a dashboard is presented visually, usually as a combination of text and graphics, but with an emphasis on graphics. Dashboards are highly graphical, not because graphics are cute or fun, but because graphical presentation, handled expertly, can often communicate more efficiently and comprehensively than text alone. How can we best present information so that human eyes can take it in quickly, and human brains can easily and accurately extract the most important meanings from it? To design dashboards effectively, we must understand something about visual perception: what works, what doesn't, and why.

Dashboards display the information needed to achieve specific objectives.

To achieve even a single objective usually requires access to a collection of facts that are not otherwise related, often coming from diverse sources related to various organizational functions. This isn't a specific type of information; it's whatever type of information one needs to do a particular job. This isn't just information that is needed by executives or even by managers; it can be needed by anyone who has objectives to meet. The information can be and often is a set of KPIs, but not necessarily so, for other facts might also be needed to do one's job.

A dashboard fits on a single computer screen.

The information should appear on a single screen, entirely available within the viewer's eye span so it can all be seen at once, at a glance. If the viewer must scroll around to see all the information, it is no longer a dashboard. If the viewer must shift from screen to screen to see it all, then we've designed multiple dashboards, not one. The objective is to have the most important information readily and effortlessly available, so the viewer can quickly absorb what he or she needs to know.

Must the information be displayed in a web browser? That might be the best medium for many dashboards today, but it isn't the only acceptable medium, and it might not be the best medium 10 years from now. Must the information be constantly refreshed in real time? Only if the objectives that it serves require real-time information. If someone is monitoring air traffic using a dashboard, she must immediately be informed when something is wrong. But if she is making strategic decisions about how to boost sales, a snapshot of information as of last night should work fine.

Dashboards are used to monitor information at a glance.

Despite the fact that information about almost anything can be appropriately displayed in a dashboard, there is at least one characteristic that describes almost all the information found in dashboards: it provides an overview. This is because the person using the dashboard cannot rapidly monitor all the details needed to achieve his objectives. A dashboard must be able to quickly point out that something deserves attention and might require action. It needn't provide all the details necessary to take action, but it should make getting to that information as easy and seamless as possible. Getting there might involve shifting to a different display beyond the dashboard or using navigational methods such as linking or drilling down. The dashboard does its primary job if it tells the viewer with little more than a glance that he should act. It serves him superbly if it directly opens the door to any additional information that's needed to take that action.

That's the essence of the dashboard. Now let's add to this definition a couple of supporting attributes that help dashboards do their job effectively.

Dashboards present information using small, concise, direct, and clear display media.

Dashboards require means of display that clearly state their messages without taking up much space, so the entire collection of information fits into the limited real estate of a single screen. If something that looks like a fuel gauge, traffic signal, or thermometer fits this requirement best for a particular piece of information, then we should use it, but if something else works better, we should use that instead. Insisting on sexy displays similar to features found in an automobile is counterproductive when other mechanisms would work better. Sacrificing effective communication for an image is a vivid example of taking a metaphor too far.

There's a term for aspects of design that emulate old-fashioned, physical objects that were used in a different context: *skeuomorphs*. Unfortunately, most dashboard products contain a large gallery of absurd skeuomorphs. Despite this fact, skeuomorphs aren't all bad. There are times when they can ease the transition from a familiar conceptual realm to one that is new. One might argue that by making dashboard gauges look like those on cars, we're making it easy for people to use monitoring displays. It is certainly true that experience driving a car has already taught us how to read those types of gauges. This would be a good argument if it took days or even hours to learn how to read more informative forms of display, but this is hardly the case. In fact, there are significantly better means to display data on a computer screen for monitoring purposes than widgets that look like fuel gauges, and people can learn to read these better means in less than a minute. A few seconds of learning is a small price to pay for a lifetime of better information that can be acquired more efficiently.

Dashboards are customized.

The information on a dashboard must be tailored specifically to the requirements of a given person, group, or function; otherwise, it won't serve its purpose.

A dashboard is a type of display, a form of presentation, not a specific type of information or technology. If we keep this distinction clear, we'll be able to focus on what really matters: designing dashboards to communicate.

In the years since 2004 when I wrote the definition above, many have adopted it, but overly broad and vague definitions, which fail to clarify how dashboards are different from other information displays, remain prevalent. According to Gartner's website when I accessed it in 2012, a dashboard is defined as follows:

> *This subset of reporting includes the ability to publish formal, Web-based reports with intuitive interactive displays of information, including dials, gauges, sliders, check boxes and traffic lights. These displays indicate the status of an item or the state of a performance metric compared with a goal or target value. Increasingly, dashboards are used to disseminate real-time data from operational applications.*

According to Gartner, what characterizes a dashboard? It is web-based, interactive, and has automobile-like mechanisms of display (for example, gauges) that reveal the status of performance metrics. Definitions such as this leave us scratching our heads in confusion.

Without a clear definition of a dashboard, I couldn't even begin to describe how one should be designed. Effective information designs differ based on what people wish to do with the information. The current trend of calling anything that includes more than one chart a dashboard is much too broad; there are many purposes for which we might need to view data in multiple charts, and each of those purposes demands differences in design. For example, in my book *Now You See It*, which teaches how graphics can be used to explore and analyze data, I talk about the usefulness of multi-chart displays. When someone is trying to make sense of a data set, he must examine it from many perspectives, sometimes simultaneously. Only then can he spot relationships that would remain hidden if each of the charts were viewed independently. When we combine multiple charts on a screen for data exploration and analysis, however, we want extreme flexibility. We need to move from one view to another as fast as each new question about the information comes to mind. We constantly add and remove charts, and change them by filtering data, sorting values in a different order, switching from one chart type to another, or doing anything else that's necessary to get to the next view that we need, as quickly and seamlessly as possible. Designers of good exploratory data analysis tools build this flexibility into the interface. In contrast, when we combine multiple charts on a screen for the purpose of monitoring performance, we want that screen to look the same from day to day, without alteration, except for changes in the data. Why? Because only then will viewers be able to update their awareness by rapidly spotting and assimilating changes in the information.

Throughout this book, we will focus on the best ways to design information displays that are used on a regular basis to monitor what's going on in a particular domain. Just as the dashboard displays in a car are used to rapidly maintain awareness of the basic facts that we need to attain our driving objectives, so an information dashboard is used to maintain awareness of the facts that we need to do our jobs, whatever they might be.

So, let's get out of the way, once and for all, what a dashboard is not. A dashboard is not any of the following:

- A display that is used for data exploration and analysis
- A portal
- A scorecard
- A report that people use to look up specific facts

Although exploration and analysis are extremely important functions enabled by data visualization, we don't use a dashboard for these tasks. As a monitoring display, a dashboard might make the viewer aware of something that she must explore and analyze a bit before responding, but she wouldn't carry out the exploration and analysis using the dashboard. Ideally, she could shift from the dashboard directly into an environment that's designed for exploration and analysis, with all of the flexibility and interaction that is required, and then easily shift back to the dashboard if more monitoring is needed, but the two activities would be serviced by differently designed interfaces.

We should not make the mistake of using the terms "dashboard" and "portal" interchangeably. Though similar in some respects, they are quite different in purpose and design. A dashboard is used to *monitor* a particular collection of information, and a portal is used to access a variety of information and tasks. A portal's purpose is to make it easy to get to the things that the viewer often needs. It might contain a list of the day's tasks along with a link to her calendar, a list of messages in her email inbox along with a link to the email system, a list of the day's top news stories with links to them, and so on. A portal is a single point of access; a dashboard is a performance monitoring display and, as such, might be one of the destinations that the portal allows the viewer to access.

A balanced scorecard is an entire system of data and activities for managing and improving an organization's performance, which is based on the methodology that was developed by Kaplan and Norton. Because the viewer must monitor performance as part of the balanced scorecard process, he might use a dashboard to do this one task. But the entire methodology of the balanced scorecard, with all of its activities, is different from a form of display that he might use to do one of those activities.

Finally, reports that people use to look up facts when needed are useful, but they are not dashboards. A report might combine several charts on the screen to display selected information, but looking up facts is not the same as performance monitoring. To look something up, people must have access to controls that will allow them to select the information that's needed in that moment for the task at hand. Ongoing performance monitoring, however, involves a defined set of information that's needed every time someone looks at the dashboard, without having to go through a series of steps to select it.

Maintaining Situation Awareness

Think of a dashboard as an information display that is designed to help people maintain *situation awareness* (SA). The term was originally applied to military pilots whose lives and missions required an especially high level of awareness of the details unfolding around them.

> *Basically, SA is being aware of what is happening around you and understanding what that information means to you now and in the future. This awareness is usually defined in terms of what information is important for a particular job or goal. The concept of SA is usually applied to operational situations, where people must have SA for a specified reason, for example in order to drive a car, treat a patient, or separate traffic as an air traffic controller. Therefore, SA is normally defined as it relates to the goals and objectives of a specific job or function.*

Mica R. Endsley, Betty Bolte, and Debra G. Jones (2003). *Designing for Situation Awareness: An Approach to User-Centered Design.* Taylor & Francis, page 13.

People have jobs to do. To do them well, in many cases they must constantly know what's going on. That awareness is informed by a particular set of facts that add up to an overview of the situation. People want those facts to be readily available, displayed in a way that makes them easy and efficient to perceive, understand, and if necessary, respond. That display is a dashboard. Obviously, for a dashboard to serve as a means for maintaining situation awareness, it must be carefully designed to present those facts in a manner that works for the viewer's eyes and brain.

Commercial airline pilots don't wait for an alarm to go off before looking at their cockpit displays. They are trained to scan those displays periodically in a particular order to maintain an overall awareness of what's going on. If they didn't do this, and an alarm suddenly went off, they would lose precious time struggling under pressure to update their overall awareness of the situation before they could begin to focus their attention on the cause of the alarm. With ongoing situation awareness, however, they already have the overall understanding that they need to focus immediately on the source of the problem in an informed manner.

Situation awareness works on three levels:

- *Level 1: perception of the elements in the environment,*
- *Level 2: comprehension of the current situation, and*
- *Level 3: projection of future status.*

Ibid., page 14.

In this book, we'll look for ways to design dashboards that support situation awareness on all of these levels. Unfortunately, few of the tools that are available for developing dashboards do this well.

> *While a clear understanding of one's situation is undoubtedly the critical trigger that allows the knowledge, skills, and creativity of the human mind to be successfully brought to bear in shaping our environment, very often people must work uphill, against systems and technologies that block rather than enhance their ability to ascertain the information they need. Knowledge in a vacuum is meaningless. Its use in overcoming human problems and achieving human goals requires the successful application of that knowledge in ways that are contextually appropriate. Yet, across a wide variety of engineered systems, people face an ever-widening information gap—the gulf between the data that [are] available and the information that they really need to know.*

Ibid., page vii.

The Goal of Performance Monitoring

More than any other activity, regardless of the nature of their work, organizations engage in decision making. As the Nobel-prize winning economist Daniel Kahneman points out in his marvelous book *Thinking, Fast and Slow* (Farrar, Straus and Giroux, 2011), organizations are *decision factories*:

> *Whatever else it produces, an organization is a factory that manufactures judgments and decisions. Every factory must have ways to ensure the quality of its products in the initial design, in fabrication, and in final inspections. The corresponding stages in the production of decisions are the framing of the problem that is to be solved, the collection of relevant information leading to a decision, and reflection and review. An organization that seeks to improve its decision product should routinely look for efficiency improvements at each of these stages. The operative concept is routine. Constant quality control is an alternative to the wholesale reviews of processes that organizations commonly undertake in the wake of disasters. There is much to be done to improve decision making.*

Daniel Kahneman (2011). *Thinking, Fast and Slow.* Farrar, Straus and Giroux, page 418.

Performance management has become a worldwide obsession, at least in principle, but most organizations still lack the skills and tools that are required to actually do it. We monitor performance—how we're doing in relation to our objectives—not only to maintain awareness but to use that awareness to keep performance on track or improve it. Information in and of itself is useless. It only has value to the degree that we use it to do something worthwhile. Whether that involves improving the quality of an organization's products or services, working to prevent the spread of disease, finding ways to improve student performance, or boosting one's physical fitness, information can be used to change the world. That's why we monitor it. Any form of information display that doesn't produce this outcome is worthless.

The Performance Monitoring Process

Monitoring information to manage performance involves four primary stages:

1. Update high-level situation awareness.
2. Identify and focus on particular items that need attention.
   a. Update awareness of this item in greater detail.
   b. Determine whether action is required.
3. If action is required, access additional information that is needed, if any, to determine an appropriate response.
4. Respond.

Dashboards must be designed to support this process. Information that cannot support action to maintain or improve performance does not belong on a dashboard. An information display that does not support this process is not an effective dashboard.

A Timely Opportunity

Several circumstances have recently combined to create a timely opportunity for dashboards to add value to the workplace, including technologies such as high-resolution graphics, emphasis on performance management and metrics, and a growing recognition of visual perception as a powerful channel for information acquisition and comprehension. Dashboards offer a unique solution to the problem of information overload—not a complete solution by any means, but one that can support the task of monitoring what's going on.

Dashboards aren't all that different from some other means of presenting information, but, when properly designed, the single-screen display of integrated and finely tuned facts can quickly update the viewer's awareness:

> *Dashboards and visualization are cognitive tools that improve your "span of control" over a lot of business data. These tools help people visually identify trends, patterns and anomalies, reason about what they see and help guide them toward effective decisions. As such, these tools need to leverage people's visual capabilities. With the prevalence of scorecards, dashboards and other visualization tools now widely available for business users to review their data, the issue of visual information design is more important than ever.*

Richard Brath and Michael Peters (October 2004). "Dashboard Design: Why Design is Important." *DM Direct.*

The final sentiment that Brath and Peters express in this excerpt from their article underscores the purpose of this book. As data visualization becomes an increasingly common form of business communication, it is imperative that we acquire expertise on this topic. This expertise must be grounded in an understanding of human perception and cognition, and of how this understanding can be effectively applied to the visual display of data. These skills are rarely found in the workplace, not because they are difficult to learn, but because the need to learn them is seldom recognized. This is true of data visualization in general, and especially of dashboards. The challenge of presenting a large assortment of information on a single screen in a way that produces immediate insight is by no means trivial. Buckle up; we're in for a fun ride.

2 THIRTEEN COMMON MISTAKES IN DASHBOARD DESIGN

Preoccupation with superficial and distracting aspects of visual design has led to a rash of problems that have undermined the usefulness of most dashboards. Thirteen design problems in particular are frequently found in dashboards, especially in examples that are featured by software vendors:

1. Exceeding the boundaries of a single screen
2. Supplying inadequate context for the data
3. Displaying excessive detail or precision
4. Expressing measures indirectly
5. Choosing inappropriate display media
6. Introducing meaningless variety
7. Using poorly designed display media
8. Encoding quantitative data inaccurately
9. Arranging information poorly
10. Highlighting important information ineffectively or not at all
11. Cluttering the display with visual effects
12. Misusing or overusing color
13. Designing an unattractive visual display

The fundamental challenge of dashboard design is squeezing a great deal of information into a small space while ensuring that the display is easily and immediately understandable. If this doesn't sound challenging, either you are an expert designer with extensive dashboard experience, or you are basking in naiveté. Attempt the task, and you will find that dashboards pose a unique data visualization challenge. And don't assume that you can look to your software vendor for help. If vendors have the necessary design talent, most of them are doing a great job of hiding it.

Sadly, it is easy to find many examples of the mistakes we should avoid by looking no further than the websites of the software vendors themselves. Let's use some of these examples to examine design that doesn't work and learn why.

Exceeding the Boundaries of a Single Screen

My insistence that a dashboard should confine its display to a single screen, with no need for scrolling or switching among multiple screens, might seem arbitrary and a bit finicky, but it is based on solid and practical rationale. After studying data visualization and visual perception for awhile, we discover that something powerful happens when we see things together, all within eye span. Likewise, something critical is compromised when we lose sight of some data by scrolling or switching to another screen to see other data. Part of the problem is that we can only hold a few chunks of information at a time in working memory. The mind's eye cannot reliably recall information that is no longer visible.

In almost every case, I've chosen to illustrate dashboard design mistakes using actual examples from vendor websites. In doing so, I am not saying that the software that produced the example is bad or commenting in any way on the quality of the software. What I am saying is that the design practice is bad. This results primarily from vendors' lack of expertise in (or inattention to) visual design. Vendors should know better, but they've chosen to focus their energies on other aspects of their products, often highlighting glitzy visual features that actually undermine effective communication. I hope that seeing their work used to illustrate poor dashboard design will be a wake-up call to them to start paying attention to the features that really matter.

One of the great benefits of a dashboard as a medium of communication is the simultaneity of perception that it offers: the ability to see everything that we need, all at once. This enables comparisons that lead to insights—those "Aha!" experiences that might not occur in any other way. Exceeding the boundaries of a single screen negates this benefit. Let's examine, one by one, the two versions of this problem: fragmenting data into separate screens and requiring the viewer to scroll.

Fragmenting Data into Separate Screens

Information that appears on dashboards is often fragmented into discrete screens to which one must navigate. Enabling navigation to different screens or to different iterations of a single screen to access additional information is not necessarily a bad practice. Allowing navigation to further detail or to a different set of information that best serves its purpose by standing alone can be a powerful dashboard feature. However, when the information should all be seen at the same time to make the desired insights possible, this type of fragmentation undermines the unique advantages of a dashboard. Fragmenting data that should be seen together is a mistake.

Let's look at an example. The dashboard below fragments data that banking executives need into 10 separate screens. This would be fine if the executive wouldn't benefit from seeing these various measures together, but that isn't the case.

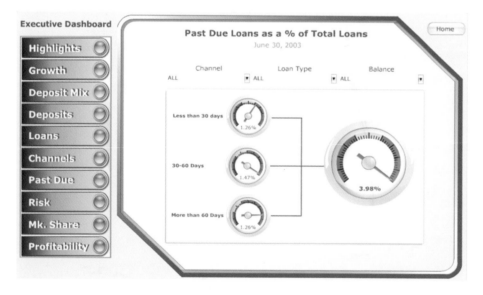

FIGURE 2.1. This dashboard fragments the data in a way that undermines the viewer's ability to see meaningful relationships.

In this example, the executive is forced to separately examine the following aspects of the bank's performance:

- Highlights
- Growth
- Deposit mix
- Deposits

- Loans
- Channels
- Past-due loans
- Risk
- Market share
- Profitability

Each of these screens presents a separate, high-level snapshot of a small set of measures that should be integrated together into a single screen. Despite what we might assume about the screen labeled "Highlights," it does not provide a consolidated overview. A banking executive needs to see these measures together to make comparisons and understand how they relate to and influence one another. Splitting the big picture into a series of separate small pictures is a mistake whenever seeing the big picture is worthwhile.

A similar example appears below. This time a picture of daily sales has been split into 20 separate dashboards for each of 20 products. If the intention is to serve the needs of product managers who are each exclusively interested in a single product and never want to compare sales of that product to others, this design doesn't fragment the data in a harmful way. If, however, any benefit could be gained by viewing the sales of multiple products together, which is almost surely the case, this design fails.

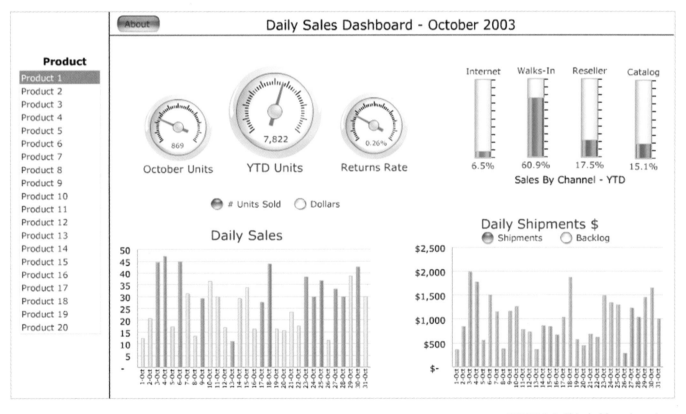

FIGURE 2.2. This dashboard requires viewers to click on and view information for only one product at a time.

Requiring the Viewer to Scroll

The next dashboard illustrates the problem that's created when scrolling is required to see all the data.

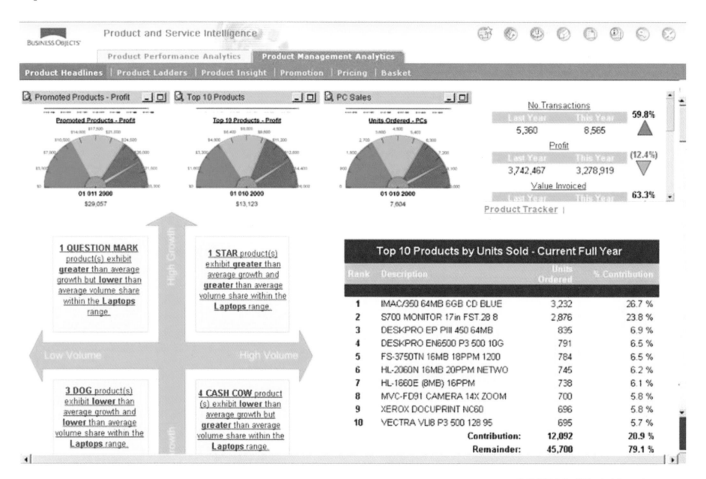

Not only is the viewer left wondering what lies below the bottom of the screen in the dashboard as a whole, but he's also given immediate access only to the first of the many metrics that appear in the scrollable box at the top right, beginning with "No. Transactions." He'd be better off reading a printed report extending across multiple pages because at least then he could lay out all of the pages at once for simultaneous viewing. People commonly assume that anything that lies beyond their immediate field of vision and requires scrolling to see is of less importance than what's immediately visible. Many viewers won't bother to look at what lies off the screen, and those who take the time will resent the unnecessary effort.

FIGURE 2.3. This dashboard demonstrates that effectiveness is sacrificed when scrolling is required to see all the information.

Supplying Inadequate Context for the Data

Measures of what's currently going on in an organization never perform well as a solo act; they need a good supporting cast to succeed. For example, to state a quarter-to-date sales total of $736,502 without any context means little. Compared to what? Is this good or bad? How good or bad? Are we on track? Are we doing better than we have in the past, or worse than we've forecasted? Supplying the right context for key measures is the difference between numbers that just dumbly sit there on the screen and those that enlighten and inspire action.

Useful context that could have been incorporated into the following gauges was neglected.

October Units   YTD Units   Returns Rate

FIGURE 2.4. These dashboard gauges fail to provide adequate context to make the measures meaningful.

For instance, the center gauge tells us only that 7,822 units have sold so far this year, and that this number is good (indicated by the green arrow—though you might not be able to tell it's green if you're colorblind). A quantitative scale on a graph, such as the radial scales of tick marks on these gauges, is meant to provide a quick approximation of the measure, but it can only do so if the scale is labeled with values, which these gauges lack. If the values had been labeled, the positions of the arrows might have been meaningful, but here the presence of the tick marks only suggests useful information that wasn't included.

These gauges use up a great deal of space to tell us little. The same information could have been communicated simply as text in much less space, without any loss of meaning:

YTD Units   7,822
October Units   869
Returns Rate   0.26%

Another failure of these gauges is that they tease us by coloring the arrows to indicate good or bad performance without telling us how good or bad it is. They could easily have done this by labeling the quantitative scales and visually encoding sections along the scales as good or bad rather than just encoding the arrows in this manner. Had this been done, we would be able to see at a glance how good or bad a measure is by how far the arrow pointed into the good or bad ranges.

The next gauge does a better job of incorporating context in the form of meaningful comparisons. Here, the potential of the graphical display is more fully realized. The gauge measures the average duration of phone calls and is part of a larger dashboard of call-center data.

FIGURE 2.5. This dashboard gauge (found in a paper entitled "Making Dashboards Actionable," written by Laurie M. Orlov and published in December 2003 by Forrester Research, Inc.) is more effective than the previous ones at communicating information.

The circular shape used by gauges like this one wastes precious space on a dashboard, as I'll explain in Chapter 6: *Achieving Eloquence Through Simplicity*. Nevertheless, I commend this gauge for displaying richer information than most.

As this gauge illustrates, supplying context for measures need not always involve choosing the single best comparison; rather, several contexts may be given. For instance, quarter-to-date sales of $736,502 might benefit from comparisons to the target of $1,000,000, sales on this day last year of $856,923, and a line graph of sales figures for the past six quarters. Such a display would provide much richer insight than a simple display of the current sales figure. We must be careful, however, when incorporating rich context such as this; we have to do so in a way that doesn't bog the viewer down in reading lots of details to get the basic message. It is helpful to provide a visually prominent display of the primary information and to subdue the supporting context somewhat so that it doesn't get in the way when a viewer is quickly scanning the dashboard for key points.

The amount of context that ought to be incorporated to enrich measures on a dashboard depends on the dashboard's purpose and the needs of its viewers. More is not always better, but when more provides real value, it should be included in a way that supports a quick overview without distraction, as well as contextual information to enrich understanding.

Displaying Excessive Detail or Precision

Dashboards should almost always display fairly high-level information to provide a quick overview. Too much detail, or measures that are expressed too precisely (for example, $3,848,305.93 rather than $3,848,306 or perhaps even $3.8M), slow viewers down without providing any benefit. In a way, this problem is the opposite extreme of the one we examined in the previous section; this is the problem of too much information rather than too little.

The next dashboard illustrates this type of excess. Let's look at the two sections that I've enclosed in red rectangles. The lower-right section displays from four to ten decimal digits for each measure, which might be useful in some contexts but not likely in a dashboard. The upper section displays time down to the level of seconds, which also seems like overkill in this context. With a dashboard, every unnecessary piece of information results in time wasted as the viewer has to filter out what's important; when time is of the essence, there's no time to waste.

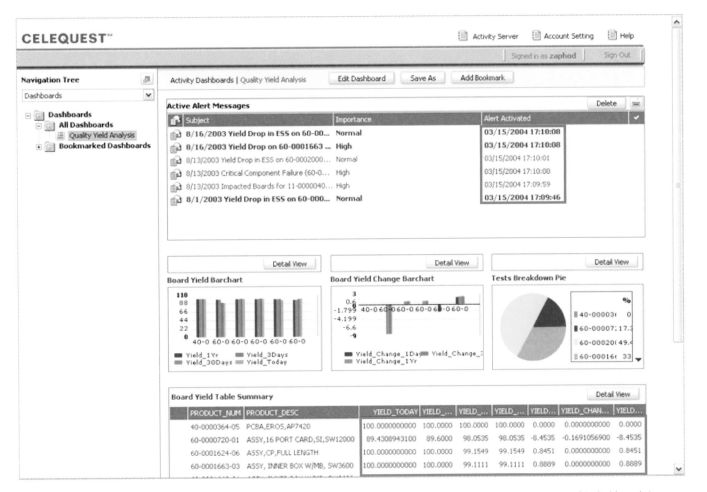

FIGURE 2.6. This dashboard shows unnecessary detail, such as times expressed to the second and measures expressed to 10 decimal places.

Expressing Measures Indirectly

For a measure to be meaningful, we must know what is being measured and the units of measure. A measure is deficient if it isn't the one that most clearly and efficiently communicates the meaning that the dashboard viewer needs. The data might be accurate but not the best choice for the intended message. For example, if the dashboard viewer only needs to know to what degree actual revenue differs from budgeted revenue, it would be more direct to simply express the variance as –9% rather than displaying the actual revenue amount of $76,934 and the budgeted revenue amount of $85,000 and leaving it to the viewer to calculate the difference (or even displaying the variance of –$8,066 as well as the other two numbers). In this case, a percentage clearly focuses attention on the variance in a manner that is directly intelligible.

The following graph, which I reproduced from a dashboard, illustrates this problem. It displays actual and budgeted revenues as separate lines even though its purpose is to communicate the variance of actual revenues from the budget.

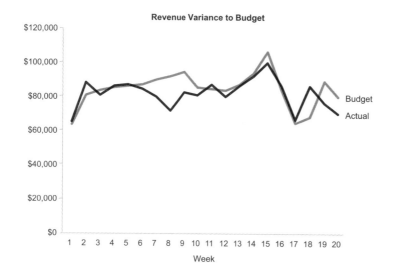

FIGURE 2.7. This graph displays measures in a way that fails to directly express the intended message.

The variance could have been displayed more clearly by encoding budgeted revenue as a reference line of 0% and the variance as a line that meanders above and below budget (expressed in units of positive and negative percentages, as shown below).

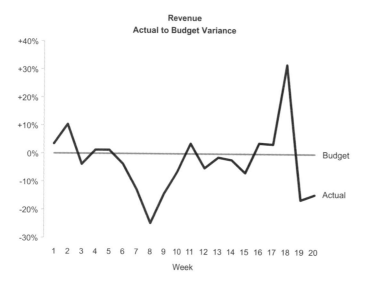

FIGURE 2.8. This graph is designed to emphasize deviation from a target, which it accomplishes in part by visually expressing the percentage difference between budgeted and actual revenues.

The point here is to always think carefully about the message that most directly supports the viewer's needs and then select the measure that most directly supports that message.

Choosing Inappropriate Display Media

Choosing inappropriate display media is one of the most common design mistakes, not just in dashboards but in all forms of quantitative data presentation. For instance, using a graph when a table of numbers would work better, and vice versa, is a frequent mistake. Allow me to illustrate using several examples.

The pie chart below is part of a dashboard that displays breast cancer statistics. Look at it for a moment and see if anything seems odd.

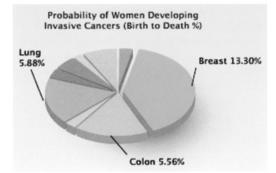

FIGURE 2.9. This chart illustrates a common problem with pie charts.

Pie charts were specifically designed to present parts of a whole, and the whole should always add up to 100%. Here, the slice labeled "Breast 13.30%" looks like it represents around 40% of the pie, a far cry from 13.3%. These slices are not parts of a whole; instead they represent the probability that a woman will develop any one of nine types of cancer (breast, lung, colon, and six types that aren't labeled). This misuse of a pie chart for things that don't add up to a whole invites confusion.

The truth is, I almost never recommend the use of pie charts. The only thing they have going for them is the fact that most people immediately know when they see a pie chart that they are (or should be) seeing parts of a whole. Beyond that, pie charts don't display quantitative data effectively. As we'll see in Chapter 5: *Tapping into the Power of Visual Perception*, humans can't compare 2-D areas or angles very accurately, and these are the two means that pie charts use to encode quantitative data. Bar graphs are a much better way to display this information.

The pie chart below shows that, even when correctly used to present parts of a whole, these graphs don't work very well. Without the value labels, we could only discern that opportunities rated as "Fair" represent the largest group, those rated as "Field Sales: 2-Very High" represent a miniscule group, and the other ratings groups are roughly equal in size.

Refer to my book *Show Me the Numbers: Designing Tables and Graphs to Enlighten*, Second Edition (Analytics Press, 2012) for a thorough treatment of the types of graphs that work best for the most common quantitative messages.

FIGURE 2.10. This example shows that even when they are used correctly to present parts of a whole, pie charts are difficult to interpret accurately.

The graph below displays the same information as shown in *Figure 2.10*, this time using horizontal bars that can be interpreted efficiently and accurately.

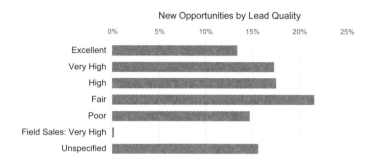

FIGURE 2.11. This horizontal bar graph does a much better job of displaying part-to-whole data than the preceding pie chart.

Other types of graphs can be equally ineffective. For example, the graph below shows little regard for the viewer's time and no understanding of visual perception. This graph compares revenue to operating costs across five months, using the size of overlapping circles (called bubbles) to encode the quantities. Like using slices of a pie, using circles to encode quantity relies on the viewer's ability to compare two-dimensional areas, which we cannot accurately do. Take the values for the month of February as an example. Assuming that operating costs equal $10,000, what is the revenue value?

FIGURE 2.12. This graph uses the two-dimensional area of circles to encode their values, which needlessly obscures the data.

Our natural tendency is to compare the sizes of the two circles using a single dimension—length or width—equal to the diameter of each, which suggests that revenue is about three times that of operating costs, or about $30,000. This conclusion is wrong, however, to a large degree. The two-dimensional area of the revenue circle is actually almost 5 ½ times bigger than that of the operating costs circle, resulting in a value of approximately $54,000. Oops! Not even close. A simple bar graph like the one below works much better.

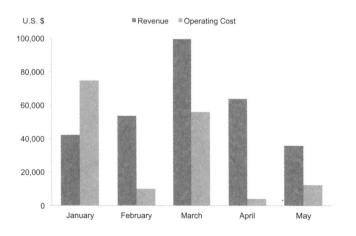

FIGURE 2.13. This bar graph does a good job of displaying a series of revenues versus operating costs.

In the next example, actual revenue versus the revenue budget is subdivided into geographical regions and displayed as a radar graph. The quantitative scale on a radar graph is laid along each of the axis lines that extend from the center to the perimeter, like radius lines of a circle. The smallest values are those that are closest to the center.

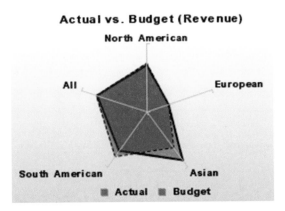

FIGURE 2.14. This radar graph obscures the straightforward data that it's trying to convey.

The lack of labeled axes in this graph limits its meaning, but choosing a radar graph to display this information in the first place is an even more fundamental error. Once again, a simple bar graph like the one below would communicate this information much more effectively. Radar graphs are rarely useful. Their circular arrangement makes comparisons difficult whereas comparisons are easy to make in a linear display such as a bar graph.

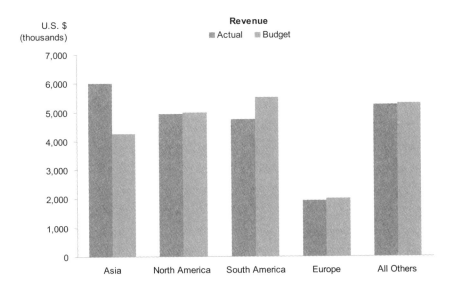

FIGURE 2.15. This bar graph effectively compares actual to budgeted revenue values.

The final example that I'll use to illustrate my point about choosing inappropriate means of display appears next. There are times when it is very useful to arrange data spatially, such as in the form of a geographical map or the floor plan of a building, but this isn't one of them. We don't derive any insight by viewing this revenue information—in this case, whether revenues are good (green light), mediocre (yellow light), or poor (red light), in the geographical regions South (burgundy), Central (orange), West (greenish tan), and East (blue)—on a map.

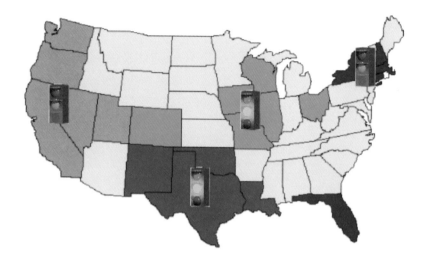

FIGURE 2.16. This display uselessly encodes quantitative values on a map of the United States.

This geospatial display takes up a lot of space to say no more than we're told in the table (see below) that appears on this same dashboard.

	Actual	Budget
East	$87,398	$78,950
West	$132,931	$119,850
South	$50,846	$49,100
Central	$129,680	$125,180

FIGURE 2.17. This table, from the same dashboard, provides the same information that appears in *Figure 2.16* more simply, precisely, and in less space.

Introducing Meaningless Variety

The mistake of introducing meaningless variety into a dashboard design is closely tied to the one we just examined. I've found that people often hesitate to use the same type of chart multiple times on a dashboard, out of what I assume is a sense that viewers will be bored by the monotony. Variety might be the spice of life, but, if it is introduced on a dashboard for its own sake, the display suffers. We should always select the display medium that works best even if that results in a dashboard filled with multiple instances of the same type of graph. If we are giving viewers the information that they desperately need to do their jobs, it won't bore them just because it's displayed in the same way. Viewers will definitely get aggravated, however, if forced to work harder than necessary to get the information they need because of arbitrary variety in the display media. In fact, wherever it's appropriate, consistency in the means of display allows viewers to use the same perceptual strategy for interpreting all of the data, which saves time and energy.

The dashboard on the following page illustrates variety run amok. This visual jumble requires a shift in perceptual strategy for each display item on the dashboard, which requires extra time and effort on the user's part.

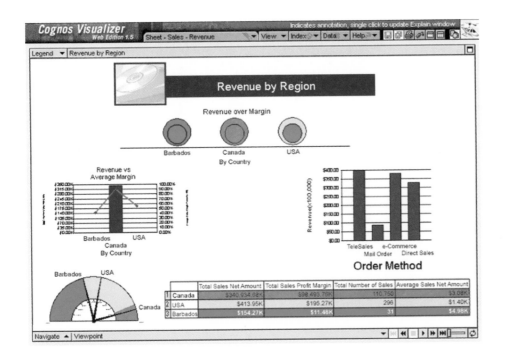

FIGURE 2.18. This dashboard exhibits an unnecessary variety of display media.

Using Poorly Designed Display Media

It isn't enough to choose the right medium to display information; we must also design the components of that medium to communicate clearly and efficiently, without distraction. Most graphs used in organizations today are poorly designed. The reason is simple: almost no one has been trained in the fundamental principles and practices of graph design. This content is thoroughly covered in my book *Show Me the Numbers: Designing Tables and Graphs to Enlighten*, so I won't repeat the details here. Instead, I'll simply illustrate the problem with a few examples.

In addition to the fact that a bar graph would have been a better choice to display the information in the pie chart below, the chart exhibits several other problems. Look at it for a moment, and see whether you can identify aspects of its design that inhibit quick and easy interpretation.

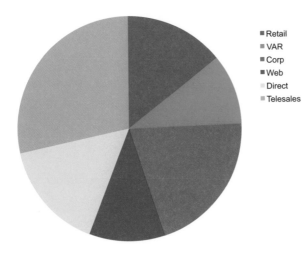

FIGURE 2.19. This pie chart illustrates several design problems.

Here are the primary problems that I see:

- **A legend was used to label and assign values to the slices of the pie.** This forces our eyes to bounce back and forth between the graph and the legend to glean meaning, which is a waste of time and effort when the slices could have been labeled directly.
- **The order of the slices appears random.** Ordering them by size would have provided useful information that could have been assimilated instantly.
- **The bright colors of the pie slices produce sensory overkill.** Bright colors ought to be reserved for specific data that should stand out from the rest.

The next pie chart also illustrates a problem with color choice. In this case, the 11 colors that were chosen are too similar. It is difficult to determine which of the hues along the yellow-orange-red spectrum in the legend corresponds to which slice of the pie. This kind of eye-straining exercise is annoying, to say the least, especially on a dashboard, which by its very nature is intended to be interpreted quickly.

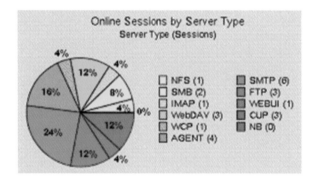

FIGURE 2.20. This pie chart uses multiple colors that are too much alike to be clearly distinguished.

Another example of an ineffective display medium is shown on the following page. These gauges attempt to be true to the metaphor of a car dashboard. Notice that the numbers look just like they would on an odometer: they lack the commas normally used to delineate every set of three digits, which help us distinguish thousands from millions, and so on. In a misguided effort to make these meters look realistic, their developers made the numbers harder to read. Software engineers designed these gauges, not people who actually use dashboards. Notice also that numbers along the quantitative scale are positioned inside rather than outside the axis, which will cause them to be obscured by the needle when it points directly to them, and that the positioning of the text at the bottom of each gauge (for example, "4382934 Amount Sold" on the "Internet Revenue" gauge) obstructs the needle for measures near the bottom or top of the scale.

FIGURE 2.21. These gauges have definitely taken the dashboard metaphor too far.

In the last section, I spoke of bar graphs as a preferable alternative to certain other display media. However, even though bar graphs can do an excellent job of displaying quantitative data, they can be misused as well. Examine the following graph, and take some time to list in the margin any problems that you notice with its design.

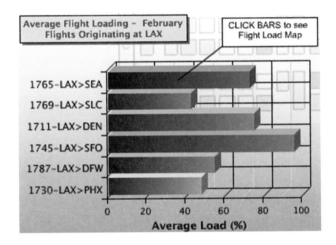

FIGURE 2.22. This bar graph, found on a dashboard, exhibits several design problems.

You might have noticed that the grid lines (not to mention the background pattern of colored rectangles) do nothing but distract from the data. Grid lines, especially when visually prominent like these, make it difficult to focus on the data. Perhaps you also noticed that the 3-D effect of the graph not only adds no value but also makes the values encoded by the bars harder to interpret. Anything else? Well, this graph illustrates a common problem with color. Why is each of the bars a different color? The colors aren't being used to identify the bars because each bar has an identifying label to its left. Differences in the color of data-encoding objects should always be meaningful; otherwise, they needlessly grab our attention and cause us to search for meaning that isn't there. They also discourage us from comparing the bars by making them differ in appearance.

The distinct colors of the bars in the next example do, thankfully, carry meaning, but here the colors are distractingly bright, and the 3-D effect makes them hard to read. However, this isn't the problem that I want you to notice most. The purpose of the graph is to compare actual to budgeted revenues for each of the four regions, but something about its design makes this difficult. Can you see the problem?

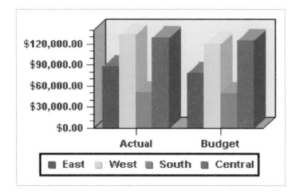

FIGURE 2.23. This bar graph, found on a dashboard, was poorly designed in a number of ways.

Given this graph's purpose, the bars for actual and budgeted revenues for each region should have been placed next to one another. As they are now, it is unnecessarily difficult to compare them. Simple design mistakes like this can significantly undermine the success of a dashboard.

Several of the examples that we've examined have been rendered in 3D even though the third dimension of depth doesn't encode any meaning, so the 3-D effect is superfluous and unnecessary. However, even when the third dimension is used to encode a separate variable, it still poses a problem. The graph below uses the third dimension of depth to represent time (the four quarters of the year 2001).

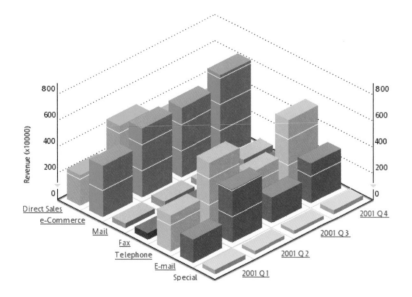

FIGURE 2.24. This 3-D bar graph illustrates the problem of occlusion.

The problem in this case isn't that the third dimension is meaningless but rather that we can't read everything on the chart. This problem is caused by *occlusion*. Displaying values along a Z-axis causes some of the bars to be hidden behind— or occluded by—others. For instance, what were fax revenues for Quarter 3? We can't tell because the bar is completely hidden. The bottom line is that we should almost always avoid 3-D graphs. Useful exceptions to this rule are rare.

Encoding Quantitative Data Inaccurately

Sometimes graphical representations of quantitative data are erroneously designed in ways that represent values inaccurately. In the following example, for instance, the quantitative scale along the vertical axis was improperly set. The height of a bar represents its quantitative value. The bars that represent values for the month of January suggest that revenue was about four times as great as costs. However, an examination of the scale reveals the error of this natural assumption: the revenue is actually less than double the costs. The problem is that the scale begins at $500,000 rather than at $0 as it always should in a bar graph.

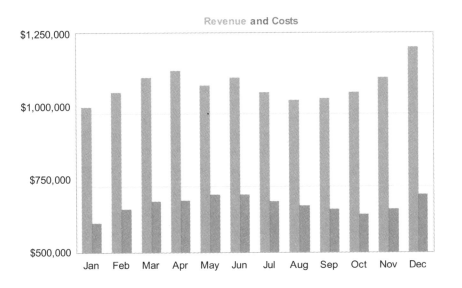

FIGURE 2.25. By failing to begin the scale at zero, these bars inaccurately encode the quantitative values.

Arranging Information Poorly

Dashboards often need to present a large collection of information in a limited amount of space. If the information isn't well organized—with data placed appropriately based on importance and proper viewing sequence and framed within a visual design that segregates information into meaningful groups rather than fragmenting it into a confusing labyrinth—the result is a cluttered mess. Most examples of dashboards found on the Web present relatively little information, yet they still often manage to look cluttered and thrown together. The goal is not simply to make the dashboard look good, but to arrange the information in a manner that fits its use. The most important information should be prominent. Information that requires immediate attention should stand out. Data that should be compared should be arranged and visually designed to encourage comparisons.

The next dashboard illustrates some of the problems that are often associated with poor arrangement of data.

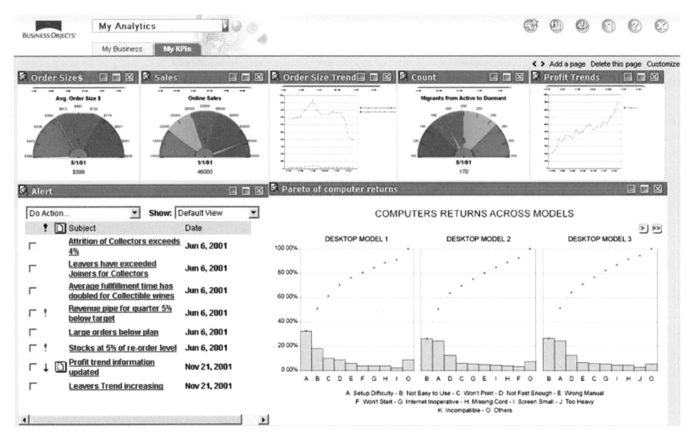

FIGURE 2.26. This dashboard exemplifies poorly arranged data.

Notice first of all that the most prominent region on this dashboard—the top left—is used to display the vendor's logo and navigational controls. What a waste of prime real estate! As we scan down the screen, the next information that we see is a gauge that presents the average order size. It's possible that average order size might be someone's primary interest, but it's unlikely that, of all the information that appears on this dashboard, this is the most important. To the right of the average order size graph appears one that features online sales, and to the right of that is a line graph that shows how the average order size changed through time leading up to the present. Why aren't the two graphs that feature average order size grouped together? The large amount of space taken up by the three graphs that present "Computers Returns Across Models" as well as the larger font sizes used in this section tend to draw attention to information that seems tangential to the rest. This dashboard lacks an appropriate visual sequence and balance based on the nature and importance of the data. Notice also that the bright red bands of color above each section of the dashboard, where the titles appear in white, are far more eye-catching than is necessary to state the meanings of the individual displays. This visually segments the space to an unnecessary degree. Lastly, note that the similarity of the line graphs that display order size and profit trends invites our eyes to compare them. This is probably a useful comparison, but the positional separation and side-by-side rather than over-under arrangement of the two graphs makes close comparison difficult. As this example illustrates, we can't just throw information onto the screen wherever we can make it fit and expect the dashboard to do its job effectively.

Highlighting Important Information Ineffectively or Not at All

When we look at a dashboard, our eyes should immediately be drawn to the information that is most important even when it does not reside in the most visually prominent areas of the screen. In Chapter 6: *Achieving Eloquence Through Simplicity*, we'll examine several visual techniques that can be used to achieve this end. For now, we'll look at what happens when this isn't done at all or isn't done well.

The problem with the next dashboard is that everything is visually prominent; consequently, nothing stands out.

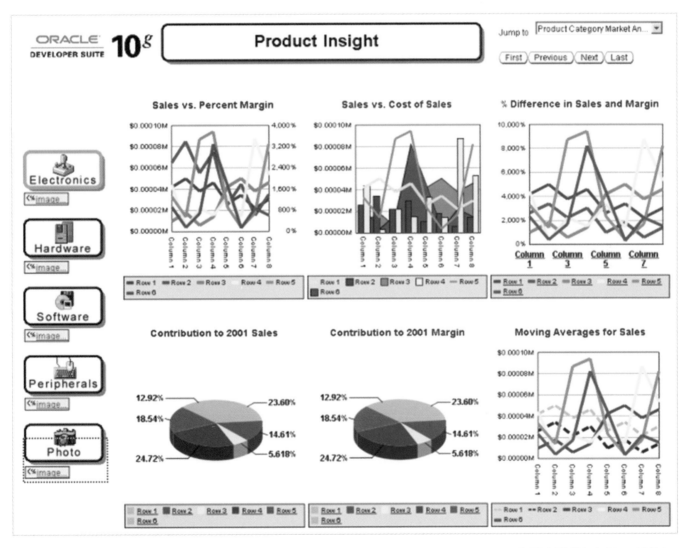

The logo and navigation controls (the buttons on the left) are prominent both as a result of their placement on the screen and the use of strong borders, but they are not data and therefore shouldn't be emphasized. In the graphs where the

FIGURE 2.27. This dashboard fails to differentiate data according to importance, giving relatively equal prominence to everything on the screen.

information resides, all of the information is equally bold and colorful, creating a wash of sameness and giving us no clue where to focus. Even the legends attract undue attention because they have a different background color than everything else. All of the information that deserves space on a dashboard is important, but not equally so; the viewer's eye should always be directed primarily to the most critical information. If everything on the dashboard shouts for attention, nothing will be heard.

Cluttering the Display with Visual Effects

Another common problem with dashboards is an abundance of useless embellishment. Developers of such dashboards must either hope that viewers will be drawn in by the artistry or assume that the decorative flourishes are necessary to entertain them. I assure you, however, that even people who enjoy the decoration on first sight will grow weary of it in a few days.

The developer of the next dashboard did an exceptional job of making it look like an electronic control panel. If its purpose were to train people in the use of some real equipment by means of a simulation, this would be great, but that isn't the purpose of a dashboard. The graphics that make the dashboard look like real equipment are pure decoration, visual content that the viewer must process to get to the data.

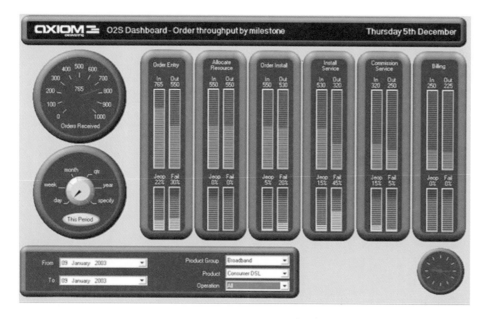

FIGURE 2.28. This dashboard is trying to look like something that it is not, by means of useless and distracting decoration.

I suspect that the following dashboard looked too plain, so its developer decided to make it look like a page in a spiral-bound notebook—cute, but a distracting waste of space.

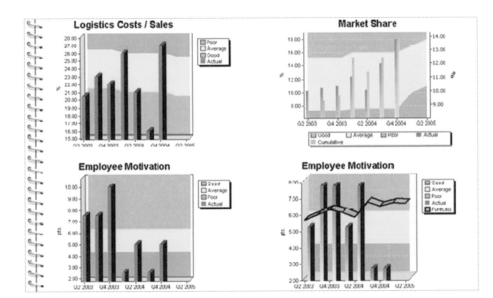

FIGURE 2.29. This dashboard is another example of useless decoration; the designer tried to make it look like a page in a spiral-bound notebook.

Likewise, I'd guess that the developer of the next dashboard—after creating a map, a bar graph, and a table that all display the same data—decided that the unused space should be filled up, so the developer went wild with an explosion of blue and gray circles. Blank space is better than meaningless decoration. Can you imagine yourself looking at this every day?

FIGURE 2.30. This dashboard is a vivid example of distracting ornamentation.

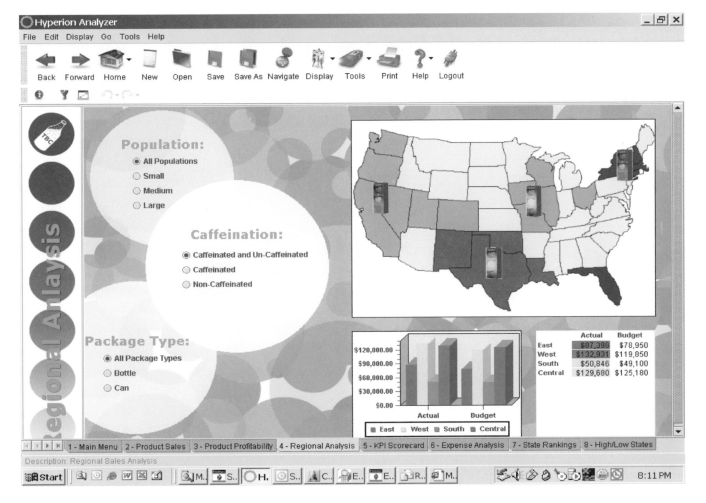

The final example in this section illustrates how a background image can distract from the data. The background image in this dashboard draws our eyes to areas that are empty of data and in some places also makes it difficult to focus on the data.

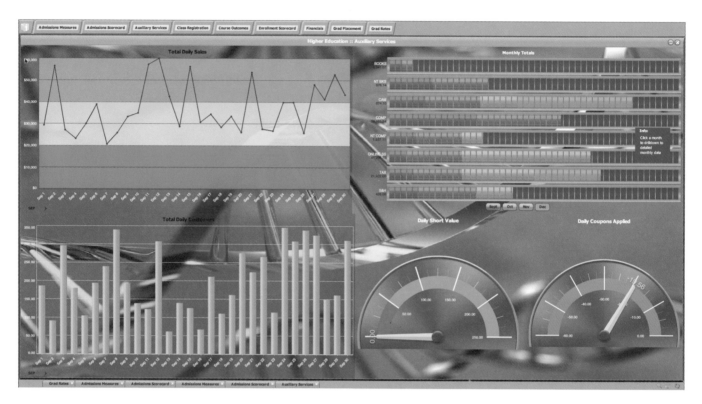

As data visualization pioneer Edward Tufte observes:

> *Inept graphics also flourish because many graphic artists believe that statistics are boring and tedious. It then follows that decorated graphics must pep up, animate, and all too often exaggerate what evidence there is in the data… If the statistics are boring, then you've got the wrong numbers.*

FIGURE 2.31. This dashboard includes a distracting background image.

Edward R. Tufte (1983). *The Visual Display of Quantitative Information.* Graphics Press, page 80.

Misusing or Overusing Color

We've already seen several examples of misused or overused color. The remaining point that I want to emphasize here is that color should not be used haphazardly.

We should make color choices thoughtfully, with an understanding of how people perceive color and the significance of color differences. Some colors are hot and demand our attention; others are cool and less salient. When any color appears as a contrast to the norm, our eyes pay attention to it, and our brains attempt to assign meaning to it. When colors in two different sections of a dashboard are the same, we are tempted to relate them to one another. We merrily assume that we can use colors such as red, yellow, and green to assign important meanings to data, but in doing so we exclude the ten percent of males and one-half a percent of females who are colorblind. In Chapter 5: *Tapping into the Power of Visual Perception*, we'll learn a bit about color and how it can be used meaningfully and powerfully.

Designing an Unattractive Visual Display

Not being one to mince words for the sake of propriety, I'll state quite directly that some dashboards are just plain ugly. When we see them, we're inclined to avert our eyes, which is hardly the desired reaction to a screen that's supposed to supply important information. You might have assumed from my earlier warning against unnecessary decoration that I have no concern for dashboard aesthetics, but that is not the case. When a dashboard is unattractive—unpleasant to look at—the viewer is put in a frame of mind that is not conducive to its use. I'm not arguing that we should add artistic touches to make dashboards pretty, but rather that we should display the information itself in attractive ways. (We'll examine the aesthetics of dashboard design a bit in Chapter 12: *Critical Design Practices*.)

The next example is an exceptionally good illustration of unattractive dashboard design. It appears that the person who created this dashboard attempted to make it look visually stunning but lacked the visual design skills needed to succeed. For instance, in an effort to fill up the space, some sections (such as the graph at the bottom right) were simply stretched. Also, although shades of gray can be used effectively as the background color of graphs, this particular shade is too dark. The image that appears under the excessively large title "Manufacturing" is clearly an attempt to redeem this dreary dashboard with a splash of decoration, but it only distracts from the data and isn't even particularly nice to look at. The guiding design principle of simplicity alone would have saved this dashboard from its current agony.

FIGURE 2.32. This is an example of a rather unattractive dashboard.

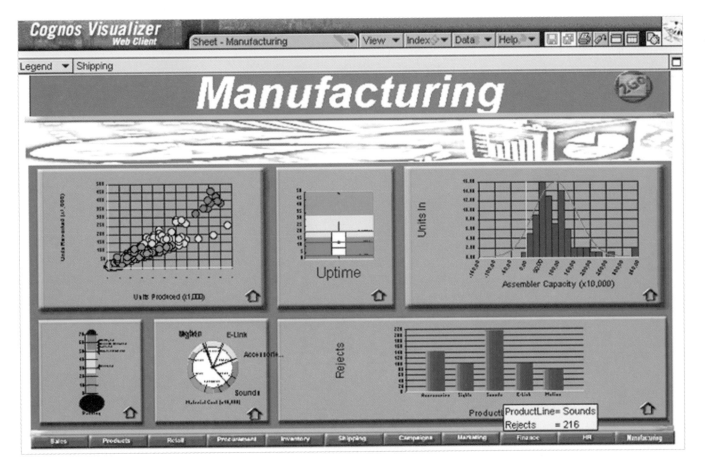

We don't need to be graphic artists to design an attractive dashboard, but we do need to understand a few basic principles about visual perception. We'll examine these in Chapter 12: *Critical Design Practices.*

Next, we'll consider ways to elicit from our clients exactly what they need in a dashboard.

3 ASSESSING WHAT'S NEEDED

It is often more challenging to assess what people truly need in a dashboard than it is to design a dashboard based on those needs. This is the case not just when developing dashboards, but when developing anything that involves human interaction with technology. Good dashboard designers must understand the relevant domain (sales, post-surgical infection prevention, classroom teaching, airplane manufacturing, etc.), and they must also know how to get into the heads of those who will use the dashboard. This requires empathy.

I won't attempt in this book to teach a comprehensive set of the skills that are needed to assess dashboard requirements. Instead, in this chapter I'll provide a few guidelines that are either unique to dashboards or especially important to dashboard effectiveness.

Begin with a Definition

When setting out to design a dashboard, we must, before anything else, clearly define the dashboard's purpose. People's understanding of what a dashboard is ranges widely. We need to make it clear to the dashboard's future users that it provides a means to rapidly monitor performance. It is not a report that they'll use to look up information from time to time. It is not a tool for exploring and analyzing data. It is an information display that will keep them aware of what's going on in their specific realm of concern. We need to help clients focus their thinking on information that measures performance. And we need to help them appreciate that, as a performance monitoring tool, the dashboard will need to be designed in particular ways, informed by perceptual and cognitive sciences, to communicate information clearly and efficiently to their eyes and brains. Once we've communicated these basic principles to them, we can then begin to meaningfully discuss their needs.

Focus on the Goals, Not on the Means

The last thing we want when trying to assess someone's dashboard requirements is to allow the discussion to wander into the realm of the dashboard's appearance. Most people have a dysfunctional set of expectations regarding dashboards. They expect dashboards that look and function like the examples they've seen. Unfortunately, most of the examples that appear in vendor product literature and on the Web are impoverished. People deserve better, but unless they've been exposed to well-designed dashboards, what they expect is not what they need. We need to keep them focused on what they hope to accomplish with the dashboard and to prepare them to welcome a dashboard that will keep them efficiently and richly informed—and that will likely end up looking quite different from what they expect.

To the enthusiastic request, "I want a bunch of bright traffic lights on my dashboard," we should respond, "If traffic lights will do the job best, then that's what you'll get, but for now let's figure out the information that's required to monitor what's going on." We must keep our clients focused on what they need to accomplish, not how it should be designed. They are the experts in what they must do to manage performance. We are the designers. The better we can help them to articulate their needs, the better we can design a monitoring solution that works.

Get into People's Heads

What we've learned over the course of our lives, from making a sandwich to calculating the trajectory of a rocket, are represented in our brains as *mental models* (also known as *conceptual models*). The better we understand something, the more detailed the mental model that represents it. The development of expertise involves constructing increasingly sophisticated and complex mental models.

People use dashboards to monitor a collection of information related to their work. Their understanding of their work exists as one or more mental models in their brains. A dashboard is used to update their awareness of what's going on, which refreshes those mental models. For this reason, a dashboard works best when it represents the information that's needed to update someone's mental model in a way that closely matches that mental model. For example, the guy who manages a particular manufacturing process has a mental model that includes each step in the process in a particular sequence. This model includes an understanding of how parts of the process relate to and affect one another and includes contingency measures that must be taken when problems occur. Because the process is sequential in nature—a series of steps that occur in a particular order—parts of the process are arranged in this manager's mental model to reflect that sequence. Consequently, a dashboard that arranges information in a way that mirrors this sequence will make it easier for the manager to assimilate the updated information that the dashboard displays into his mental model.

This means that, to design an effective dashboard, we must get into the clients' minds and examine the mental models for the activities that the dashboard will help them monitor. Yes, we must to some extent play the role of a psychologist to assess someone's dashboard requirements. Fortunately, this particular role doesn't need to be finely honed to get the job done.

One of the best ways that I know to elicit the elements and structure of a mental model is to work with the person to draw it. Simple drawings that include containers such as circles or rectangles to represent parts of the process and lines to connect parts that are related, perhaps with arrows to show direction, are usually all that's needed. As the model is emerging on paper or on a white board, ask questions such as "How does this relate to that?" and "If a problem occurs here, what does it affect and how?" The model might go through several revisions, reflecting the evolution and refinement of the client's description of the process that the dashboard will monitor.

Now, let's consider a real-world scenario that can complicate things. If you've worked with people to assess their requirements in the past, you have perhaps encountered people who don't possess good mental models or whose mental models have become so deeply ingrained, automatic, and intuitive that they struggle to consciously describe them. The lack of good mental models is common among novices, who simply haven't had enough experience to develop one. We can help these clients think through the parts and relationships of the processes that need monitoring to develop a simple model. The very act of thinking this through will deepen their expertise. The latter situation—someone who possesses a complex mental model and can no longer articulate it—can be handled by assuming the role of the novice sitting at the feet of the expert, helping her pull into focus each part of the model that she can no longer clearly see because it's become second nature. Asking her to teach us what she does in simple terms will help her coax to the surface what has settled deep into the underlying strata of her mind. Not only will we gain an understanding of her needs, but she will benefit as well by looking afresh at a model that was forged when she knew less than she does now.

By gaining an understanding of the client's mental model, we will be able to assess an important characteristic of that person: the degree of complexity that she can rapidly process. This should influence the way we design the dashboard. People vary significantly in the degree of complexity that they can quickly assimilate when viewing a dashboard. Experts with complex mental models can process a lot of information quickly if it's presented well. Novices in a particular job can process much less information at one time and therefore need simpler dashboards. We must get a sense of the amount and complexity of information that the client can handle, so we can design a dashboard that is neither overly packed and complex nor anemically scant and simplistic. People benefit most from dashboards that are well-matched to their abilities.

Ask the Right Questions

To some extent each assessment of a client's dashboard needs will lead us to ask different questions, but I've found that a few questions are useful in every case:

- How frequently should the information be updated?
- Who will use the dashboard? Is it for a single person, a single group, or people in several different departments?
- What will the dashboard be used to monitor, and what objectives will it support?
- What questions should the dashboard answer? What actions will be taken in response to these answers?

- What specific items of information should be displayed on the dashboard? What does each of these items tell you, and why is that important? At what level of summary or detail should the information be expressed to provide the quick overview that's needed?
- Which of these items of information are most important for achieving your objectives?
- What are the logical groupings that could be used to organize items of information on the dashboard? In which of these groups does each item belong?
- What are the useful comparisons that will allow you to see these items of information in meaningful context? For instance, if one of the measures that your dashboard displays is revenue, do you have targets or historical data that could also be displayed to make current revenue more meaningful?

This list of questions is not comprehensive. I generally begin with it, and, in every case, after I review the answers to these questions, other questions emerge that must be answered to gain the full understanding of the client's requirements that I need. Even later, during the dashboard design process itself, new questions will arise, so it's important to keep the dialog going. I've never had anyone complain when I continue to ask them questions that show that I'm thinking deeply about their needs.

Identify Information that Really Matters

We ask several of the questions in the list above to determine the items of information that must be monitored and to understand how that information will be used. A dashboard should only include information that actually influences performance. People are often accustomed to reports that include information that they never use for anything. Perhaps they used the information at one time in the past, but they haven't for years; even so, they're afraid to give it up. They will often ask for these items to appear on the dashboard. We should beware of this. Placing this information on the dashboard will steal space that could be used for information that actually matters, and it will waste people's time—not just once, but on every occasion the dashboard is used.

Here's a request that we can make to winnow out useless information: "Describe a situation when this information would lead you to do something." Perhaps follow it up with, "Give me an example of the actual data that would appear and the action that you would take in response." If no example comes to the person's mind, then this information doesn't belong on the dashboard. Dashboards aren't just for keeping up to date; they're for maintaining the awareness that's needed to prevent problems, take advantage of opportunities, and to take any other steps that will maintain good performance or improve it.

Identify Useful Context for Measures

One of the questions in the list above asked for useful comparisons that could be displayed along with measures to provide meaningful context. Measures—numbers—in and of themselves, are useless. They only come alive when compared to related values, such as targets, standards, measures of the norm, or past data. Without context, measures cannot be used to manage performance. I cannot stress this enough. Most of the dashboards that I've seen in my work suffer from this problem: they present information that will never inform action because the context that's needed is missing. Edward Tufte once wisely said that the fundamental question we should always ask when trying to make sense of numbers is "Compared to what?"

Edward Tufte (1990). *Envisioning Information*. Graphics Press, page 67.

Dashboards can support a broad spectrum of monitoring needs, spanning all tasks that benefit from an immediate overview of what's going on. To create a dashboard that does the job, we must consider from the outset a few characteristics of the tasks the dashboard must support, the information that informs those tasks, and the people who perform them, which will direct us to design the dashboard in particular ways.

The following six features of how dashboards will be used and by whom affect the way they should be designed:

Feature	Items
Update Frequency	Daily Hourly Real time
User Expertise	Novice Journeyman Expert
Audience Size	One person Multiple people with the same requirements Multiple people who need to monitor different data subsets
Technology Platform	Desktop/laptop Web server/browser Mobile device
Screen Type	Extra-large screen Standard screen Small screen Variable screens
Data Type	Quantitative Non-quantitative

Let's consider each feature in turn to understand the design choices that it determines.

Update Frequency

- Daily
- Hourly
- Real time

The frequency at which a dashboard's information is refreshed can have significant influence on the way it should be designed. One obvious difference is that if a dashboard is updated more often than daily, it must post the time of the latest update, so the viewer knows how recent the information is. Another less obvious example is that a dashboard that is refreshed in real time throughout the day must be simpler, containing less information, than one that is only updated daily. Why? Because the need for updating awareness over and over again throughout the day increases the need for speed, and there is a limit to the amount of information that people can take in at a glance.

Notice that the list does not include update frequencies less often than daily. Information displays that are accessed less often than daily don't qualify as dashboards because they're not being used to maintain situation awareness and therefore don't need to be monitored at a glance. They might be similar in design to a dashboard, but the reduced need for speed relaxes some design requirements. For example, a monthly report might be critically important, but it isn't something that the user reviews at a glance to rapidly update his awareness. He takes his time in reading it. Unlike with a dashboard, which he views every day, he doesn't become as intimately familiar with a monthly report's layout, and he doesn't really need to. Instructions for using a dashboard often don't need to be placed on the screen but can be kept in a separate document that can be easily accessed when needed because, once he's read them, he remembers them, so why have them cluttering the dashboard and robbing space that can be used for additional information? In contrast, a web page that the general public accesses every once in a while to catch up on current information must include instructions right there on the screen because people don't access it often enough to become familiar with its use. Most of what's taught in this book can be applied to other types of reports, but if a report is updated less often than daily, we won't call it a dashboard.

User Expertise

- Novice
- Journeyman
- Expert

One of the keys to successful communication of all types is often expressed as "know your audience." This is certainly true of the communication that dashboards support. Beyond the obvious, that we must know who our audience is before we can determine what should be displayed on a dashboard and how it should be displayed to most directly serve their needs, details about the audience influence the dashboard's design as well. One of these is the audience's level of expertise. As mentioned earlier, someone with a high level of expertise in a particular domain can handle a high degree of complexity in a data display, assuming that we don't introduce unnecessary complications through poor design. Someone who is new to the job can handle relatively little complexity, so, for the novice, the display must be simpler but can increase in complexity as he gains experience.

Audience Size

- One person
- Multiple people with the same requirements
- Multiple people who need to monitor data subsets

The more we can customize a dashboard to specifically meet the audience's needs, the more effective it will be. When we design a dashboard for an individual, we can customize it to fit that person's needs precisely. Designing a dashboard for a group of people is more challenging, even when they need to monitor the same information for the same purpose, because they themselves are different. For example, they might differ in expertise. In this case, we are forced to either design different versions of the dashboard for those with significantly different levels of expertise or to design a single dashboard that is compromised in its ability to work for some but better serves the needs of others. This challenge is increased when different people share the same basic monitoring requirements but are concerned with different subsets of data. For example, sales managers in different geographic regions might all share the same performance monitoring requirements, but each is only concerned with sales data for her particular area. When this is the case, a single dashboard might work, but each manager must have a means to view only her data. We wouldn't want to accommodate the need for data selection by populating the dashboard with filter controls, in part because it will waste valuable space on the screen and will force the manager to make a series of choices each time she views the dashboard. Ideally, intelligence should be built into the system to populate the dashboard with relevant data based on the identity of the manager who accesses it.

Technology Platform

- Desktop/laptop
- Web server/browser
- Mobile device

Three distinct technology platforms host dashboards today. The earliest examples ran on individual desktop or laptop computers, and the software that ran them also resided on those machines. This is still a viable platform today. As the platform of the Web matured to support rich displays and efficient performance, dashboard software emerged that was hosted on a server and viewed through Web browsers, to the delight of IT departments because it was easier to maintain and control and was often less expensive for large deployments. With the introduction of Apple's iPad in 2010, mobile devices became a viable platform for dashboards as well. Although the iPhone, introduced in 2007, preceded the iPad, the phone's small screen, no matter how highly resolved, provides insufficient space to support rich performance monitoring. With tablets, however, especially those with high-resolution screens, mobile displays became large and clear enough to support rich dashboards.

Each of these platforms is viable, but they vary in ways that demand differences in design. At this time, the greater maturity of the desktop/laptop platform still provides the best potential for rich dashboard development. Applications that run directly on individual computers with Windows, Mac OS, or other operating systems have the fewest constraints. Browser-based dashboards can offer many advantages, which often make them desirable, but developing applications for the Web can impose constraints, which is why products that come in both desktop and Web versions usually differ, with the latter offering less functionality and a less elegant interface. Dashboards that are viewed on tablet devices come in two basic flavors: those that run on the device's native operating system (for example, iOS on the iPad) and those that are viewed through a Web browser. Those that run in Web browsers share the same constraints of any Web-based application, but to this is added the unique benefits (sometimes limitations) of the tablet interface—chiefly, input via touch. The advantage is that the dashboard can be viewed on any device that can access the Web. Dashboards that run using the native operating system of a particular tablet device are usually limited to that device only, which is a considerable constraint in organizations that use diverse devices. Whether the dashboard is Web-based or runs natively on a tablet device, it has to meet particular demands imposed by touch interfaces if interaction is required. Fortunately, a true monitoring display requires relatively little interaction, but one action that is particularly useful—selecting a specific item, such as a point along a line in a line graph, to view more information—is difficult to do with the fat tip of a finger. The act of hovering, which on non-touch platforms can cause information to appear in a small tooltip window, is not available in touch platforms. Software vendors can overcome these difficulties with thoughtful design, but few have managed to do this so far.

Screen Type

- Extra-large screen
- Standard screen
- Small screen
- Various screens

The type of screen on which a dashboard will be viewed has significant impact on the way the dashboard should be designed. For our purpose, screens can be broken into categories based on four characteristics: size, viewing distance, aspect ratio (the ratio of the screen's width and height), and resolution. Let's look at the four characteristics that define screen type first, and then we'll consider the individual types.

Dashboard screens vary significantly in size, ranging from large wall-mounted displays measured in feet rather than inches to small tablet devices. Although size matters, it is not true that bigger is necessarily better, at least not beyond a certain point. No matter how large a screen is, there is only so much of it that we can see at any one moment. Because of how our eyes work, we must think of the viewable space in terms of angle, not size. If we look straight ahead, hold our arms out to our sides, and wiggle our fingers, we might be able to barely notice our fingers moving. We perceive motion in the periphery of vision better than static objects. This 180° angle of vision, however, is far greater than the angle on which we can view the content of a dashboard. Only a fairly small angle at the center of our gaze can be seen clearly because only a small section of densely packed receptors in an area of the retina called the fovea is designed for focused sight. A slightly larger section of receptors is useful for the kinds of viewing tasks that we typically do when looking at dashboards: the parafovea, which spans an angle of six degrees only, centered on the fovea. When a screen is positioned 57 centimeters (approximately 22.5 inches) from your face (the typical distance between our eyes and a desktop screen), the parafovea can see with adequate clarity a space approximately 6 centimeters (2.36 inches) wide. This is less than one-fifth the width of my 15-inch laptop screen. This doesn't mean that we can't benefit from larger screens; however, we can't view any more than this at any one moment with the level of clarity that is needed for reading text and viewing graphs. To view more, we must shift our focus back and forth, which we can do to a certain degree without moving our heads and to greater degree by moving them, but movement takes time. To see everything, we would need to sit much farther away, but the increase in distance would require screen content to be larger; otherwise, it would be too small to discern. This leads to our next consideration regarding the screen: viewing distance.

According to Colin Ware, a good rule of thumb for estimating the width of the viewing area when looking at a display that is approximately 57 centimeters away is that 1 degree of angle roughly equals 1 centimeter of width.

With a flat screen (that is, one that doesn't wrap around your head such that it is always at the same distance from your eyes when you turn your head to the right or left), the distance from your eyes to objects on the screen increases when you look to the left or right rather than directly ahead. This means that, when we design dashboards for a flat screen, there's a practical limit to their useful size. A 60-inch screen would greatly exceed what's practical if you're sitting only 22.5 inches from it.

FIGURE 4.1. A large display wall designed by Mechdyne for BP

The primary point we must keep in mind about the distance between a person's eyes and a dashboard is that greater distances force us to make things larger, which means that designing for a large screen does not necessarily mean that we can place more content on the dashboard. In fact, it often means the opposite. For instance, imagine a large wall-mounted screen that is positioned where all members of a telesales group can see it to keep in touch with the team's performance. Text and graphs must be large enough for the person who sits farthest from the screen to discern them. This means that we'll be forced to make everything so large that the total amount of content will be less than we could fit on screens that sit on each person's desktop. Clients should keep this in mind before investing in one of those huge, expensive screens or a large array of screens that fills an entire wall.

The aspect ratio of a screen (that is, the ratio of the screen's width to its height, such as 4:3) must also be considered when designing a dashboard. We ideally want to take full advantage of the available screen space, so if the person using the dashboard has a widescreen display, we should design for that.

The final screen characteristic that we'll consider is resolution (the number of pixels per inch), which is becoming less of a concern as screens improve. The screen that I'm using as I type these words packs in 220.5 pixels per inch. Ideally, we can check the resolution of the screen that will be used for viewing a particular dashboard and design for that, making sure that everything can be seen crisply and cleanly. We rarely live in this ideal world, however, so we must sometimes design for multiple resolutions.

The screen types that I've described oversimplify the possibilities that we encounter. We've already considered how screen sizes, distance, aspect ratio, and resolution affect design. What's worth further consideration is the complexity of real-world dashboard development when multiple people with screens of various types will use them. I wish I had a simple solution to this challenge, but I don't. In the real world we are sometimes forced to make compromises. Therefore, we should determine the degree to which we're willing to sacrifice effective design to accommodate diversity in screen types. If the diversity that we face on a particular project forces a level of sacrifice that exceeds our limit on compromise, then we must either change our standards or develop more than one version of the dashboard.

Data Type

- Quantitative
- Non-quantitative

Dashboards are useful for work of many types. A well-designed dashboard can serve anyone from a meteorologist monitoring the weather to an intelligence analyst monitoring terrorist chatter, a CEO monitoring the performance and opportunities of a multi-billion dollar corporation, a financial analyst monitoring the stock market, a medical doctor monitoring the health of a patient, or a teacher monitoring the progress of her students. Because of the nature of monitoring, most of the information that fills a dashboard is quantitative; that is, it measures what's happening. There are exceptions, however, especially when people must monitor the status of activities and events.

Quantitative Data

Despite their diverse applications, dashboards in most cases primarily display quantitative measures of what's currently going on. Dashboards are used to monitor the critical information needed to do a job or meet one or more particular objectives, and most of the information that does this best is quantitative.

The following table lists several typical measures of "what's currently going on":

Category	Measures
Sales	Bookings Billings Pipeline (anticipated sales) Number of orders Order amounts Selling prices
Marketing	Market share Campaign success Customer demographics
Finance	Revenues Expenses Profits
Technical Support	Number of support calls Resolved cases Customer satisfaction Call durations
Fulfillment	Number of days to ship Backlog Inventory levels
Manufacturing	Number of units manufactured Manufacturing times Number of defects
Human Resources	Employee satisfaction Employee turnover Count of open positions Count of late performance reviews
Information Technology	Network downtime System usage Fixed application bugs
Web Services	Number of visitors Number of page hits Visit durations
Training	Number of students Learning outcomes Course ratings
Consulting	Number of projects Employee utilization Share of revenues

These measures are usually expressed in summary form, typically as totals, counts, rates (such as rate of return), or averages (such as average selling price). Summary expressions of quantitative data are particularly useful because dashboards are used to monitor an array of data at a glance. The limited real estate of a single screen requires concise communication of the type that summaries provide.

VARIATIONS IN TIMING

Measures of what's currently going on can be expressed in a variety of time frames. A few typical examples include:

- This year to date
- This quarter to date
- This month to date
- This week to date
- Yesterday
- Today so far

The appropriate time frame is determined by the nature of the objectives that the dashboard supports. If the viewer needs to respond immediately when things go wrong, she'd better be monitoring information that's being updated in real time throughout the day. If she must respond today to significant changes that occurred yesterday, then daily aggregates are necessary. If activity varies significantly from day to day and the patterns of longer periods of time, such as weeks or months, are more meaningful, then week-to-date or month-to-date summaries, along with several weeks or months of historical context, would make more sense.

ENRICHMENT THROUGH COMPARISON

To be meaningful and useful, measures must be understood in context, which comes primarily in the form of comparisons. Here are perhaps the most typical comparative measures.

Comparative Measure	Example
The same measure at the same point in time in the past	The same day last year
The same measure at some other point in time in the past	The end of last year
The current target for the measure	A budgeted amount for the current period
Relationship to a future target	Percentage of this year's budget so far
A prior prediction of the measure	Forecast of where we expected to be today
Relationship to a future prediction of the measure	Percentage of this quarter's forecast
Some expression of the norm for this measure	Average, typical range, or a benchmark, such as the number of days it usually takes to ship an order

Comparative Measure	Example
An extrapolation of the current measure in the form of a probable future, either at a specific point in the future or as a time series	Projection into the future, such as to the coming year end
Someone else's values for the same measure	A competitor's measure, such as revenues
A separate but related measure	Order count compared to order revenue

These comparisons can be expressed graphically to clearly communicate the differences between the values, which might not leap out as dramatically when expressed only as text. However, text alone is sometimes adequate, especially when the value is a rate or percentage that contains a built-in comparison. For example, 119% of budget, 7% below performance on this day last year, or 36% of sales all express comparisons in and of themselves.

Measures of what's currently going on might be displayed either as a single measure combined with one or more comparative measures, or with one of the following:

- Multiple instances of a measure, each representing a categorical subdivision of the whole (for example, sales subdivided into regions or a count of orders subdivided into numeric ranges in the form of a frequency distribution)
- Temporal instances of a measure (that is, a time series, such as monthly instances of the measure)

Time series, in particular, offer rich context for understanding what's really going on and how well it's going.

Whenever we display a measure on a dashboard, we must make sure that the context that is required to determine how well things are going is right there with it. We should test this with those who will use the dashboard to confirm that enough context and the right context has been provided. To do so, we can ask the question, "In looking at this information, can you tell me how well what you're monitoring is performing?" We can follow this question up in various ways to confirm whether we have provided the needed context:

- "Do you see anything abnormal?"
- "Are the relative magnitudes of these measures (for example, sales revenues among several regions) what you would expect?"
- If everything is judged as fine, ask: "Can you describe what might be different that would cause you to think that something's abnormal or wrong?"
- If something is judged as good (or bad), ask: "What is it that tells you that it's good (or bad)?" "How good (or bad) is it?" "Is it getting better or worse?"

If inquiries such as these suggest that adequate context is missing, we can brainstorm a little, to imagine what could be added to bring the measures alive.

ENRICHMENT THROUGH EVALUATION

Because a great many facts must be evaluated quickly when someone is viewing a dashboard, it is also useful at times to explicitly declare whether something is good or bad based on defined criteria. Such evaluative or qualitative information is often encoded in the form of special visual objects (for example, a traffic light) or as visual attributes (for example, by displaying the measure in bright red to indicate a serious condition). When designed properly, simple visual indicators can effectively alert users to the state of particular measures without altering the overall design of the dashboard. Evaluative indicators need not be limited to binary distinctions between good and bad, but if indicators exceed the limit of more than a few distinct states (for example, very bad, bad, acceptable, good, and very good), they'll become too complex to be perceived efficiently.

People often think of dashboards and key performance indicators (KPIs) as essentially connected. It is certainly true that dashboards are a powerful medium for presenting KPIs, but not all quantitative information that might be useful on a dashboard belongs to a list of defined KPIs. In fact, not all information that is useful on dashboards is even quantitative; the critical information needed to do a job cannot always be expressed numerically.

ANTICIPATION THROUGH PREDICTION

We cannot drive a car by looking only in the rearview mirror. What's behind us—the past—is most informative when it can help us anticipate the future. Performance management is most effective when we're able to prevent bad things from happening and improve opportunities for good things to occur. So we look for ways to develop good predictive models based on historical data and an understanding of probability. If we lack the statistical training that's required to build reliable predictive models, we must ask for help. We should not trust naïve models, which are worse than none at all. For example, we can't merely extend time-series values on a line graph into the future in the same general direction that it's been going in the past and expect people to rely on that for good decisions. When good predictions can be built, we should incorporate them into the dashboard. We should encourage the use of dashboards for shaping the future.

Non-Quantitative Data

Although most information that typically finds its way onto a dashboard is quantitative, some types of non-quantitative data, such as simple lists, are not unusual. Here are a few examples:

- Top 10 customers
- Issues that need to be investigated
- People who need to be contacted

Other non-quantitative information occasionally found on dashboards relates to schedules; examples are tasks, due dates, the people responsible, and similar information. These types of data are commonly used when the dashboard supports people who manage projects or processes.

We've now covered some of the preliminaries, but we're not quire ready to focus on designing dashboards. First, we must consider two more characteristics of our audience that varies little from person to person, but influences the design of dashboards more than all other characteristics combined: how people see and think.

5   TAPPING INTO THE POWER
OF VISUAL PERCEPTION

Vision is by far our most powerful sense. Seeing and thinking are intimately connected. To display data effectively, we must understand a bit about visual perception, gleaning from the available body of scientific research the findings that can be applied directly to dashboard design: what works, what doesn't, and why.

It isn't accidental that when we begin to understand something we say, "I see." Not "I hear" or "I smell," but "I see." Vision dominates our sensory landscape. As a sensophile, I cherish the rich abundance of sounds, smells, tastes, and textures that inhabit our world, but I experience the richest volume, bandwidth, and nuance of information through vision. This isn't a matter of preference; it is built into the structure of our brains. Even though my natural style of thinking is more verbal than visual, 50% of my brain's resources, and yours as well, support visual processing. Approximately 70% of the sense receptors in our bodies are dedicated to vision. How we see is closely tied to how we think.

I've learned about visual perception from many sources, but Colin Ware's books stand out above the others in their applicability to information visualization. Ware expresses beautifully the importance of studying visual perception:

> *Why should we be interested in visualization? Because the human visual system is a pattern seeker of enormous power and subtlety. The eye and the visual cortex of the brain form a massively parallel processor that provides the highest-bandwidth channel into human cognitive centers. At higher levels of processing, perception and cognition are closely interrelated… However, the visual system has its own rules. We can easily see patterns presented in certain ways, but if they are presented in other ways, they become invisible… The more general point is that when data is presented in certain ways, the patterns can be readily perceived. If we can understand how perception works, our knowledge can be translated into rules for displaying information. Following perception-based rules, we can present our data in such a way that the important and informative patterns stand out. If we disobey the rules, our data will be incomprehensible or misleading.*

Colin Ware (2012). *Information Visualization: Perception for Design*, Third Edition. Morgan Kauffman, page xxi.

For our current purpose—to develop expert skills in dashboard design—we'll focus on the following aspects of visual perception:

- The limits of working memory
- Encoding data for rapid perception
- Gestalt principles of visual perception

Each of these topics offers useful insights that can be applied directly to dashboard design.

The Limits of Working Memory

In truth, we don't see with our eyes; we see with our brains. Our eyes are the sensory mechanisms through which light enters and is sensed and then translated into electro-chemical information that is passed on to our brains. It is in our brains that perception—the process of interpreting what our eyes register— actually occurs.

Our eyes do not sense everything that is visible in the world around us. Only a portion of what our eyes take in becomes an object of focus, and only through focus does what we see become more than a vague sense. Further, only a fraction of what we focus on becomes the object of attention, and only a portion of that is further processed as conscious thought. Finally, only a little bit of what we attend to gets stored in memory for future use. Without these limits and filters, what we perceive would overwhelm us.

Our memories store information starting the moment we see something, continuing as we consciously process the information, and potentially accumulating over years in a permanent (or nearly permanent) storage area where information remains ready for use if ever needed again—that is, until access to that information eventually begins to atrophy.

Memory comes in three fundamental types:

- Iconic memory
- Working memory
- Long-term memory

Iconic memory (also known as the sensory register) is a lot like the keyboard memory buffer of a computer: a place where input is briefly held until it can be moved into random access memory (RAM), where it resides while being processed by the CPU. A preconscious form of information processing known as *preattentive processing* occurs at this early stage. Certain attributes of what we see are recognized during preattentive processing at an extraordinarily high speed, which results in certain objects and their attributes standing out, and particular sets of objects being grouped together, all without conscious thought. Preattentive processing plays a powerful role in visual perception, and we can intentionally design our dashboards to take advantage of this function if we understand a bit about it.

Working memory is where information resides during conscious processing. Information remains in working memory from a few seconds to as long as a few hours if periodically rehearsed; then it is wiped. If rehearsed in a particular way, information is moved from working memory to long-term memory where it is stored more permanently for later recall. When information is recalled from long-term memory, it is temporarily moved once again into working memory where it is consciously processed.

When we design dashboards, we need to be particularly concerned with working memory. Three important facts to know about working memory are:

- It is temporary.
- A portion of it is dedicated to visual information.
- It has limited capacity.

We can only store up to three or four chunks of visual information at a time in working memory. When that capacity is full, something has to either be moved out into long-term memory or removed altogether (forgotten) for something new to be brought into working memory. What constitutes a "chunk" of visual information varies depending on the nature of the objects we are seeing, aspects of their design, and our familiarity with them. For instance, individual numbers on a dashboard are stored as one or more discrete chunks, depending on the size of the number, but a well-designed graphical pattern, such as the pattern formed by a line in a line graph, can represent several numeric values as a single chunk. This is one of the great advantages of graphs (when used appropriately and skillfully designed) compared to text. Dashboards should be designed in a way that supports optimal chunking together of information so that it can be perceived and understood efficiently, in big visual gulps.

The limited capacity of working memory is also the reason why information that belongs together should never be fragmented into multiple dashboards, and scrolling shouldn't be required to see it all. Once the information is no longer visible, unless it is one of the few chunks stored in working memory, it is no longer available. If the viewer must scroll or page back to see it again, he'll lose access to the information that he was previously viewing. As long as everything he needs remains within eye span on a single dashboard, however, he can rapidly exchange information in and out of working memory at lightning speed.

Encoding Data for Rapid Perception

The difference between what preattentive and attentive processing do is easy to demonstrate. Take a moment to examine the four rows of numbers in following figure and try to determine as quickly as you can the number of times the number five appears in the list.

98734979027564790289472862409240603707057027907208320802900730250127023700837408207872027200708324780260270379377570970737797066746209709470278092797970972309723097959275092727979873497260802

FIGURE 5.1. How many fives are in this list? Note the slow speed at which we take in visual stimuli that must be processed sequentially, in this case one number at a time.

How many did you find? The correct answer is six. Whether you got the answer right or not, the process took you a while because it involved sequential attentive processing. The fives did not exhibit any preattentive attributes that could be used to distinguish them from the other numbers. Now try it again, this time using the list of numbers on the next page.

9873497902756479028947286240924060370705702790072
8032080290073025012702370083740820787202720207083
24780260270379377570970737797066746209709470702780
92797970972309723097959275092727979873497260802027

FIGURE 5.2. How many fives do you see now? Note the fast speed at which we process preattentive visual stimuli, in this case greater color intensity.

Much easier this time, wasn't it? In this figure the fives could easily be distinguished from the other numbers because of their greater color intensity (one of the preattentive attributes we'll discuss below): the fives are black, and all the other numbers are gray, which causes the fives to stand out in clear contrast. Why couldn't we easily distinguish the fives in the first set of numbers (Figure 5.1) based purely on their unique shape? Because the complex shapes of the numbers are not attributes that we perceive preattentively. Simple shapes such as circles and squares are distinguishable when we are processing information preattentively, but the shapes of numbers are too elaborate.

In *Information Visualization: Perception for Design*, Colin Ware describes 17 preattentive attributes of visual perception and suggests that they can be organized into four categories: color, form, spatial position, and motion. For our current topic, dashboard design, I've reduced his larger list of preattentive attributes to the following 11:

Category	Attribute	Illustration
Color	Hue	
	Intensity	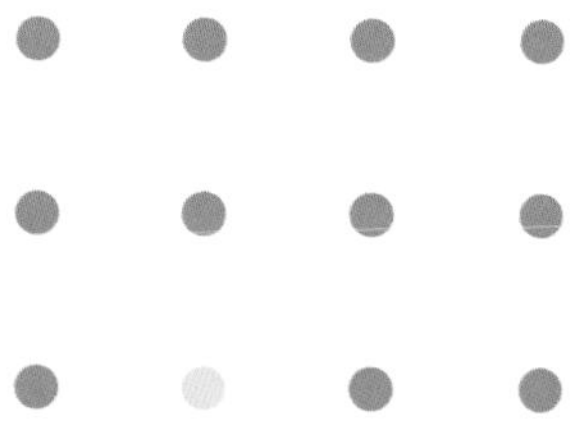
Form	Line length	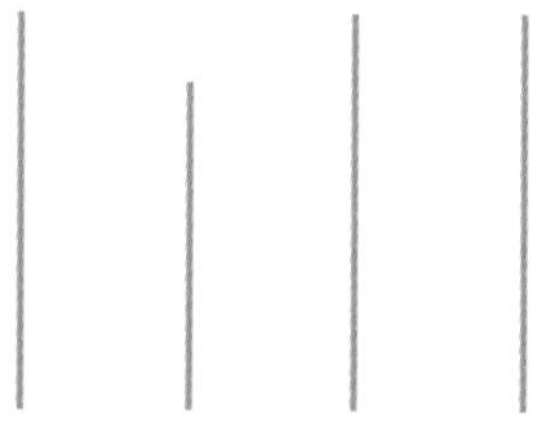
	Line width	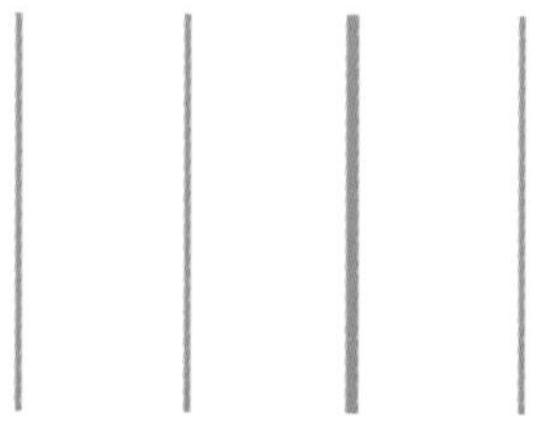

Category	Attribute	Illustration
Form *(continued)*	Orientation	
	Size	
	Shape	
	Added marks	
	Enclosure	
Position	2-D location	
Motion	Flicker	A visual attribute of an object, such as color, that continuously changes back and forth between two values, or the entire object itself repeatedly appears and then disappears

Each of these visual attributes can be consciously applied to dashboard design to group or highlight information. Some can also be used to encode quantitative information, as we'll see below.

Attributes of Color

A common way to describe color combines three attributes: hue, saturation, and lightness/brightness. This is sometimes referred to as the HSL or HSB system of describing color. *Hue* is a more precise term for what we normally think of as color (red, green, blue, purple, etc.). *Saturation* measures the degree to which a particular hue exhibits its full, pure essence. The saturation of the red hue below ranges from 0% saturation on the left to 100% saturation on the right.

FIGURE 5.3. The full range of color saturation, in this case of the hue red, with 0% saturation on the left and 100% saturation on the right

Lightness (or brightness) measures the degree to which any hue appears dark or light, ranging from fully dark (black) to fully light (white). The full range of lightness is shown for the red hue below.

FIGURE 5.4. The full range of color lightness, in this case of the hue red, with 0% lightness on the left (black) and 100% lightness on the right (pure red)

I'm using the term *intensity* in reference to both saturation and lightness together. In the example below, one of the circles differs from the others, not by hue but as a lighter version of the same hue; the light red circle is the same hue as dark red, just a less intense version. Both are different points along a continuum that ranges from fully light to fully dark.

FIGURE 5.5. Each of these circles is red. They vary not by hue but by intensity.

It isn't necessary to completely understand the technical distinction between saturation and lightness, so we'll refer to them both simply as intensity.

One of the interesting (but hardly intuitive) things about color is that we don't perceive it in an absolute way. What we see is dramatically influenced by the context that surrounds it. Take a look at the gray squares in the figure below. They appear to vary in intensity, but in fact they are all exactly the same as the lone square that appears against the white background in the row underneath.

FIGURE 5.6. Context affects our perception of color intensity. All of the small squares are actually the exact same shade of gray though they appear different because of the different background.

All five squares have a color value of 50% black, yet the surrounding grayscale gradient, ranging from light on the left to dark on the right, alters our perception of the squares. This perceptual illusion applies not only to intensity, but also to hue. In the next figure, the word "Text" appears against three backgrounds: blue, white, and red. In all cases, the color of the word "Text" is the same. However, it not only looks different in all three cases, but it's also much less visible against the red background.

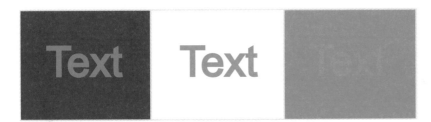

FIGURE 5.7. Context also affects our perception of hue. The word "Text" is exactly the same hue in all three cases.

We must use color with a full awareness of context. We not only want information to be fully legible, but also to appear the same when sameness will best communicate, and to appear different when difference will best communicate.

Attributes of Form

Some visual attributes of form have no obvious connection to dashboard design, but their relevance should become clear with a little explanation. *Line length* is especially useful for encoding quantitative values as bars in a bar graph. *Line width*, in contrast, can be useful for highlighting. Think of line width as the thickness or stroke weight of a line. When lines are used to underscore content or, in the form of boxes, to form borders around content, we can draw more attention to that content by increasing the thickness of the lines.

The most common application of *orientation* is in the form of italicized text, which is reoriented from straight up and down to a slight slant to the right. Orientation can also be used to encode quantitative values, such as the orientation of a pointer (needle) in a fuel gauge (see below) although a better alternative than a gauge like this is almost always available on an information dashboard.

FIGURE 5.8. Fuel gauges on car dashboards display the amount of gasoline in the tank, using the orientation of the needle in relation to a quantitative scale ranging from "empty" to "full."

The relative *sizes* of objects that appear on a dashboard can be used to visually rank importance. For instance, larger titles, tables, graphs, or icons can be used to signal the greater importance of the associated data. Simple *shapes* can be used in graphs to differentiate data sets and, in the form of icons, to assign distinct meanings, such as different types of alerts. *Added marks* are most useful on dashboards in the form of simple icons that appear next to items that need attention. Any simple mark (such as a circle, a square, an asterisk, or an X), if placed next to information only when that information must be highlighted, works to draw attention. Last on the list of form attributes is *enclosure*, which is a powerful means of grouping sections of data or, when used sparingly, of highlighting content as important. To create the visual effect of enclosure, we can use either a border around or a fill color behind the content.

Attributes of Position

The preattentive attribute of *2-D position* is the primary means that we use to encode quantitative data in graphs (for example, the position of data points in relation to a quantitative scale). The primacy of this strategy isn't arbitrary. Of all the preattentive attributes, differences in 2-D position are the most easily and accurately perceived.

Attributes of Motion

As I type these words, I am aware of my cursor flickering on and off on the screen. Flicker was chosen as the means to help us locate the cursor because something rapidly and repeatedly appearing and disappearing is a powerful attention-getter. Evolution has equipped us with a heightened sensitivity to something that suddenly appears within our field of vision. Our ancient ancestors found it very valuable to become instantly alert when a saber-toothed tiger suddenly sprang into their peripheral vision. As most of us are aware, flickering objects on a screen can be quite annoying and thus should usually be avoided. Still, there are occasions when flicker is useful. This is especially true for dashboards that are constantly updated with real-time information and are used to monitor operations that require immediate responses.

Encoding Quantitative Versus Categorical Data

Some of the preattentive attributes that we examined above can be used to communicate quantitative data, but others can be used only to communicate categorical data. That is, some attributes allow us to perceive one thing as greater than others in some way (bigger, taller, more important), and others merely indicate that items are distinct from one another without any sense of quantitative difference. For example, different shapes can be perceived as distinct, but only categorically: squares are not greater than triangles or circles; they're just different. The following table lists each of the preattentive attributes again and indicates which are perceived quantitatively:

Category	Attribute	Quantitative
Color	Hue	No
	Intensity	Yes, but with little precision

Perhaps it stands out that I've specified "2-D" position—an object's location relative to the vertical and horizontal dimensions only—and have ignored 3-D position, also known as *stereoscopic position*. 3-D position is also a preattentive attribute, but it is less powerful than most others, especially when simulated by the pseudo-3-D effects that can be produced on the flat surface of a computer screen. Because, as noted earlier in the book, 3-D elements are so rarely useful for representing quantitative information, I recommend avoiding them altogether.

Category	Attribute	Quantitative
Form	Line length	Yes
	Line width	Yes, but with little precision
	Orientation	Yes, but only when displayed in the context of a quantitative scale
	Size	Yes, but with little precision
	Shape	No
	Added marks	No
	Enclosure	No
Position	2-D position	Yes
Motion	Flicker	Yes, based on speed, but with little precision

We can use the attributes qualified above as "Yes, but with little precision" when only an approximate sense of differences is needed. For example, in the figure below, it's obvious that the circle on the right is bigger than the circle on the left, but how much bigger? If the small circle has a size of one, what is the size of the bigger circle?

There is no natural association of greater or lesser value with different orientations. For example, which is greater, a vertical or horizontal line? We perceive orientation quantitatively only when we associate it with a quantitative scale.

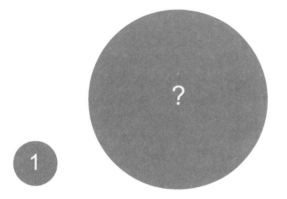

FIGURE 5.9. This figure illustrates our inability to assign precise quantitative values to objects of different sizes.

The correct answer is 16, but it's likely that you guessed a lower number. We tend to underestimate differences in 2-D areas, so we must be wary of using areas of different sizes to encode quantitative values, especially on a dashboard, where speed of perception is essential.

It is important to understand the different ways that the preattentive attributes can be used to group and encode data, but by splitting them into quantitative and categorical classes, I do not mean to imply that only attributes that enable viewers to make quantitative comparisons are of use to dashboard designers. Our inability to perceive certain preattentive attributes quantitatively does not render those attributes useless on dashboards. Each can be used to divide data into distinct categories, to visually link items together even when they are separated spatially, and to highlight data.

Limits to Perceptual Distinctness

When designing dashboards, we must bear in mind that there is a limit to the number of distinct expressions of a single preattentive attribute that viewers can quickly and easily distinguish. For example, when using varying grayscale intensities to distinguish data sets in a line graph, we must make sure that the color of each line is different enough to stand out clearly as distinct. When we vary lines in a line graph by color intensity, if we want the lines to be easily distinguishable, we're limited to about five lines of different intensities. In the next figure, we can see that it would be difficult to include more gray lines that would stand out as distinct without requiring careful, conscious, and thus slow examination on the part of the viewer.

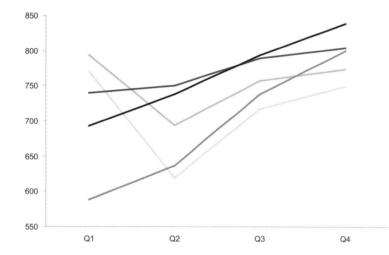

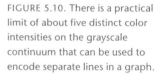

FIGURE 5.10. There is a practical limit of about five distinct color intensities on the grayscale continuum that can be used to encode separate lines in a graph.

Similar limits apply to every one of the preattentive attributes except line length (such as the length of a bar on a graph) and 2-D location (such as the location of a data point on a graph). When organizing data into distinct groups using different expressions of any preattentive attribute, we should be careful not to exceed five distinct expressions. When using the shape attribute, in addition to this limit, we must also be careful to choose shapes that are simple, such as circles, squares, triangles, dashes, and crosses (or X's) because complex shapes, including most icons, are not perceived preattentively. When using hue, we must keep in mind that even though viewers can easily distinguish more than five hues, working memory can't simultaneously retain the meaning of more than three or four. Also, the use of too many hues results in a dashboard that looks cluttered and is visually taxing because it has too many distinctions for the viewer to be able to sort quickly. When designing dashboards, it helps to prepare standard sets of hues, color intensities, shapes, and so on, and then stick to them. This will keep the display perceptually simple and will eliminate the need to select visual attributes from scratch each time one is required.

Using Vivid vs. Soft Colors Appropriately

Color is so often misused in dashboard design that I'm compelled to emphasize one more relevant principle: some colors are soothing, and some take hold of us and shake us up. Knowing the difference is important. There are times that particular information needs to grab the viewer's attention in an unavoidable way, but using color for this purpose works only if it's done sparingly. We should reserve the use of bright, fully saturated colors for these special cases. Colors that are common in nature, such as soft grays, browns, oranges, greens, and blues, work very well as a standard color palette for dashboards. They allow the viewer to peruse the dashboard calmly with an open mind, rather than stressfully, with pinpoint attention in response to assaulting colors. The following figure displays examples of soft and bold color palettes.

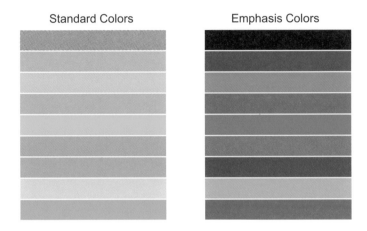

FIGURE 5.11. Examples of two color palettes: one for standard use and one for emphasizing data

Gestalt Principles of Visual Perception

Back in 1912, the Gestalt school of psychology began its efforts to understand how we perceive pattern, form, and organization in what we see. The German term "gestalt" simply means "pattern." The Gestalt researchers recognized that we organize what we see in particular ways to make sense of it. Their work resulted in a collection of Gestalt principles of perception that reveal the visual characteristics that incline us to group objects together. These principles of visual perception are still respected today and offer several useful insights that we can apply directly in our dashboard designs to intentionally tie data together, separate data, or make some data stand out as distinct from the rest.

We'll examine the following six Gestalt principles:

- Proximity
- Similarity
- Enclosure
- Closure
- Continuity
- Connection

The Principle of Proximity

We perceive objects that are located near one another as belonging to the same group. The figure on the next page clearly illustrates this principle. Based on their relative locations, we automatically see the dots as belonging to three separate groups. This is the simplest way to link data that we want viewers to perceive together on a dashboard. White space alone is usually all we need to separate groups from the other information that surrounds them.

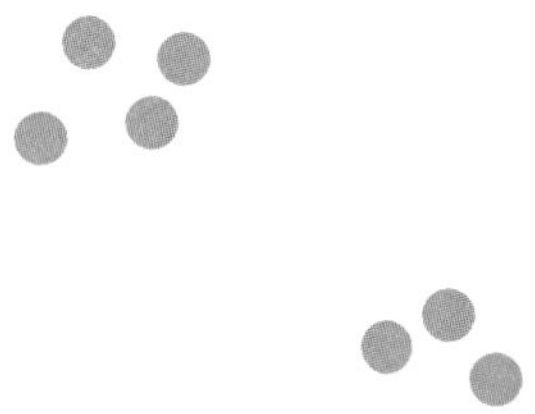

FIGURE 5.12. The Gestalt principle of proximity explains why we see three groups instead of just ten dots in this image.

The principle of proximity can also be used to direct viewers to scan data on a dashboard predominantly in a particular direction: either left to right or top to bottom. Placing sections of data closer together horizontally encourages viewers' eyes to group the sections horizontally and thus to scan from left to right. Placing sections of data closer together vertically achieves the opposite effect. Notice how subtly this works in the figure below. We are naturally inclined to scan the small squares that appear on the left horizontally as rows and the ones on the right vertically as columns because of the way they are positioned in relation to each other.

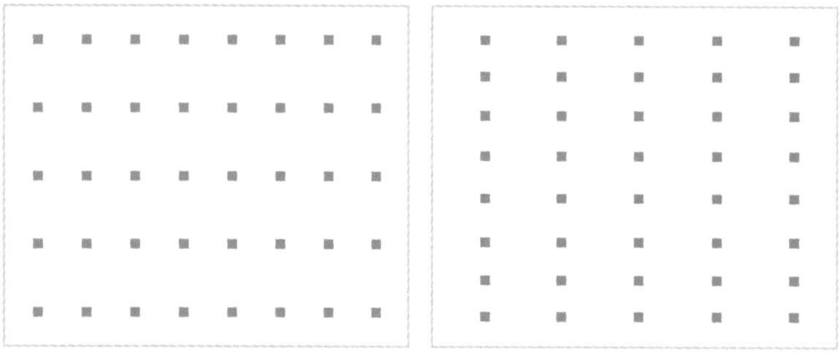

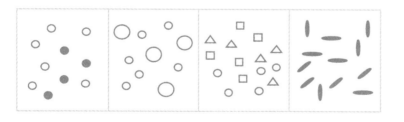

FIGURE 5.13. The Gestalt principle of proximity can be used to encourage either horizontal or vertical scanning.

The Principle of Similarity

We tend to group objects that are similar in color, size, shape, and orientation. The figure below illustrates this tendency.

FIGURE 5.14. When objects share a visual attribute in common, we tend to see them as belonging to the same group.

This principle reinforces what we've already learned about the usefulness of color (both hue and intensity), size, shape, and orientation to segregate information into categorical groups. Even when the information that we wish to link resides in separate locations on a dashboard, the principle of similarity can be applied to establish a link. For instance, if we wish to tie together revenue information that appears in various graphs, we can do so by using the same color to encode it wherever it appears. This technique can be useful for encouraging comparisons of closely related values that appear in various places, for example order count, order size, and order revenue.

The Principle of Enclosure

We perceive objects as belonging together when they are enclosed by anything that forms a border around them (for example, a line or a common field of background color). Enclosure sets the objects within apart from the rest. Notice how strongly we're induced to group the enclosed objects in the figure below.

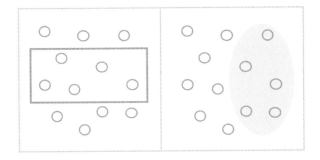

FIGURE 5.15. The Gestalt principle of enclosure points out that any form of visual enclosure causes us to see the enclosed objects as a group.

The arrangement of the two sets of circles in the figure above is exactly the same, yet the differing enclosures direct us to group the circles in different ways. This principle is exhibited frequently in tables and graphs when borders and fill colors or shading are used to group information and set it apart. As we can see here, it does not take a strong enclosure (for example, bright, thick lines or dominant colors) to create a strong perception of grouping.

The Principle of Closure

We humans are uncomfortable with loose ends. When faced with ambiguous visual stimuli—objects that could be perceived either as open, incomplete, and unusual forms or as closed, whole, and regular forms—we naturally perceive them as the latter. The principle of closure asserts that we perceive open structures as closed, complete, and regular whenever there is a way that we can reasonably do so. The following figure illustrates this principle.

FIGURE 5.16. The Gestalt principle of closure explains why we see these as closed shapes even though they are not.

It is natural for us to perceive what appears on the left as a rectangle with a break in the middle rather than as two sets of three lines connected at right angles. We perceive the object on the right as an oval instead of a curved line even though a portion of the line required to form an oval outline is missing.

We can apply this tendency to perceive whole structures in dashboards, especially in the design of graphs. For example, we can group objects such as points, lines, or bars in a graph into visual regions without using complete borders or background colors to define the space. This is preferable, because when we need to display a large collection of data in a small amount of space we must avoid clutter by eliminating all visual content that is not absolutely necessary. As shown in the following figure, it is sufficient to define the area of a graph through the use of a single set of X and Y axes rather than by lines that form a complete rectangle around the graph.

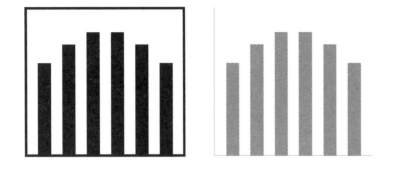

FIGURE 5.17. The Gestalt principle of closure explains why only two axes, as illustrated on the right, are required to define the space in which the information appears, rather than full enclosure shown on the left.

The Principle of Continuity

We perceive objects as belonging together, as part of a single whole, if they are aligned with one another or appear to continue one another. In the next figure, for instance, we tend to see the individual lines as a continuation of one another—as a dashed line rather than separate lines.

FIGURE 5.18. The Gestalt principle of continuity explains why we see these segments as a single wavy line.

The other result of the principle of continuity is that things that are aligned with one another appear to belong to the same group. In the table below, it is obvious which items are division names and which are department names based on their distinct alignment. Divisions, departments, and headcounts are clearly grouped, without any need for vertical grid lines to delineate them. Even though the division and department columns overlap with no white space in between, their distinct alignment alone makes them easy to distinguish. This same technique can be used to tie together separate data sections on a dashboard.

Division/Department	Headcount
G&A	
Finance	15
Purchasing	5
Information Systems	17
Sales	
Field Sales	47
Sales Operations	10
Engineering	
Product Development	22
Product Marketing	5

FIGURE 5.19. The Gestalt principle of continuity explains how the indentation of text works as a means to group information.

The Principle of Connection

We perceive objects that are connected, such as by a line, as part of the same group. In the following figure, even though the dots are nearer to one another vertically than horizontally, the lines that connect them create a clear perception of two horizontally attached pairs.

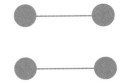

FIGURE 5.20. The Gestalt principle of connection explains why we see these dots grouped by rows rather than columns.

The perception of grouping produced by connection is stronger than that produced by proximity or similarity (color, size, and shape); it is weaker only than that produced by enclosure. The principle of connection is especially useful for tying together non-quantitative data—for example, to represent relationships among steps in a process or employees in an organization.

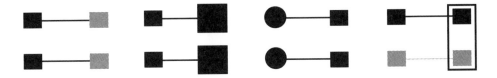

FIGURE 5.21. Connecting objects, such as by the lines in these examples, groups the objects together more powerfully than just about any other visual means. Only the enclosure in the example on the far right groups the two squares more strongly than the connections formed by the lines.

Applying an Understanding of Visual Perception to Dashboard Design

Two of the key challenges that we face in dashboard design are 1) making the most important data stand out from the rest, and 2) arranging what is often a great deal of disparate information in a way that makes sense, gives it meaning, and supports its efficient perception. An understanding of the preattentive attributes and Gestalt principles of visual perception is a useful conceptual foundation for approaching these challenges. It is more helpful to understand *how* and *why* something works than to simply understand *that* something works. If we understand the how and why, then, when we're faced with new challenges, we'll be able to determine whether or not the principles apply and how to adapt them to the new circumstances. If we've simply been told that something works in a specific situation, we'll be stuck when faced with conditions that are even slightly different.

As we proceed into the coming chapters, we'll have several opportunities to reinforce our grasp of visual perception by applying what we've learned to real-world dashboard design problems.

6 ACHIEVING ELOQUENCE THROUGH SIMPLICITY

Now that we're familiar with some of the science behind dashboard design, it's time to examine a few effective strategies for creating performance monitoring displays. My guiding principle of dashboard design is "eloquence through simplicity": eloquence of communication through simplicity of design. In earlier chapters, we examined design approaches that don't work. It's now time to shift our focus to those that do, resulting in dashboards that inform rapidly, with impeccable clarity.

Characteristics of a Well-Designed Dashboard

The fundamental challenge of dashboard design, as we've observed before, is squeezing a great deal of useful and often disparate information into a small amount of space, all the while preserving clarity. This certainly isn't the only challenge—others abound, such as selecting the right data in the first place—but it is the primary challenge that is particular to dashboards. Limited to a single screen to keep all the data within eye span, dashboard real estate is extremely valuable: we can't afford to waste an inch. Fitting everything in without sacrificing meaning doesn't require muscles, it requires finesse.

Unless we know what we're doing, we'll end up with a cluttered mess. Think for a moment about the cockpit of a commercial jet. Years of effort went into its design to ensure that despite the many things pilots must monitor, they can update their awareness at a glance. Every time I board a plane, I'm grateful that skilled designers worked hard to present this information effectively. Similar care is needed for the design of dashboards, but, unlike aircraft cockpit designers, few of those who create dashboards have actually studied the science of dashboard design. We can become exceptions to this unfortunate and costly norm. It is unlikely that people will lose their lives if we fail, but organizations do crash and burn—and frequently lose money—because of failed communication of just this sort.

Henry David Thoreau once penned the same word three times in succession to emphasize an important quality of life: "Simplicity, simplicity, simplicity!" Though I often fail, I strive to live my life according to Thoreau's sage advice to keep things simple. Simplicity is especially important for clear communication. Too often we smear a thick layer of gaudy makeup over data in an effort to impress or entertain, rather than focusing on communicating the truth of the matter in the clearest possible way.

Henry David Thoreau (1864). *Walden.*

To Thoreau's advice I'd like to add another insightful quotation: "Simplicity is the ultimate sophistication." These words are usually attributed to Leonardo da Vinci, but we actually don't know who uttered them first. They are profound regardless of the source. Anyone can complicate things. However, finding the simplest possible way to express information without sacrificing anything of value isn't easy; it takes skill.

When designing dashboards, we must reduce the content that's displayed to the essence of what's necessary for performance monitoring. As Antoine de Saint-Exupery said so well: "Perfection is achieved, not when there is nothing more to add, but when there is nothing left to take away." We must condense content in ways that don't decrease its meaning, and we must present it using visual display media that, even when quite small, can easily be read and understood. Well-designed dashboards deliver information that is:

- Exceptionally well organized
- Condensed, primarily in the form of summaries
- Specific to the task at hand and customized to communicate clearly to those who will use it
- Displayed using concise and often small media that communicate the information in the clearest and most direct way possible

Dashboards are for telling people what's happening. They must accomplish this task in a way that immediately highlights anything that needs the viewer's attention. Just like the dashboard of a car, which provides easy and efficient measures of speed, fuel, oil level, battery strength, engine trouble, and so on, an information dashboard provides an overview that can be assimilated quickly. It doesn't necessarily provide all of the information that might be needed to respond to any problems or opportunities that are revealed. A full diagnosis to determine how to respond often requires additional information. This is as it should be because a dashboard that tried to give the viewer everything she needed to do her job, including all the details, would be unreadable. Instead, dashboards should provide a high-level overview that informs the viewer instantly about the state of things. They should also provide quick and easy access to the additional information that's needed to respond, but that journey extends beyond the dashboard itself.

The best way to condense a broad spectrum of information to fit onto a dashboard is by summarizing. This is a process of reduction. *Summaries* represent a set of numbers (often a large set) as a single number. The three most common summaries that appear on dashboards are sums, averages, and rates. Summary measures of distribution and correlation are sometimes appropriate, but these are relatively rare.

Given the purpose of a dashboard—to help people monitor what's going on—some measures are only critical when something unusual is happening: something that falls outside the realm of normality into the realm of problems and opportunities. Why make someone wade through hundreds of values when only one or two require attention? We call these critical values *exceptions*.

We need to beware of taking the useful practice of managing by exception too far, however. Situation awareness requires constant updates even about things that are operating within normal parameters. As I mentioned in Chapter 1, *Clarifying the Vision*, because pilots scan their cockpit controls on a periodic basis in a particular sequence rather than waiting for an alarm to go off before updating their awareness, when an alarm does go off they already have an overall awareness of what's going on and can shift their attention to the problem without delay. Without an ongoing awareness of the aircraft's status, they wouldn't be able to focus on the problem without first gathering information about the overall context.

I received an email once from an executive of a software company that specializes in dashboards. We were discussing my definition of a dashboard, and, in the course of this discussion, he reported that a customer once asserted that his ideal dashboard would display a single traffic signal to indicate whether everything was all right or whether anything needed attention. The customer didn't want to be bothered by unnecessary information if all was well, and, when something was wrong, he could drill down from that single alert to additional, more detailed dashboards or reports to determine exactly what was wrong before taking action. For a moment, I found myself attracted to the Spartan simplicity of this idea, but only for a moment. The next moment my mind was haunted by visions of executives trying to run their businesses in ignorant bliss, completely out of touch unless a threshold built into the software determined that they ought to be informed. Anyone who has a job to do needs to maintain a basic awareness of what's going on even when all is well. Too often leaders—whether in business, academia, religion, or politics—forge ahead with their agendas, relying entirely on someone else to tell them what that person thinks the leaders should know. Only after the dust of some destructive event settles do these leaders discover that they knew far too little to lead effectively.

The best dashboards are designed to address information needs related to a particular objective or set of objectives. The information should be narrowed to that which directly applies and should be expressed using terms that are familiar. We wouldn't express the relationship between the costs of marketing and resulting revenues as a *linear correlation coefficient* if the audience has no idea what that is or how to make sense of it. A familiar style of graph would do a better job. Likewise, we wouldn't break the data into months if the audience were composed of sales managers who think in terms of weeks. Customization is vital to the success of a dashboard.

An aspect of customization that is often overlooked is expressing quantitative data at a level of precision that is appropriate to the task at hand. The greater the numeric precision, the more time it will take viewers to absorb the data. When examining financials, most executives rarely need to see numbers down to the level of cents or even beyond the nearest thousand, ten thousand, hundred thousand, or even million dollars. However, the manager of accounting might need to see every penny.

Display media must be designed to say exactly what's needed—no more or less—directly, clearly, and without any form of distraction, in a way that communicates the maximum meaning in the minimum amount of space. If a chart that looks like a fuel gauge, thermometer, or traffic signal communicates the necessary information in this manner, and does so in a minimum amount of space, then that's what we should use. If, however, it fails any of these tests, it should be replaced with something that does the job better. Insisting on cute charts when another means would work better is counterproductive even if everyone seems to be in love with them. This love is fickle. The appeal of cuteness will fade quickly, and, when it does, the only thing that will matter is how well the means of display works: how efficiently and effectively it communicates.

Two fundamental principles should guide the selection of the ideal display medium for a dashboard:

- It must be the best way to display a particular type of information that is commonly found on dashboards.
- It must be able to serve its purpose even when sized to fit into a small space.

In the upcoming chapters, we'll examine an ideal library of dashboard display media that fulfill these requirements. For now, let's examine other important design principles.

Key Goals in the Visual Design Process

Edward R. Tufte introduced a concept in his 1983 classic *The Visual Display of Quantitative Information* that he calls the "data-ink ratio." When quantitative information is displayed in printed form, some of the ink that appears on the page presents data, and some presents visual content that is not data (also known as *non-data*). The following figure shows two displays of quantitative data: one in the form of a table and the other in the form of a graph. Take a minute to examine them, and try to differentiate the data ink from the non-data ink.

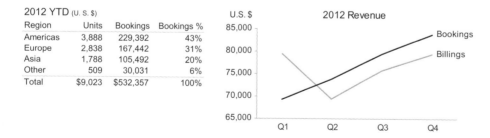

FIGURE 6.1. This table and graph consist of both data ink and non-data ink.

There isn't much non-data ink in either the table or the graph because they were intentionally designed to keep it to a minimum. The following figure shows the same table and graph, this time with the non-data ink featured in red.

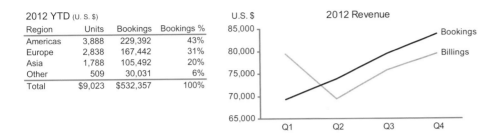

2012 YTD (U. S. $)			
Region	Units	Bookings	Bookings %
Americas	3,888	229,392	43%
Europe	2,838	167,442	31%
Asia	1,788	105,492	20%
Other	509	30,031	6%
Total	$9,023	$532,357	100%

FIGURE 6.2. Here, the non-data ink is highlighted in red.

Tufte defines the data-ink ratio in the following way:

A large share of ink on a graphic should present data-information, the ink changing as the data change. Data-ink is the non-erasable core of a graphic, the non-redundant ink arranged in response to variation in the numbers represented.

Edward R. Tufte (1983). *The Visual Display of Quantitative Information.* Graphics Press, page 93.

Tufte offers this design principle:

Maximize the data-ink ratio, within reason. Every bit of ink on a graphic requires a reason. And nearly always that reason should be that the ink presents new information.

Ibid., page 96.

This principle applies perfectly to dashboard design, with one simple revision: because dashboards are always displayed on computer screens, I've changed the word "ink" to "pixel" Across the entire dashboard, non-data pixels—any pixels that are not used to display data, excluding a blank background—should be reduced to a reasonable minimum. Take a moment to examine the following dashboard, and try to identify the non-data pixels that can be eliminated without sacrificing anything meaningful.

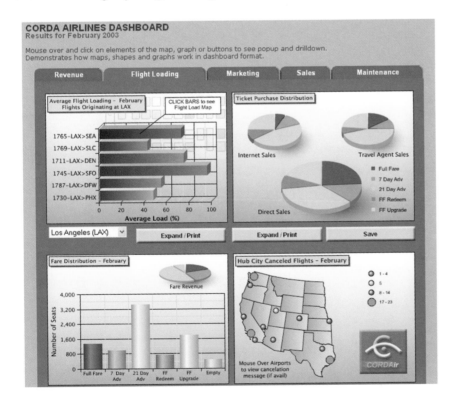

FIGURE 6.3. This dashboard displays an excessive percentage of non-data pixels.

The non-data pixels we could easily eliminate without any loss of useful information include:

- The third dimension of depth on all the pie charts and on the bars in the upper bar graph
- Lighting effects on the green, yellow, and red legend symbols to make them look three dimensional
- Drop shadows on the rectangles that contain the titles (for example, the rectangle labeled "Fare Distribution – February")
- The grid lines in the bar graphs
- The decoration in the background of the upper bar graph
- The color gradients in the backgrounds of the graphs, which vary from white at the top through shades of blue as they extend downward

Some of the data pixels on this dashboard could also be removed without loss; we'll come back to that in a moment.

Reducing the non-data pixels to a reasonable minimum places us firmly on the path to effective dashboard design. Much of visual dashboard design revolves around two fundamental goals:

1. Reduce the non-data pixels.
2. Enhance the data pixels.

We start by reducing the non-data content as much as possible and then proceed to enhance the data content with as much clarity and meaning as possible, working to make the most important data stand out above the rest.

1. Reduce the non-data pixels

   A. Eliminate all unnecessary non-data pixels.

   B. De-emphasize and regularize the non-data pixels that remain.

2. Enhance the data pixels

   A. Eliminate all unnecessary data pixels.

   B. Highlight the most important data pixels that remain.

FIGURE 6.4. Key goals and steps of visual dashboard design

Reduce the Non-Data Pixels

Reducing non-data pixels can be broken into two sequential steps:

1. Eliminate all unnecessary non-data pixels.
2. De-emphasize and regularize the non-data pixels that remain.

ELIMINATE ALL UNNECESSARY NON-DATA PIXELS

Dashboard design is an iterative process. We begin by mocking up a sample dashboard, and then we improve it through a series of revisions, each followed by a fresh evaluation leading to another redesign, until we have it right. As we get better and better at this, the number of iterations that will be required will decrease, partly because we won't be including unnecessary non-data pixels in the first place. No matter how far we advance, looking for unnecessary non-data pixels will never stop yielding results.

Here are a few examples of non-data pixels that often find their way onto dashboards and can usually be eliminated without loss:

Graphics that are merely decorative

FIGURE 6.5. We should eliminate graphics that provide nothing but decoration.

Variations in color that don't encode any meaning

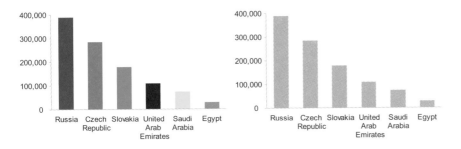

FIGURE 6.6. The bars on the left vary in color for no meaningful reason.

Borders that are used to delineate sections of data when white/blank space alone would work as well

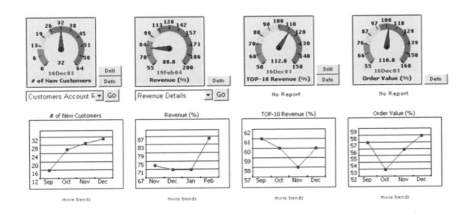

FIGURE 6.7. Borders were used, unnecessarily, to separate the sections of the display from one another. This fragments the display.

Fill colors that are used, when a neutral background would work as well, to delineate sections of content such as a title, the data region of a graph, the legend of a graph, the background of a table, or an entire section of data

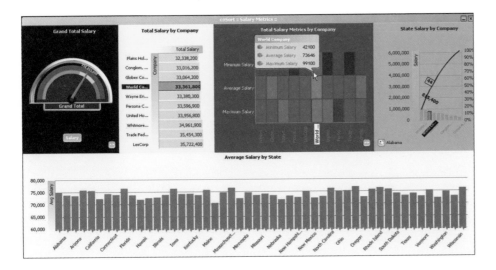

FIGURE 6.8. Unnecessary fill colors to separate sections of the display are an example of distracting non-data pixels.

Gradients of fill color

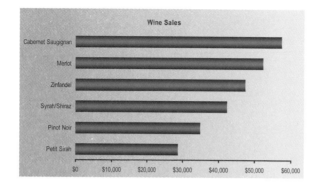

FIGURE 6.9. Gradients of color, both on the bars of this graph and across the entire background, add distracting non-data pixels.

Grid lines in graphs

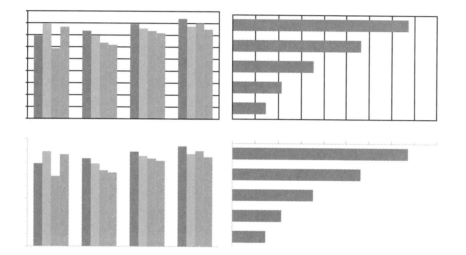

FIGURE 6.10. Grid lines in graphs are rarely useful as we can see in the comparison between these two graphs with and without grid lines. Grid lines are one of the most prevalent forms of distracting non-data pixels found on dashboards.

Grid lines in tables, which divide the data into individual cells or divide the rows or columns, when white space alone would do the job as well

Salesperson	Jan	Feb	Mar
Robert Jones	2,834	4,838	6,131
Mandy Rodriguez	5,890	6,482	8,002
Terri Moore	7,398	9,374	11,748
John Donnelly	9,375	12,387	13,024
Jennifer Taylor	10,393	12,383	14,197
Total	$35,890	$45,464	$53,102

Salesperson	Jan	Feb	Mar
Robert Jones	2,834	4,838	6,131
Mandy Rodriguez	5,890	6,482	8,002
Terri Moore	7,398	9,374	11,748
John Donnelly	9,375	12,387	13,024
Jennifer Taylor	10,393	12,383	14,197
Total	$35,890	$45,464	$53,102

FIGURE 6.11. Grid lines in tables, especially thick, dark ones, can make otherwise simple displays difficult to look at, as we can see by comparing these two versions of the same table.

Fill colors in the alternating rows of a table to delineate them when white space alone would work as well

Salesperson	Jan	Feb	Mar
Robert Jones	2,834	4,838	6,131
Mandy Rodriguez	5,890	6,482	8,002
Terri Moore	7,398	9,374	11,748
John Donnelly	9,375	12,387	13,024
Jennifer Taylor	10,393	12,383	14,197
Total	$35,890	$45,464	$53,102

Salesperson	Jan	Feb	Mar
Robert Jones	2,834	4,838	6,131
Mandy Rodriguez	5,890	6,482	8,002
Terri Moore	7,398	9,374	11,748
John Donnelly	9,375	12,387	13,024
Jennifer Taylor	10,393	12,383	14,197
Total	$35,890	$45,464	$53,102

FIGURE 6.12. Fill colors should be used to delineate rows in a table only when this is necessary to help the viewer's eyes track across wide rows. The two versions of this table make clear that the fill colors on the left are unnecessary non-data pixels.

Complete borders around the data region of a graph when one horizontal and one vertical axis would sufficiently define the space

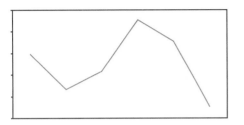

FIGURE 6.13. A complete border around the data region of a graph should be avoided when a single set of axes would adequately define the space, as we can see in the two versions of this graph.

3-D effects in graphs

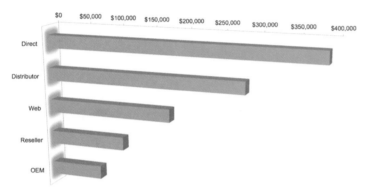

FIGURE 6.14. 3-D should be avoided.

Visual components or attributes of a display medium that serve no purpose but to make it look more like a real physical object or more ornate

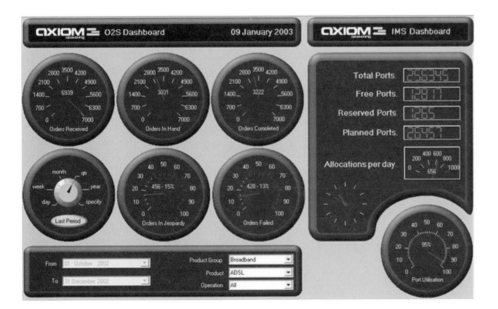

FIGURE 6.15. This dashboard is filled with visual components and attributes that serve the sole purpose of simulating real physical objects but add nothing to the actual data content.

This list is by no means comprehensive, but it includes much of the non-data content that I routinely run across on dashboards. When we find that we've included useless non-data pixels such as those in any of the previous examples, we simply remove them.

DE-EMPHASIZE AND REGULARIZE THE NON-DATA PIXELS THAT REMAIN

Not all non-data pixels can be eliminated without losing something useful. Some support the structure, organization, or legibility of the dashboard. For instance, when information is tightly packed, sometimes it is necessary to use lines or fill colors instead of just white space to distinguish one section from another. In these cases, rather than eliminating these useful non-data pixels, we should simply mute them visually so that they do their job without attracting attention to themselves. The viewer's focus should always be drawn to the information. The trick is to de-emphasize non-data pixels by making them just visible enough to do their job, but no more.

Here are a few examples of non-data pixels that are either always or occasionally useful. I've shown each of these examples in two ways: 1) a version that is too visually prominent, which illustrates what we should avoid; and 2) a version that is just visible enough to do the job, which is the objective.

Axis lines that are used to define the data region of a graph

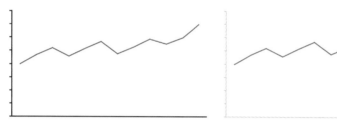

FIGURE 6.16. Axis lines used to define the data region of a graph are almost always useful, but they can be muted, like those on the right.

Lines, borders, or fill colors that are used to delineate sections of data when white space is not enough

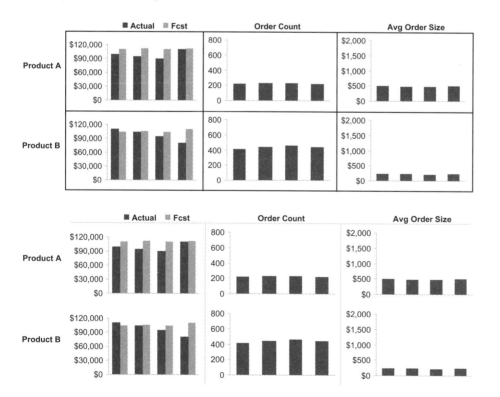

FIGURE 6.17. Lines can be used effectively to separate adjacent sections of the display from one another, but the stroke weight and color intensity of these lines can be kept to a minimum, as shown in the second version of the graph at the bottom of the figure.

Grid lines in graphs when useful

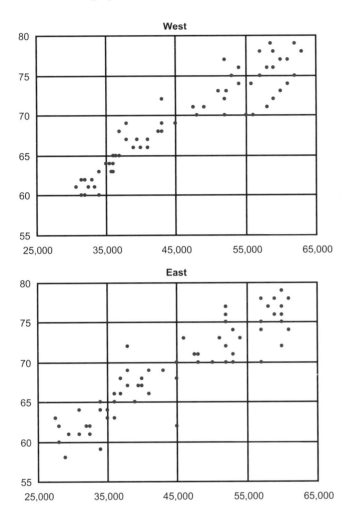

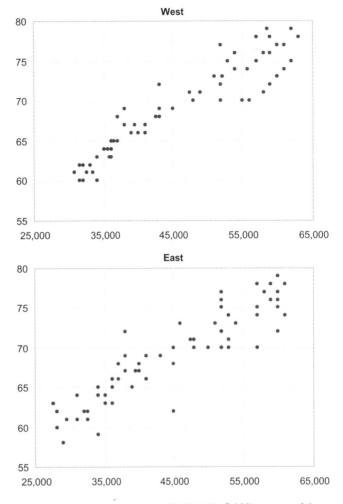

FIGURE 6.18. Grid lines are useful when they help viewers compare specific subsections of graphs, such as the range of values that fall within 65 to 75 on the vertical scale and 35,000 to 45,000 on the horizontal scale. The grid lines in the pair of graphs on the right are sufficient to do the job without being too prominent.

FIGURE 6.19. Grid lines and fill colors can be used in tables to clearly distinguish some columns from others, but this should be done in the muted manner seen in the second version of the table at the bottom of the figure rather than the heavy-handed manner seen at the top of the figure.

Grid lines and/or fill colors in tables when white space alone cannot adequately delineate columns and/or rows

Product	Jan	Feb	Mar	Q1 Total	Apr	May	Jun	Q2 Total	YTD Total
Product A	93,993	84,773	88,833	267,599	95,838	93,874	83,994	273,706	541,305
Product B	87,413	78,839	82,615	248,867	89,129	87,303	78,114	254,547	503,414
Product C	90,036	81,204	85,093	256,333	91,803	89,922	80,458	262,183	518,516
Product D	92,737	83,640	87,646	264,023	94,557	92,620	82,872	270,048	534,072
Product E	83,733	75,520	79,137	238,390	85,377	83,627	74,826	243,830	482,220
Total	447,913	403,976	423,323	1,275,212	456,705	447,346	400,264	1,304,314	2,579,526

Product	Jan	Feb	Mar	Q1 Total	Apr	May	Jun	Q2 Total	YTD Total
Product A	93,993	84,773	88,833	267,599	95,838	93,874	83,994	273,706	541,305
Product B	87,413	78,839	82,615	248,867	89,129	87,303	78,114	254,547	503,414
Product C	90,036	81,204	85,093	256,333	91,803	89,922	80,458	262,183	518,516
Product D	92,737	83,640	87,646	264,023	94,557	92,620	82,872	270,048	534,072
Product E	83,733	75,520	79,137	238,390	85,377	83,627	74,826	243,830	482,220
Total	447,913	403,976	423,323	1,275,212	456,705	447,346	400,264	1,304,314	2,579,526

Fill colors in the alternating rows of a table when white space alone cannot adequately delineate them

Product	Jan	Feb	Mar	Apr	May	Jun	Jul	Aug	Sep	Oct	Nov	Dec	Total
Product 01	93,993	84,773	88,833	95,838	93,874	83,994	84,759	92,738	93,728	93,972	93,772	99,837	$1,100,111
Product 02	87,413	78,839	82,615	89,129	87,303	78,114	78,826	86,246	87,167	87,394	87,208	92,848	$1,023,103
Product 03	90,036	81,204	85,093	91,803	89,922	80,458	81,191	88,834	89,782	90,016	89,824	95,634	$1,053,796
Product 04	92,737	83,640	87,646	94,557	92,620	82,872	83,626	91,499	92,476	92,716	92,519	98,503	$1,085,410
Product 05	86,245	77,785	81,511	87,938	86,136	77,071	77,773	85,094	86,002	86,226	86,043	91,608	$1,009,432
Product 06	88,833	80,119	83,956	90,576	88,720	79,383	80,106	87,647	88,582	88,813	88,624	94,356	$1,039,714
Product 07	82,614	74,511	78,079	84,236	82,510	73,826	74,498	81,511	82,382	82,596	82,420	87,751	$966,934
Product 08	85,093	76,746	80,421	86,763	84,985	76,041	76,733	83,957	84,853	85,074	84,893	90,384	$995,942
Product 09	87,646	79,048	82,834	89,366	87,535	78,322	79,035	86,475	87,399	87,626	87,440	93,095	$1,025,821
Product 10	90,275	81,420	85,319	92,047	90,161	80,672	81,406	89,070	90,021	90,255	90,063	95,888	$1,056,595
Total	$884,886	$798,085	$836,307	$902,255	$883,765	$790,751	$797,953	$873,070	$882,391	$884,688	$882,805	$939,903	$10,356,860

Product	Jan	Feb	Mar	Apr	May	Jun	Jul	Aug	Sep	Oct	Nov	Dec	Total
Product 01	93,993	84,773	88,833	95,838	93,874	83,994	84,759	92,738	93,728	93,972	93,772	99,837	$1,100,111
Product 02	87,413	78,839	82,615	89,129	87,303	78,114	78,826	86,246	87,167	87,394	87,208	92,848	$1,023,103
Product 03	90,036	81,204	85,093	91,803	89,922	80,458	81,191	88,834	89,782	90,016	89,824	95,634	$1,053,796
Product 04	92,737	83,640	87,646	94,557	92,620	82,872	83,626	91,499	92,476	92,716	92,519	98,503	$1,085,410
Product 05	86,245	77,785	81,511	87,938	86,136	77,071	77,773	85,094	86,002	86,226	86,043	91,608	$1,009,432
Product 06	88,833	80,119	83,956	90,576	88,720	79,383	80,106	87,647	88,582	88,813	88,624	94,356	$1,039,714
Product 07	82,614	74,511	78,079	84,236	82,510	73,826	74,498	81,511	82,382	82,596	82,420	87,751	$966,934
Product 08	85,093	76,746	80,421	86,763	84,985	76,041	76,733	83,957	84,853	85,074	84,893	90,384	$995,942
Product 09	87,646	79,048	82,834	89,366	87,535	78,322	79,035	86,475	87,399	87,626	87,440	93,095	$1,025,821
Product 10	90,275	81,420	85,319	92,047	90,161	80,672	81,406	89,070	90,021	90,255	90,063	95,888	$1,056,595
Total	$884,886	$798,085	$836,307	$902,255	$883,765	$790,751	$797,953	$873,070	$882,391	$884,688	$882,805	$939,903	$10,356,860

The previous examples demonstrate how the visual prominence of non-data pixels can usually be de-emphasized by using light, unsaturated colors, such as light grays, and minimal stroke weights (thin lines).

The prominence of non-data pixels can also be reduced if we *regularize* them (that is, make them consistent). If the axis lines of all graphs look the same—say, if we use the same light gray lines wherever they appear—no one graph is likely to catch a viewer's eye more than the others. Differences seldom go unnoticed and therefore have the potential to create distraction even when they are expressed in muted tones. We shouldn't vary the color, weight, or shape of non-data pixels that serve the same purpose in the dashboard.

Another category of content that is often found on dashboards and can be considered non-data pixels is content that supports navigation and data selection. Buttons and selection boxes are used to allow viewers to navigate to another screen or to choose which information appears on the dashboard (for example, by selecting a subset, such as hardware or software). These navigational elements might serve a purpose, but they don't display information, so they should not be given prominence. If they must be on the dashboard, we should place them in an out-of-the-way location such as the bottom-right corner of the screen, and mute them visually, so they won't compete for attention with the data. Notice how much of the following dashboard is dedicated to buttons and data selection controls, which I've highlighted with red borders. These elements take up far more valuable and prominent real estate on the dashboard than is required.

FIGURE 6.20. Fill colors can be used to delineate rows in a table when necessary to help viewers' eyes scan across the rows, but this should always be done in the muted manner seen in the version at the bottom of the figure rather than the visually weighty manner seen in the version at the top of the figure.

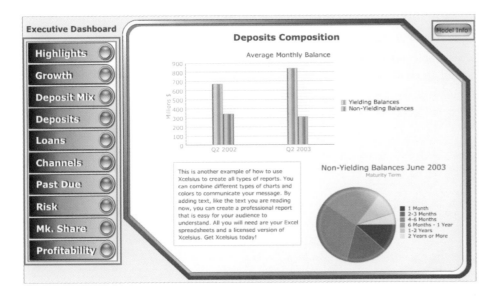

FIGURE 6.21. This dashboard gives navigational and data selection controls far more prominence and space than they deserve.

Some products encourage us to clutter the dashboard with a standard set of controls that are rarely useful for performance monitoring, such as the *Save*, *Save to Excel*, and *Save to PDF* controls that appear in the form of icons in the upper right in the example below. Sections such as the blue band at the top that displays the chart's title on the left and file controls on the right cannot be turned off in some products even though these elements would rarely be needed on a dashboard. Imagine an entire dashboard, consisting of several charts, each of which displays the blue title band and controls, resulting in useless clutter.

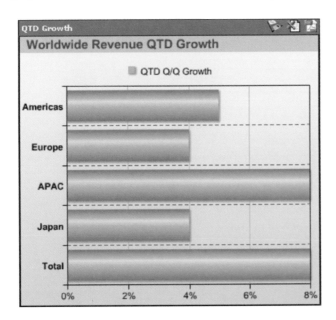

FIGURE 6.22. Standard controls, such as those on the top right for saving a copy of the chart in this example, create a great deal of clutter.

Similarly, although it might sometimes be necessary to include instructions on the dashboard, any nonessential text takes up space that could be used by data, attracts attention away from the data, and clutters the dashboard's appearance.

It usually works best to place most instructional or descriptive content either on a separate screen that can easily be reached when needed or, if possible, in the form of pop-ups that can be accessed when necessary with a click of the mouse. Notice how much prime real estate is wasted on the following dashboard to provide instructions that viewers will probably only need the first time they use the dashboard.

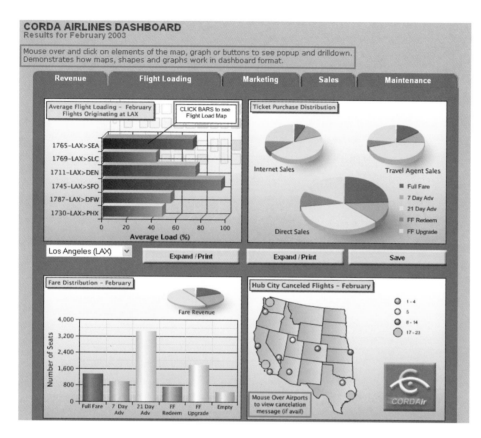

FIGURE 6.23. As we can see in the three areas highlighted in red, this dashboard is cluttered with instructions that most people would only need to read once.

Enhance the Data Pixels

Similar to the process we just examined, the process of enhancing the data pixels can be broken into two sequential steps:

- Eliminate all unnecessary data pixels.
- Highlight the most important data pixels that remain.

ELIMINATE ALL UNNECESSARY DATA PIXELS

It is tempting to throw everything we think anyone could ever possibly want onto a dashboard. Those of us who have worked in the field of business intelligence for a while have grown weary of being asked for more (always more!), so it can be appealing to anticipate this demand by giving folks everything. On a dashboard, however, where immediate insight is the viewer's goal, this is a costly mistake. I'm not suggesting that we force people to get by with less than they need, but that we firmly draw the line at what they *really* need for the task at hand. Eliminating information that isn't necessary automatically increases the attention that is given to the information that remains.

We can reduce unnecessary data pixels not only by removing irrelevant data but also by summarizing data so that the level of detail that's displayed doesn't exceed what's necessary. For most applications, it would be absurd to include detailed information such as transaction-level sales data on a dashboard. Some level of summarization is needed, and it is often up to us to determine what that level is.

HIGHLIGHT THE MOST IMPORTANT DATA PIXELS THAT REMAIN

All of the information that's displayed on a dashboard should be important, but not all information is created equal: some information is more important than other information for the task at hand. Important information can be divided into two categories:

- Information that is always important
- Information that is only important at the moment

When we consider the entire collection of information that belongs on a dashboard, we should be able to prioritize it according to what is usually of greatest interest to viewers. For instance, a dashboard that serves the needs of a corporation's executives might display several categories of financial, sales, and personnel data. On the whole, however, the executives usually care about some key measures more than others.

The other category of important information is important only when it reveals something that needs attention. A measure that has fallen far behind its target, an opportunity that has just arisen and won't last for long, or an operational condition that demands immediate attention all fall into this category.

These two categories of important information require special means of highlighting on a dashboard. The first category—information that is always important—can be emphasized using static means, but the second category—information that is important only at the moment—requires a dynamic means of emphasis.

The location of information on the screen—the layout—is an aspect of a dashboard's appearance that doesn't, or at least shouldn't, change dynamically. This is true not only because it would be technically difficult to dynamically rearrange the data on the screen, but also because, after using the dashboard for a time, viewers will come to expect specific data to appear in specific locations. This expectation is good because it helps them to scan the dashboard quickly. Because location is static, this is a variable that we can leverage to highlight information that is always important. Just as with real estate, the value of information is primarily based on "location, location, location."

Few aspects of visual design emphasize some information above the rest as effectively as location. The following figure identifies the emphasizing effect that different regions of a dashboard provide. The top-left region is the area of greatest emphasis, all else being equal. The greater emphasis tied to the upper left is probably a result of the conventions of Western written languages, which sequence words on a page from left to right and top to bottom. Speakers of these languages usually begin scanning the screen at the top left.

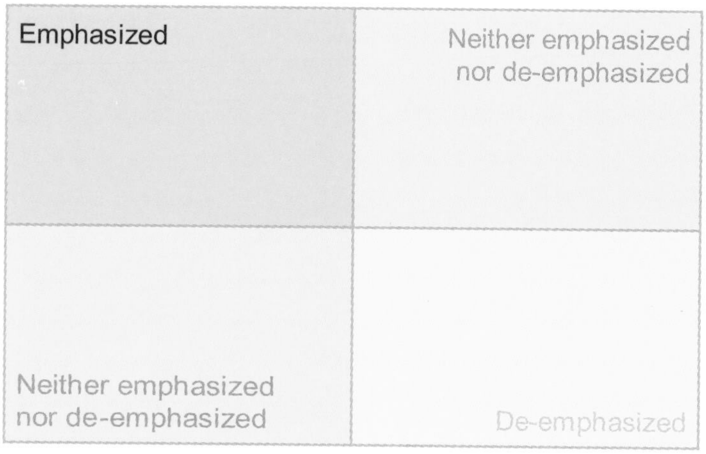

FIGURE 6.24. Different degrees of visual emphasis are associated with different regions of a dashboard.

As much as possible, we place the information that is always of great importance in the upper-left region of the dashboard. We should never waste this valuable real estate by placing a company logo or controls for navigation or data selection in this area. The following example provides a vivid but all-too-common example of what we should avoid when designing the layout of a dashboard.

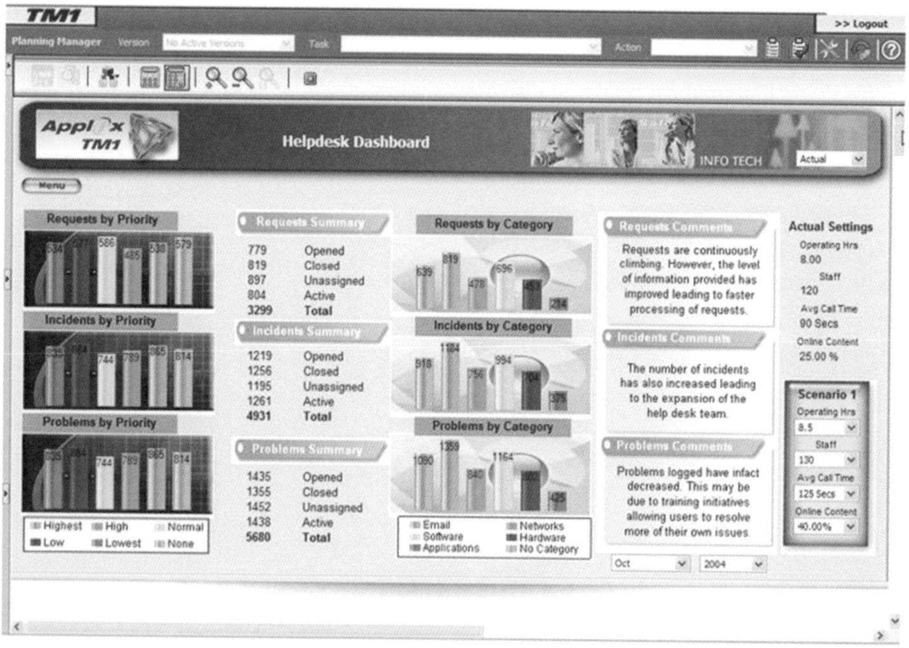

FIGURE 6.25. The most valuable real estate on this dashboard is wasted.

Information that is of relatively little importance (for example, the company's logo if we must include it) can be placed in the bottom right section of the dashboard to give it less prominence.

Visual attributes other than location are usually easy to manipulate in a dynamic manner on a dashboard. Therefore, dynamic techniques can be used to highlight information that is of great importance only at particular times. These techniques can also be used to highlight information that is always important once we've used up the prime screen locations to display other important data.

Many of the visual attributes that we examined in Chapter 5, *Tapping into the Power of Visual Perception*, can be used effectively to highlight data, both statically and dynamically. Here are two approaches that we can take:

- Use visual attributes that are greater or more intense than the norm (for example, brighter or darker colors).
- Use visual attributes that simply contrast with the norm (for example, blue text when the norm is black or gray).

Visual attributes don't need to be expressed in a way that is greater or more intense than others to stand out; contrast from a predominant pattern is all it takes. Visual perception is highly sensitive to differences and vigilant to assign meaning to them when they are detected.

Some useful visual attributes that can be expressed in ways perceived as greater or more intense than others include the following:

Visual attribute	Useful expressions	Illustrations
Color intensity	A darker or more fully saturated version of any hue is naturally perceived as greater than a lighter or less-saturated version.	
Size	Bigger things clearly stand out as more important than smaller things.	Item Item Item Item **Item** Item Item Item
Line width	Thicker lines stand out as more important than thinner lines.	Item Item **Item** Item Item Item Item Item

Some ways of expressing visual attributes that stand out merely by contrast to the norm include the following:

Visual attribute	Useful expressions	Illustrations
Hue	Any hue that is distinct from the norm will stand out.	
Orientation	Anything oriented differently than the norm will stand out.	*Item* Item Item Item Item Item Item Item
Enclosure	Anything enclosed by borders or surrounded by a fill color will stand out if different from the norm.	Item Item Item ...
Added marks	Anything with something distinctly added to it or adjacent to it will stand out.	Item Item Item *Item Item Item Item Item Item

Note that red does not signify that something is important, urgent, or a problem in all cultures. For example, in China, red relates to happiness. Also bear in mind when choosing symbolic colors that approximately 10% of males and 0.5% of females are colorblind.

Any of the previous visual attributes can be used to make the most important information stand out from the rest on a dashboard. Color is especially useful because distinct differences in color stand out very clearly and because color is a variable that dashboard software normally permits us to change dynamically based on predefined data conditions.

I've also found that one of the best ways to draw attention to particular items, especially those expressed as text, involves the use of an added mark that has a distinct color. For example, causing a simple symbol such as a circle, check mark, or asterisk to appear next to items that need attention does the job nicely. Choosing one color and varying its intensity to indicate varying degrees of importance or urgency works better than using different colors because even those who are colorblind can detect distinct intensities of the same color. The figure below illustrates this practice. Different symbols could also be used to indicate different levels of importance or urgency and eliminate the need to vary colors, but increasing color intensities corresponding to increasing levels of importance or urgency are understood more intuitively.

FIGURE 6.26. Simple symbols can be used along with varying color intensities to highlight data dynamically.

Color can be effectively used to highlight items on a dashboard only if we don't overuse color for other purposes. The figure below contains the same information as the one above, but colors have been used for purposes other than highlighting; the result is that the highlighting effect of color is lost.

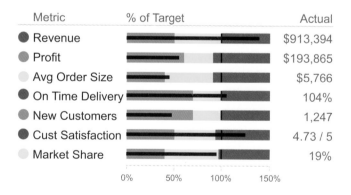

FIGURE 6.27. When color is overused, it loses its highlighting ability.

Notice how this overuse of color makes it impossible to spot the red icons immediately in a preattentive search. Instead, we can only find them by performing a slow, conscious search. For this reason, we should never introduce colors gratuitously. We use color only when it is meaningful and necessary.

When highlighting important information, we must be careful to restrict the definition of what's important. If we highlight too much information, nothing will stand out, and the dashboard's effort to communicate will fail. When used with discretion, however, visual highlighting can achieve the goal of immediate recognition and quick response.

When information is presented well, people can rapidly assimilate and understand a great deal of it. When information is presented poorly, people will struggle to assimilate even a little. The essential design principle that differentiates effective dashboards from those that fail is simplicity. By understanding how human eyes and brains process information, we can display it in ways that are finely tuned to human abilities. More than anything else, simplicity is the key.

Dashboards must be able to condense a great deal of information onto a single screen and present it at a glance without sacrificing anything important or compromising clarity. Consequently, they require display media that communicate effectively under these conditions. Every section of information on a dashboard should be displayed using the clearest, most informative and efficient means possible in a small amount of space. This requires an available library of display media that have been selected, customized, and in some cases created especially for dashboards, and an understanding of the circumstances in which each medium should be applied.

We'll begin this chapter with some basic guidelines for matching data and message to the right form of display, and then proceed to the heart of the chapter: a full library of display media that are ideal and routinely useful for dashboards.

Select the Best Display Medium

The best medium for displaying data should always be based on the nature of the information, the intended message, and the needs of the audience. A single dashboard generally displays a variety of information and therefore requires a variety of display media. In the next section we'll pair specific information and messages with the graphical media that display them best, but let's begin here with a more fundamental question: "Should the information be encoded as text, graphics, or both?" The appropriateness of each medium for a given situation— either verbal language in written form (text) or visual language (graphics)—isn't arbitrary.

Verbal language is processed serially, one word at a time. Some people are faster readers than others—an ability that I envy—but everyone processes language serially. Especially when communicating quantitative information, the strength of written words and numbers compared to graphics is their precision. If our sole purpose is to precisely communicate current year-to-date expenses of $487,321, for example, nothing works better than a simple display like this:

YTD Expenses $487,321

Displaying individual values does not require graphics; indeed, their use would only retard communication. Let's continue to enhance this information to see whether there is a point at which adding graphics will provide benefit.

Sometimes just providing an individual number and label is appropriate, but usually we must say more. Let's enhance the information with a simple evalua-tive remark that year-to-date expenses are higher than they ought to be:

YTD Expenses $487,321

Coloring the number red certainly isn't the only way to express this evaluative information, but it is sufficient. As long as only measures in this condition are displayed in red boldfaced numbers, with the rest displayed in black or gray, even people who are colorblind will be able to recognize that we are calling attention to this expense amount.

Now let's add the criterion that was used to determine that expenses are higher than they should be, which in this case is the target for year-to-date expenses:

	Actual	Target
YTD Expenses	$487,321	$450,000

At this stage we're beginning to venture into the territory where a graphical display might be useful, but it is not yet imperative. The viewer must do a little math to interpret the extent of the expense overage, but in this case the math can be done simply and quickly. We could even remove the need for the viewer to do the calculation by adding the amount of variance from the target, or perhaps by displaying the variance alone, without the actual expense amount, if the variance is all that's needed. Here are a few examples of ways we could do this:

	Actual	Target	Variance
YTD Expenses	$487,321	$450,000	+$37,321

	Actual	Target	Variance %
YTD Expenses	$487,321	$450,000	+8%

	Actual	Variance to Target
YTD Expenses	$487,321	+$37,321

	Actual	Variance to Target %
YTD Expenses	$487,321	+$37,321

YTD Expenses Variance $487,321

YTD Expenses Variance   +8%

Any one of the above approaches might be appropriate for a single measure that has been enhanced with contextual data such as a target and some indication of whether the value is good or bad.

An entire display full of individual measures expressed textually in this manner would work fine if its purpose was to draw attention to individual measures one at a time, but what if we want a bigger picture of the whole or comparisons among multiple measures to emerge? Text alone doesn't support this.

Text, especially when organized into tables (that is, as rows and columns of data), is a superb medium for looking up information. Bus schedules, tax rate tables, and the indexes of books, to name but a few examples, are all organized as tables to support this use. If we need to look up the Consumer Price Index (CPI) rate for September 1996 using the table below, for example, we can easily find the precise value of 157.8. Graphs don't support looking up individual values as efficiently and certainly not as precisely.

Year	Jan	Feb	Mar	Apr	May	Jun	Jul	Aug	Sep	Oct	Nov	Dec	Annual
1990	127.4	128.0	128.7	128.9	129.2	129.9	130.4	131.6	132.7	133.5	133.8	133.8	130.7
1991	134.6	134.8	135.0	135.2	135.6	136.0	136.2	136.6	137.2	137.4	137.8	137.9	136.2
1992	138.1	138.6	139.3	139.5	139.7	140.2	140.5	140.9	141.3	141.8	142.0	141.9	140.3
1993	142.6	143.1	143.6	144.0	144.2	144.4	144.4	144.8	145.1	145.7	145.8	145.8	144.5
1994	146.2	146.7	147.2	147.4	147.5	148.0	148.4	149.0	149.4	149.5	149.7	149.7	148.2
1995	150.3	150.9	151.4	151.9	152.2	152.5	152.5	152.9	153.2	153.7	153.6	153.5	152.4
1996	154.4	154.9	155.7	156.3	156.6	156.7	157.0	157.3	157.8	158.3	158.6	158.6	156.9
1997	159.1	159.6	160.0	160.2	160.1	160.3	160.5	160.8	161.2	161.6	161.5	161.3	160.5
1998	161.6	161.9	162.2	162.5	162.8	163.0	163.2	163.4	163.6	164.0	164.0	163.9	163.0
1999	164.3	164.5	165.0	166.2	166.2	166.2	166.7	167.1	167.9	168.2	168.3	168.3	166.6
2000	168.8	169.8	171.2	171.3	171.5	172.4	172.8	172.8	173.7	174.0	174.1	174.0	172.2
2001	175.1	175.8	176.2	176.9	177.7	178.0	177.5	177.5	178.3	177.7	177.4	176.7	177.1
2002	177.1	177.8	178.8	179.8	179.8	179.9	180.1	180.7	181.0	181.3	181.3	180.9	179.9
2003	181.7	183.1	184.2	183.8	183.5	183.7	183.9	184.6	185.2	185.0	184.5	184.3	184.0
2004	185.2	186.2	187.4	188.0	189.1	189.7	189.4	189.5	189.9	190.9	191.0	190.3	188.9
2005	190.7	191.8	193.3	194.6	194.4	194.5	195.4	196.4	198.8	199.2	197.6	196.8	195.3
2006	198.3	198.7	199.8	201.5	202.5	202.9	203.5	203.9	202.9	201.8	201.5	201.8	201.6
2007	202.4	203.5	205.4	206.7	207.9	208.4	208.3	207.9	208.5	208.9	210.2	210.0	207.3
2008	211.1	211.7	213.5	214.8	216.6	218.8	220.0	219.1	218.8	216.6	212.4	210.2	215.3
2009	211.1	212.2	212.7	213.2	213.9	215.7	215.4	215.8	216.0	216.2	216.3	215.9	214.5
2010	216.7	216.7	217.6	218.0	218.2	218.0	218.0	218.3	218.4	218.7	218.8	219.2	218.1

Now look at the CPI table again, but this time try to determine the shape of the values as they change through the course of the year 1996. Text doesn't support this use of the data, but look at how well the following graph does the job. Notice also that the previous task of looking up the index value for September is not supported well by the graph.

FIGURE 7.1. This CPI table illustrates the strength of tables as a means to look up precise individual values.

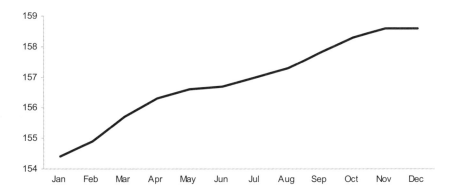

FIGURE 7.2. This graph of the CPI for the year 1996 illustrates how well graphs reveal the shape of data, in this case as they change through time.

When, in the late 18th century, the Scottish social scientist William Playfair invented many of the graphs that we still use today, he promoted a powerful language for communicating quantitative information. Giving values shape through the use of grid coordinates along two perpendicular axes enabled us to visualize entire sets of numbers, which dramatically extended our ability to think quantitatively. This is the strength of graphs: they give shape to numbers and, in doing so, bring patterns to light that would otherwise remain undetected.

Let's see some of these concepts at work on a dashboard. Look at the predominantly text-based dashboard below. Notice how the textual medium primarily supports the process of lookup. Each measure is isolated from the rest, and comparisons are difficult.

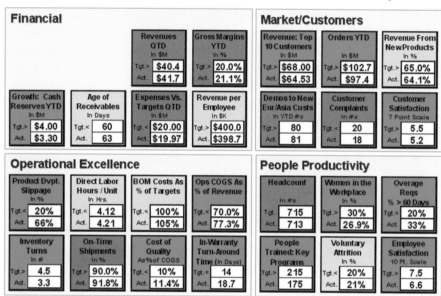

FIGURE 7.3. A predominantly text-based dashboard

The only big-picture information that's provided on the above dashboard is conveyed through the visual attribute of hue. Assuming that we are not color-blind and can distinguish these hues, a quick scan of the many red and yellow boxes reveals that much is wrong. Beyond that, however, we are forced to consider each measure individually. If no comparisons or patterns are useful for this dashboard, the predominance of text is fine. But even if this is the case, which is unlikely, the textual display of this information could be less fragmented, such as in the following redesign where the measures are arranged in tables to make scanning easier. The red, yellow, and green color coding has been replaced with boldface, black, and gray text, respectively, to enable perception by people who are colorblind. Note that this redesign has improved the dashboard's use for lookup but not for gleaning additional meaning.

RealTime Balanced Scorecard (April 2004)

Financial

Metric	Actual	Target
Revenue QTD (millions)	$41.7	$40.4
Gross Margins YTD (%)	21.1%	20.0%
Growth: Cash Reserves YTD (millions)	**$3.3**	**$4.0**
Age of Receivables (days)	63	60
Expenses vs. Targets QTD (millions)	$20.0	$20.0
Revenue per Employee (thousands)	$398.7	$400.0

Market Customers

Metric	Actual	Target
Revenue: Top 10 Customers (millions)	**$64.5**	**$68.0**
Orders YTD (millions)	**$97.4**	**$102.7**
Revenue from New Products (%)	64.1%	65.0%
Demos to New Eur/Asia Customers (count)	81	80
Customer Complaints (count)	18	20
Customer Satisfaction (7-point scale)	**5.2**	**5.5**

Operational Excellence

Metric	Actual	Target
Product Development Slippage (%)	**66.0%**	**20.0%**
Direct Labor Hours per Unit (hours)	4.21	4.12
BOM Costs as % of Target (%)	105%	100%
Ops COGS as % of Revenue (%)	**77.3%**	**70.0%**
Inventory Turns (count)	**3.3**	**4.5**
On-Time Shipments (%)	91.8%	90.0%
Cost of Quality as % of COGS (%)	**11.4%**	**10.0%**
In-Warranty Turnaround Time (days)	**18.7**	**14.0**

People Productivity

Metric	Actual	Target
Headcount (count)	713	715
Women in the Workplace (%)	**26.9%**	**30.0%**
Overage Requisitions > 60 days (%)	**33%**	**20%**
People Trained: Key Programs (count)	**175**	**215**
Voluntary Attrition (%)	21%	20%
Employee Satisfaction (10-point scale)	**6.6**	**7.5**

FIGURE 7.4. Redesign of the text-based dashboard in *Figure 7.3*, arranged in tables to better support lookup

Effective dashboards need to present a rich and meaningful display, along with the required level of quantitative precision, that can be efficiently perceived. With each measure or set of related measures, we must ask what the viewer needs, how the measures will be used, and what message the measures must convey, and then select between text or graphics to achieve these communication objectives. Whenever information lends itself to graphical display, it almost always makes sense to present it in this way because more can be communicated in the available space, and information presented graphically can be perceived more efficiently than information presented as text. Notice when viewing the two expressions of values below—one that uses text and one that uses graphics—how quickly you can scan and compare the values using the graphical version on the right.

Metric	% of Target
Revenue	140%
Profit	47%
Avg Order Size	54%
On Time Delivery	105%
New Customers	81%
Customer Satisfaction	125%
Market Share	95%

FIGURE 7.5. Values that are expressed as text on the left provide precision but not an efficient means for scanning and comparison, which is provided by the graphical display on the right.

When efficiency and comparisons are needed, which is always the case when viewing a dashboard, graphics should be used whenever possible.

A poorly chosen graph can completely obscure otherwise clear data. In this section, we'll compile a library of the best graphs for displaying quantitative information on a dashboard.

Two fundamental principles have guided the selection of each graph in this library:

- It must be the best means to display a particular type of quantitative information that is commonly found on dashboards.
- It must be able to serve its purpose even when sized to fit into a small space.

All of the items in this category display quantitative data in the form of a 2-D graph. Most of these are familiar types of graphs, but one or two will probably be new to you because they were designed or adapted specifically for use in dashboards. Here's the list:

- Bullet Graphs
- Bar Graphs
- Dot Plots
- Line Graphs
- Sparklines
- Box Plots
- Scatter Plots
- Spatial Maps
- Heat Maps
- Tree Maps

Bullet Graphs

The *bullet graph* is probably the least familiar means of display in this library, because, until 2005, it didn't exist. I know this because it is a simple invention of my own, created specifically for dashboards. It is my answer to the problems exhibited by most of the gauges that have become synonymous with dashboards. Gauges typically display a single key measure, sometimes compared to a related measure such as a target, and sometimes in the context of quantitative ranges with qualitative labels that declare the measure's state (such as good or bad).

Below are several examples of the gauges that are typically found in dashboard products, both radial (circular) and linear in design.

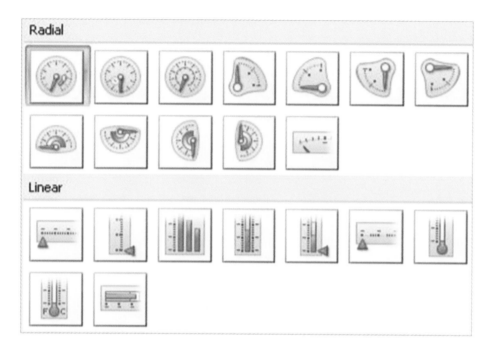

FIGURE 8.1. These are examples of the gauges and meters that are typically found in dashboard products. These are found in Microsoft Visual Studio.

When considering gauges, we should ask: "Do they provide the clearest, most meaningful presentation of the data in the least amount of space?" In my opinion, gauges like these do not. The circular shape of radial gauges, such as the examples on the top, wastes a great deal of space. This problem is magnified when we have many of these gauges on a single dashboard, for they cannot be arranged together in a compact manner. The linear nature of the thermometer style of gauge means it can be displayed more compactly, but in displays such as this, space still tends to be wasted, often on meaningless attempts at realism. If dashboard display media were designed by expert communicators, they would look different.

How much research do you think went into determining that quantitative displays on a dashboard should look like traffic lights, thermometers, speedometers, and fuel gauges? Believe it or not, none whatsoever. Back when dashboards were first introduced, some software engineer had the brilliant idea that, because we're calling this form of computer-based display a dashboard, it should display information in ways that look like gauges and meters on an car dashboard. Once one engineer did it this way, they all began to do it this way. Soon, the race was on to create the cutest, most dazzling, and realistic gauges they could imagine. They took the dashboard metaphor too far. The metaphor is only useful to the extent that it compares computer-based displays that are used for rapid performance monitoring to dashboard displays that are used for quickly monitoring driving conditions. Similarity in purpose does not mean that we should display information on a computer screen in the same manner that we display it in a car. Different purposes and conditions require different forms of display.

FIGURE 8.2. An assortment of typical dashboard gauges.

No matter how beautiful the details of the gauges, from the reflection of light on the glass to the intricate design of the needle, the cuteness will wear off after a day or two, and those who use the dashboard will care about one thing only: their ability to acquire the information that they need in the fullest, clearest, most meaningful, and efficient way possible.

Because software vendors didn't consider the unique requirements of a dashboard and devise an effective way to display a single measure of something that is going on, I stepped in to fill the gap. The bullet graph achieves this objective without the problems that usually plague gauges. The bullet graph is designed to display, in a compact manner, a single key measure along with a comparative measure and qualitative ranges to instantly signal whether the measure is good, bad, or in some other state. Here's a simple example.

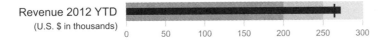

FIGURE 8.3. A simple horizontally oriented bullet graph

A bullet graph is just a bar graph with a single bar, an additional mark for a quantitative comparison, and shades of color in the background. Although simple, this combination of graphical features works exceptionally well on dashboards. Here's the same bullet graph, this time with its components labeled.

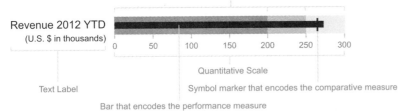

FIGURE 8.4. A simple bullet graph with each of its components labeled

Because bullet graphs are so often useful on dashboards, I've dedicated an entire chapter to them. We'll learn their many uses and design variations in Chapter 9, *Designing Bullet Graphs*.

Bar Graphs

Unlike bullet graphs, bar graphs were specifically created to display multiple rather than single instances of a measure. In fact, every graph in this chapter other than the bullet graph is designed to display more than one instance of one or more measures. Bar graphs are great for displaying measures that are associated with discrete items in a category, such as multiple regions or departments. The following example is typical of bar graphs that appear on dashboards. It displays two key measures, bookings and billings revenue, subdivided into sales regions.

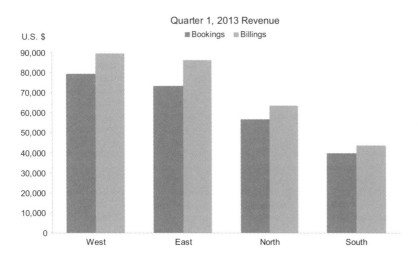

FIGURE 8.5. A typical bar graph

I use the term "bar graph" to refer to all graphs that use bars to represent quantitative data, whether the bars are oriented vertically or horizontally. The following is another example of a typical bar graph, this time with the bars running horizontally.

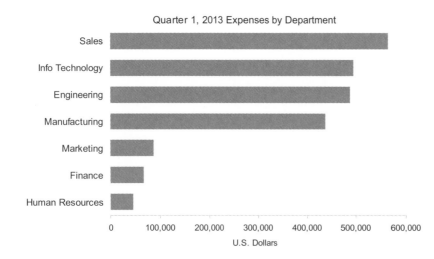

FIGURE 8.6. A bar graph with horizontally oriented bars

To fully understand when it is appropriate to encode data in a graph as bars rather than as lines (as is done in a line graph), we must understand a little about the three types of categorical scales that appear commonly in graphs:

Nominal: Nominal scales consist of discrete items that belong to a single category but really don't relate to one another in any particular way. They differ in name only (that is, nominally). The items in a nominal scale, in and of themselves, have no particular order and don't represent quantitative values in any way. Typical examples in dashboards include regions (for example, The Americas, Asia, and Europe) and departments (for example, Sales, Marketing, and Finance).

Ordinal: Ordinal scales consist of items that, unlike the items in a nominal scale, do have an intrinsic order but in and of themselves still do not correspond to quantitative values. Typical examples involve rankings, such as "A, B, and C," "small, medium, and large," and "poor, below average, average, above average, and excellent."

Interval: Interval scales, like ordinal scales, consist of items that have an intrinsic order, but they also represent quantitative values. An interval scale starts out as a quantitative scale that is then converted into a categorical scale by subdividing the range of values in the entire scale into a sequential series of smaller ranges of equal size; each range is given a label. This explanation will make more sense when illustrated with an example. Consider the quantitative range made up of values extending from 55 to 80. This range could be converted into an interval scale consisting of the following sequence of intervals:

- Greater than 55 and less than or equal to 60
- Greater than 60 and less than or equal to 65
- Greater than 65 and less than or equal to 70
- Greater than 70 and less than or equal to 75
- Greater than 75 and less than or equal to 80

The following illustrates each type of scale.

FIGURE 8.7. The three types of categorical scales found in graphs

Here's a quick (and somewhat sneaky) test to see how well you've grasped these concepts. Can you identify the type of categorical scale that appears in the example below?

January   February   March   April   May   June

FIGURE 8.8. This is a categorical scale that is commonly used in graphs. Can you determine which of the three types it is?

Months of the year obviously have an intrinsic order, which raises the question: "Do the items in a time series correspond to quantitative values?" In fact, they do. Units of time such as years, quarters, months, weeks, days, hours, and so on are measures of quantity, and the individual items in any given unit of measure—for example, years—represent equal intervals. (Months aren't exactly equal, and even years vary in size occasionally because of leap years, but they are close enough in size to constitute an interval scale for most reporting purposes.)

Bar graphs—never line graphs—are the best means to display measures associated with discrete items along a nominal or ordinal scale. The visual weight of bars places emphasis on the individual values in the graph and makes it easy to compare individual values to one another by simply comparing the heights of the bars.

Line graphs are useful for encoding values along an interval scale, but there are occasions when it is preferable to use a bar graph to display such measures. For example, when we wish to emphasize the individual values rather than the overall patterns, or when we wish to enable close comparisons of values that are located next to one another, a bar graph is a better choice. The following figure displays the same set of interval values in two ways: as a bar graph and as a line graph. Notice the differences in what the two images emphasize even though they display precisely the same data. The bar graph emphasizes the individual values in each interval and makes it easy to compare those values to one another whereas the line graph does a much better job of revealing the overall shape of the distribution.

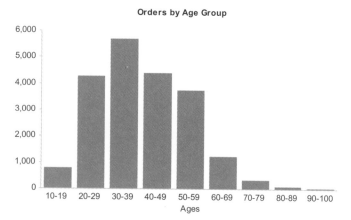

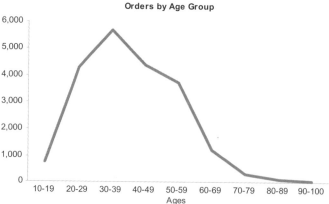

FIGURE 8.9. These two graphs—one a bar graph and one a line graph—display exactly the same information but highlight different aspects of it.

Because bar graphs emphasize individual values, they also enable easy comparisons between adjacent values. This next example illustrates the ease with which we can compare measures—in this case the productivity of the daytime and the nighttime crews in any given month—using this type of graph.

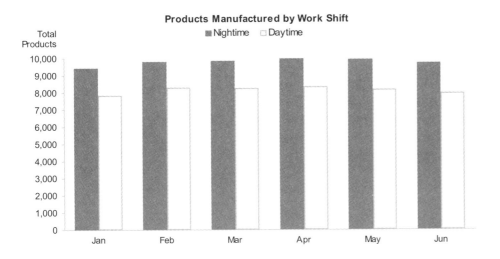

FIGURE 8.10. Bars are preferable to lines for encoding data along an interval scale—in this case, a time series divided into months—when the graph is intended to support comparisons of individual measures.

Even when we wish to display values that represent parts of a whole, we should use a bar graph rather than the ever-popular pie chart. A bar graph will present the data much more clearly as long as we indicate that the bars represent parts of a whole (for example, in the graph's title). Below is an example of a pie chart and a bar graph that both present the same part-to-whole values. Notice how much easier it is to make accurate visual judgments of the relative sizes of each part in the bar graph.

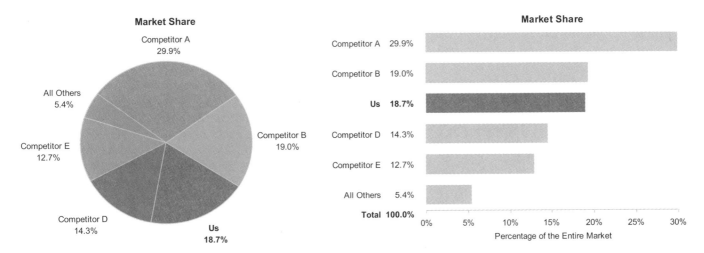

A variation of the bar graph is the *stacked bar graph*. This type of graph is useful at times, but it can easily be misused. I recommend against ever using a stacked bar graph to display a single series of part-to-whole data. A regular bar graph

FIGURE 8.11. We can use a bar graph to more clearly display the same part-to-whole relationship that is commonly displayed using a pie chart.

works much better. As we can see, it is much harder and more time-consuming to read the stacked bar graph below than the bar graph showing the same data.

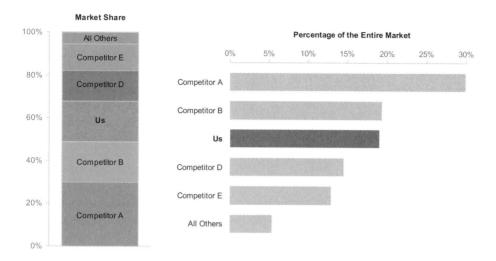

FIGURE 8.12. A stacked bar graph is not the best way to display a single series of part-to-whole data.

Stacked bar graphs are the right choice only when we must display multiple instances of a whole and its parts, with emphasis on the whole. The following example displays separate instances of sales revenue per region, each subdivided by sales channel.

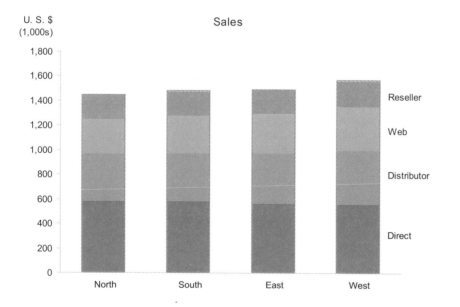

FIGURE 8.13. The only circumstance in which a stacked bar graph is useful is when we must display multiple instances (for example, one for each region) of a whole (for example, total sales) and its parts (in this case, per sales channel), with a greater emphasis on the whole than the parts.

Differences in a sales channel from region to region are difficult to detect for all but the one that appears at the bottom of each bar (in this case, "Direct" sales), which is why a stacked bar graph should not be used if these differences must be shown more precisely. Notice the proportions of sales per channel and region that can easily be seen in the following bar graphs.

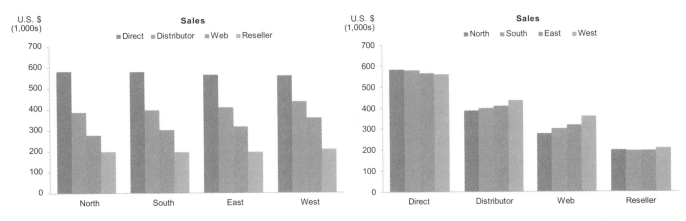

What's lacking in the bar graphs above, however, is a representation of total sales per region on the left and channel on the right. When we want to emphasize totals but also provide an approximate representation of the parts, a stacked bar graph will do the job nicely.

FIGURE 8.14. These bar graphs reveal the differences in the proportions of sales among the four channels much more clearly than the stacked bar graph in *Figure 8.13* does.

Dot Plots

It's likely that you've never heard of a *dot plot* until now. It's a shame that they're not well known because they're quite useful. They're used for the same purposes as bar graphs: as a simple way to compare one or more sets of discrete values. I use them primarily when I want use a quantitative scale that doesn't begin at zero. In the following example, notice that it's difficult to see differences in the values because they are relatively close to one another.

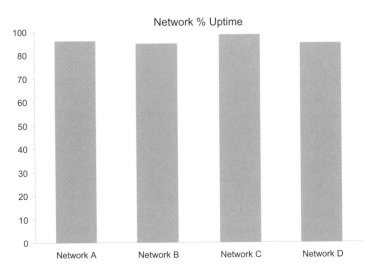
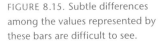

FIGURE 8.15. Subtle differences among the values represented by these bars are difficult to see.

In a case such as this, if all of the values range between 90% and 100%, and small differences are significant, we would want to scale the graph to begin at 90% to spread the differences in value across more space. We cannot do this with bars, however, because bars encode values based not only on the position of their ends but also on their heights. For the heights of bars to accurately represent differences in their values, they must begin at zero. In the example below where the axis does not begin at zero, notice that the Network C bar is almost twice the height of the Network A bar, yet its value is only slightly larger.

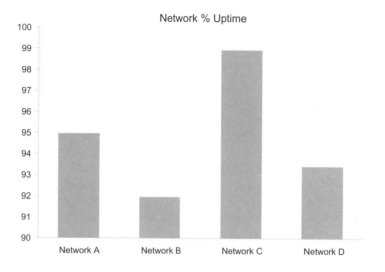

FIGURE 8.16. The heights of bars do not accurately represent their values when the scale does not begin at zero.

We can resolve this problem by replacing the bars with dots, which will allow us to narrow the scale because dots represent values based on position alone, not height. Here are the same values as before, this time displayed as a dot plot.

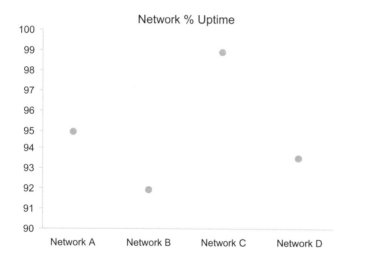

FIGURE 8.17. Small differences among these values are easy to see when the quantitative scale is narrowed in a dot plot.

Dot plots may be used rather than bar graphs even when the scale begins at zero. This is often useful on dashboards because bars have more visual weight than dots, and a dashboard with many bars can look cluttered.

Line Graphs

Lines emphasize the overall shape of an entire series of values. By connecting the individual values, lines give a sense of continuity from one value to the next throughout the entire series. This sense of connection among the values is appropriate only along an interval scale, which subdivides a continuous range of quantitative values into equal, sequential sections; it's not appropriate along a nominal or ordinal scale where the values are discrete and not intimately connected. The next figure shows examples of inappropriate and appropriate uses of lines.

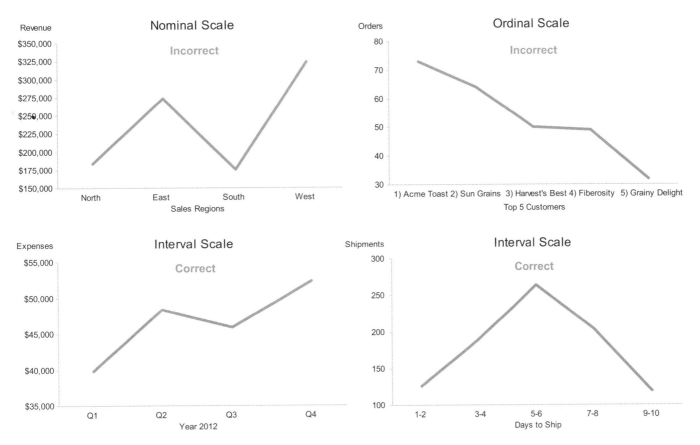

Line graphs are especially useful for showing the shape of change through time. Any time that we wish to emphasize patterns in time-series values, such as trends, fluctuations, cycles, rates of change, and how two or more sets of values change in relation to one another, line graphs are the best vehicle to use. Keep in mind that when we display time-series data on a dashboard, we want to emphasize the information's shape ("Is it going up or down?" "Is it volatile?" "Does it go through seasonal cycles?") rather than the individual values as in bar graphs. In the context of dashboards, line graphs are often the best means to present a quick overview of a time series.

The next example shows the same time-series data in two ways: on the left using a bar graph and on the right using a line graph. Notice how much more quickly and clearly the overall shape of the data comes through in the line graph. Unlike a bar graph, the quantitative scale of a line graph need not begin at zero; it can be narrowed to a range beginning just below the lowest and ending just above the highest values in the data set, thereby filling the data region of the graph and revealing greater detail. We must always be sure to make

FIGURE 8.18. Examples of inappropriate (top two) and appropriate (bottom two) uses of lines to encode data in graphs.

the lines that encode the data more prominent than any other part of the graph so that the information stands out above all else.

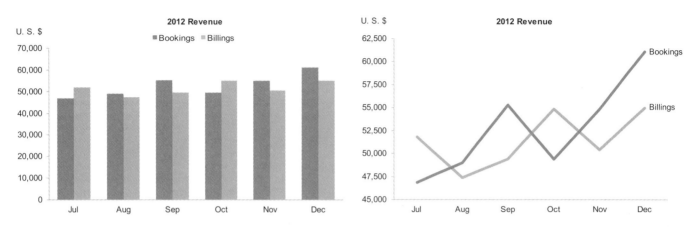

FIGURE 8.19. Two graphs of the same time-series data: a bar graph on the left and a line graph on the right; notice how the overall shape of the data is much easier to see in the line graph.

Sparklines

Sparklines are the brainchild of Edward R. Tufte. He dedicated a chapter to them in his book *Beautiful Evidence*. Here's a simple example:

$137,384.28   Savings Balance on 05/20/2013

FIGURE 8.20. A simple sparkline that displays the 12-month history of a savings account balance.

Tufte created the sparkline to provide a bare-bones and space-efficient historical context for measures. Assuming that the sparkline above encodes a rolling 12-month history of an account balance, the ups and downs are instantly available to the viewer who wishes to consider the meaning of the current balance in light of its history.

Tufte describes sparklines as "data-intense, design-simple, word-size graphics." As such, they are ideal for dashboards and anything else that requires highly condensed forms of data display, such as medical diagnostic reports that include patient histories.

You might be wondering, "Where's the quantitative scale?" It's nowhere to be seen, and that's intentional. Sparklines are not meant to provide the quantitative precision of a normal line graph. Their whole purpose is to provide a quick sense of historical context to enrich the meaning of the measure. This is exactly what's required in a dashboard. Instead of details, we must display a quick view that can be assimilated at a glance. The details can come later, if needed, in the form of supplemental graphs and reports.

There's a lot to learn about sparklines and the various ways that they can be used, designed, and enhanced, which we'll focus on in Chapter 10, *Designing Sparklines*.

Edward R. Tufte (2006). *Beautiful Evidence*. Graphics Press, page 47.

Box Plots

The box plot was invented in the 1970s by an extraordinary statistician named John Wilder Tukey. Box plots show how multiple sets of values are distributed across a quantitative range in a way that makes it possible to compare their centers, spreads (lowest to highest values), and shapes to one another.

It is often inadequate to describe a set of values as a single summarized measure such as a sum or average. At times it is important to describe how values are distributed across the entire range. For instance, to fully understand the nature of employee compensation in each of the salary grades in a company (that is, specified levels of compensation with prescribed ranges), we would certainly need to see more than the sum of salaries for each salary grade. Even a measure of average compensation, such as the mean or median, wouldn't tell us enough. Let's look at a few different ways that this information could be presented. The following figure presents the median salary in each grade.

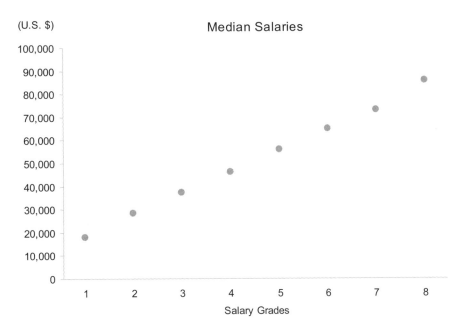

FIGURE 8.21. This graph displays employee salaries per salary grade as a single median value for each grade.

The adequacy of this display depends on the viewer's purpose. If her purpose requires a sense of how salaries are distributed across each range, this display won't tell enough of the story. The median expresses the center of the range but not how the values are distributed around that center. The next figure shows several examples of salary distributions that all have the same medians and spreads from low to high but quite different shapes. As we can see, the median alone tells a limited story, so it is often useful to display the data in a way that reveals more about how the values are distributed.

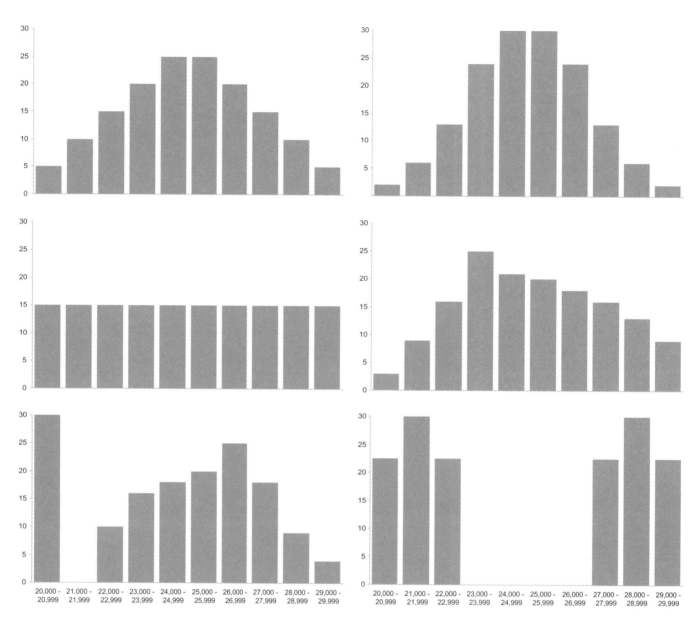

The following graph illustrates the simplest (and least informative) way to display how sets of values are distributed. It uses range bars to display two values for each salary grade: the lowest and the highest. Although it is useful to see the full range of each salary grade, this simple approach still tells us nothing about how individual values are distributed within those ranges. Do the values cluster near the bottom, center, or top, or are they evenly distributed?

FIGURE 8.22. Six examples of how a set of salaries with the same median value and spread might be differently distributed; the scales on the vertical axes represents the number of employees whose salaries fall into each of the ranges that run along the scales on the horizontal axes.

FIGURE 8.23. This is the simplest but least informative way to display ranges of values. It uses range bars that encode the lowest and highest salaries in each salary grade.

With a combination of range bars and a measure of the median, as shown in the following figure, a bit more insight begins to emerge. Knowing that, by definition, half of the values are larger than or equal to the median and half are smaller than or equal to the median, we know that when the median is closer to the low end of a range of values, more values fall into the lower half than the upper half of the spread. The closer the median is to the bottom of the range, the more skewed the values are toward the top of the range. The opposite is true when the median lies closer to the top of the range. The understanding of the distribution that is revealed by this relatively simple display certainly isn't complete, but it's definitely getting better and is probably sufficient for many purposes on a dashboard.

FIGURE 8.24. This graph combines a range bar for the spread with a mark for the median for each salary grade.

We can think of the combination of range bars with data points to mark the medians as a simplistic version of a box plot. A true box plot, as introduced by Tukey, provides more information. The box portion of a box plot is simply a rectangle with or without a fill color. As with a range bar, the bottom of the box represents a value and the top represents a value, but these are usually not the lowest and highest values in the range. The following figure illustrates a full-grown version of a single box plot with "whiskers" (also known as a *box-and-whisker* plot). This is just one of the many variations that are commonly used.

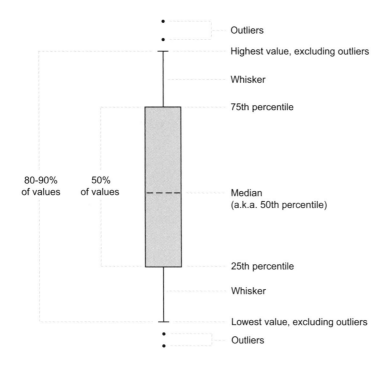

FIGURE 8.25. An individual box plot with whiskers; outliers are individual data values that fall outside the normal range. The normal range is represented by the whiskers.

A graph with boxes like this conveys a rich picture of data distribution—perhaps too rich for most dashboards and most of the folks who use them. A simpler version of the box plot, such as the one below, might be preferable for dashboard use.

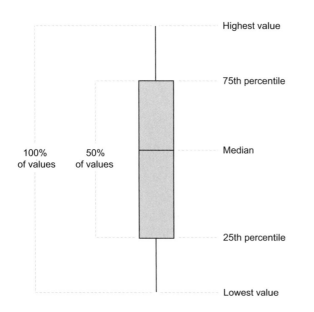

FIGURE 8.26. A simplified version of a box plot such as this one is usually more appropriate for dashboards than the one shown in *Figure 8.25*.

Scatter Plots

A scatter plot does only one thing, but it does it quite well: it displays correlations. That is, in a scatter plot, we can see whether or not, in what direction, and to what degree two paired sets of quantitative values are correlated. For instance, if we want to show that there is a relationship between the number of broadcast ads and sales revenues, a scatter plot such as the one below would work nicely.

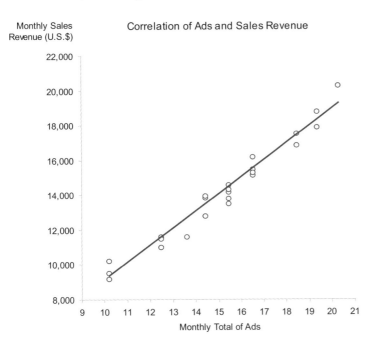

FIGURE 8.27. This scatter plot displays the correlation between the number of ads and the amount of sales revenue for 24 months.

In this case, the number of times ads were aired and the sales revenues for each month were collected as a paired set of values for 24 months. This graph tells us the following:

- There is a correlation between ads and sales revenue, indicated by the fact that a change in the number of ads almost always corresponded to a change in sales revenue.
- The correlation is positive (upward sloping from left to right), indicating that as the number of ads increased the sales revenue usually also increased.
- The correlation is fairly strong. This is indicated by the tight grouping of the data values around the trend line, showing that an increase or decrease in ads from one measure to another almost always corresponded to a similar amount of increase or decrease in sales revenue.

Given that each pair of measures was collected monthly for 24 consecutive months, this information could have been displayed as a pair of time-series line graphs, but the nature of the correlation would not have stood out as clearly.

The scatter plot will still work nicely if we split the measures into multiple sets. For instance, we could split the ads into two types, radio and television, as shown on the following page. A quick examination of this display tells us that the correlation of television ads to sales revenue is more positive (upward sloping) than that of radio ads though the strength of each correlation (the proximity of the data values to the trend line) appears to be about the same.

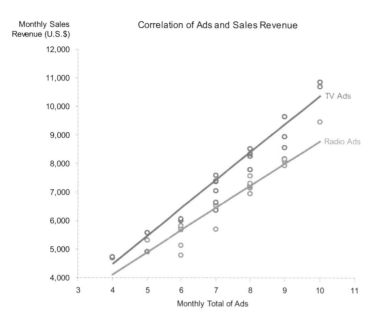

FIGURE 8.28. This scatter plot displays the correlation between the number of radio and television ads and the corresponding sales revenue for 24 months.

Scatter plots are sometimes rendered in 3D to display the correlation among three quantitative variables, rather than only two. Other methods are sometimes also used to increase the number of correlated variables in a single scatter plot. I recommend against using any of these approaches on a dashboard, however, because even when they are designed as well as possible, they require too much study to understand; they take time that dashboard viewers don't have.

One other point I'd like to mention is that the use of a *linear trend line* (also known as a *straight line of best fit*) in a scatter plot makes the direction and strength of the correlation stand out more than is possible when we see the individual data points by themselves. The graph below is precisely the same as the one in *Figure 8.28* except that it lacks trend lines. It is easy to see that the strength of the correlations would require more time to discern without the trend lines. Lines of best fit come in several types, some of which are curved, and each works best for data sets that exhibit particular patterns.

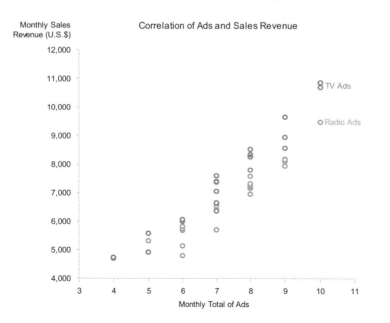

FIGURE 8.29. This scatter plot displays the correlation between the number of radio and television ads and their respective amount of sales revenue for 24 months, this time without the trend lines that appear in *Figure 8.28*.

Even though the scatter plot was primarily created for showing a correlation (or lack of one) between two quantitative variables, it and its close cousin the bubble plot may also be used for the simpler purpose of showing how a set of items relate to one another in terms of two or three quantitative variables, including how those items fall into different categories that are based on those variables. In the following example, a bubble plot is divided into meaningful quadrants.

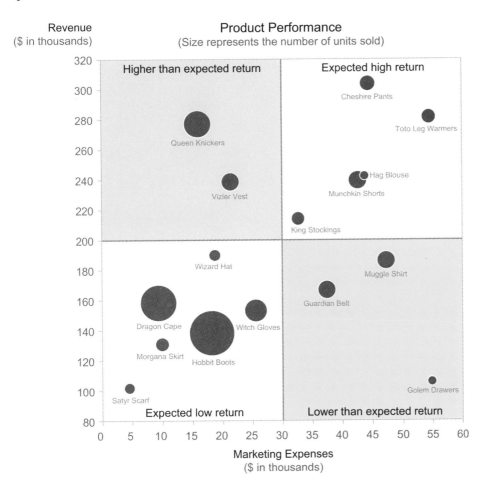

FIGURE 8.30. Scatter plots and bubble plots may be used in dashboards to show where items fall within qualitative ranges based on two quantitative variables associated with the X and Y axes.

Spatial Maps

Spatial maps can be used to associate information—both categorical and quantitative—with physical space. When the location of items must be known to understand what's going on, spatial maps are useful.

The most common form of spatial display is a geographic map. This doesn't mean, however, that any time measures can be displayed on a map, they should be; only when the meaning of the information is tied to geography and that meaning cannot easily be understood without actually seeing the measures on a map should this approach be taken. For example, sales revenue can be understood in relation to a small number of sales regions without displaying the data on a map (see below).

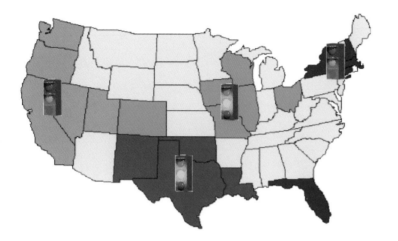

FIGURE 8.31. Spatial maps can be useful when they add to our understanding of the data, but, as in this case, they are often used unnecessarily.

Some information demands a geospatial display. For example, the path and intensity of storms on a weather-monitoring dashboard could not be displayed effectively without a map.

FIGURE 8.32. When location is an important part of what's being tracked, geospatial displays are priceless.

The next-most-useful type of spatial map on a dashboard is probably the floor plan of a building. For the manager who has to monitor temperatures throughout a large, multi-story building and respond whenever particular areas exceed established norms, seeing the temperatures arranged on a floor plan, as illustrated on the following page, could bring to light relationships among adjacent areas that he might miss otherwise.

FIGURE 8.33. Air temperatures are being monitored spatially using variation in color on a simple floor plan.

Heat Maps

Whenever quantitative values are represented as variation in color, we call the display a *heat map*. We're all familiar with heat maps in the form of geographic displays in which colors represent various air temperatures or amounts of precipitation. The following map uses varying intensities of red to display rates of traumatic brain injury in the United States from 2004-2006.

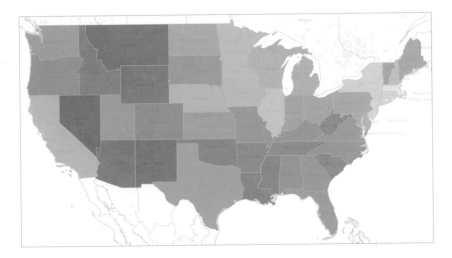

FIGURE 8.34. Heat maps arranged geographically are familiar.

It is also common and useful to arrange heat map colors in tabular fashion as a matrix of columns and rows. The following example based on data from the World Health Organization (WHO) displays a proportional breakdown of alcohol consumption as of the year 2005, by type, per country in a heat map arranged as a matrix.

Country	Spirits	Beer	Wine	Other
India				
Philippines				
Nicaragua				
Cuba				
El Salvador				
Russian Federation				
Ukraine				
Honduras				
China				
Guatemala				
Japan				
Ecuador				
Costa Rica				
Brazil				
Romania				
Turkey				
Colombia				
Panama				
Chile				
Poland				
USA				
Finland				
Peru				
Paraguay				
Canada				
Greece				
Puerto Rico				
Czech Republic				
Hungary				
Venezuela				
Australia				
Bolivia				
Mexico				
United Kingdom				
Norway				
France				
Germany				
Singapore				
Iceland				
Ireland				
Uruguay				
Switzerland				
Sweden				
Netherlands				
Denmark				
New Zealand				
Spain				
Austria				
Portugal				
Argentina				
Belgium				
Italy				

FIGURE 8.35. Heat maps may also be arranged as a matrix of columns and rows.

Representing the values using variation in color intensity does not provide the precision that could be seen using a series of horizontal bars in this case, but many more small color-coded objects can be placed in the limited space that we might have on a dashboard.

Treemaps

Treemaps were developed in the 1990s by Ben Shneiderman of the University of Maryland to display large sets of hierarchically or categorically structured data in the most space-efficient way possible. Shneiderman is one of the most inspiring researchers and innovators working in information visualization; he has played a major role in defining the domain. Treemaps fill the available space with a set of contiguous rectangles that have each been sized to encode a quantitative variable. Hierarchies and categories are represented as rectangles contained within larger rectangles. In addition to the quantitative variable that is associated with rectangle size, color can also be used to encode a second quantitative variable and thus provide a richer, multi-variate display.

The purpose of treemaps is not to make fine quantitative comparisons or to rank items but rather to spot particular conditions of interest within a huge set of values. We should never use treemaps when we can use a form of display that supports easier and more accurate comparisons, such as a bar graph. The sizes of rectangles and variations in color do not support easy, efficient, or accurate value comparisons, but when there are too many values to display in a bar graph, a treemap can be used to make rough comparisons that are good enough for high-level performance monitoring.

Because of their space-efficient design, treemaps can be used quite effectively on dashboards but should be reserved for the circumstances for which they were developed, and, when used, should be designed with care. The next example illustrates an appropriately applied and effectively designed treemap for a business dashboard. It displays stocks by sectors of the stock market (financial, health care, technology, etc.) with the market capitalization of each stock encoded as rectangle size and percentage change in the stock's price today compared to yesterday encoded as color ranging from dark red for the greatest losses to dark blue for the greatest gains. Notice how your eyes are especially drawn to the large dark red and dark blue rectangles, which represent stocks with large market capitalizations that either lost or gained a lot of value. Notice also how easy it is to spot sectors of the market that decreased in price on this particular day (especially technology) as well as those that increased (for example, consumer, cyclical). Exceptions to the norm also pop out, such as the fact that Dell's stock price did exceptionally well (the fairly large dark blue rectangle in the technology sector) when most of the technology sector did poorly.

FIGURE 8.36. This treemap, created using software from Panopticon, displays two quantitative variables for the entire stock market.

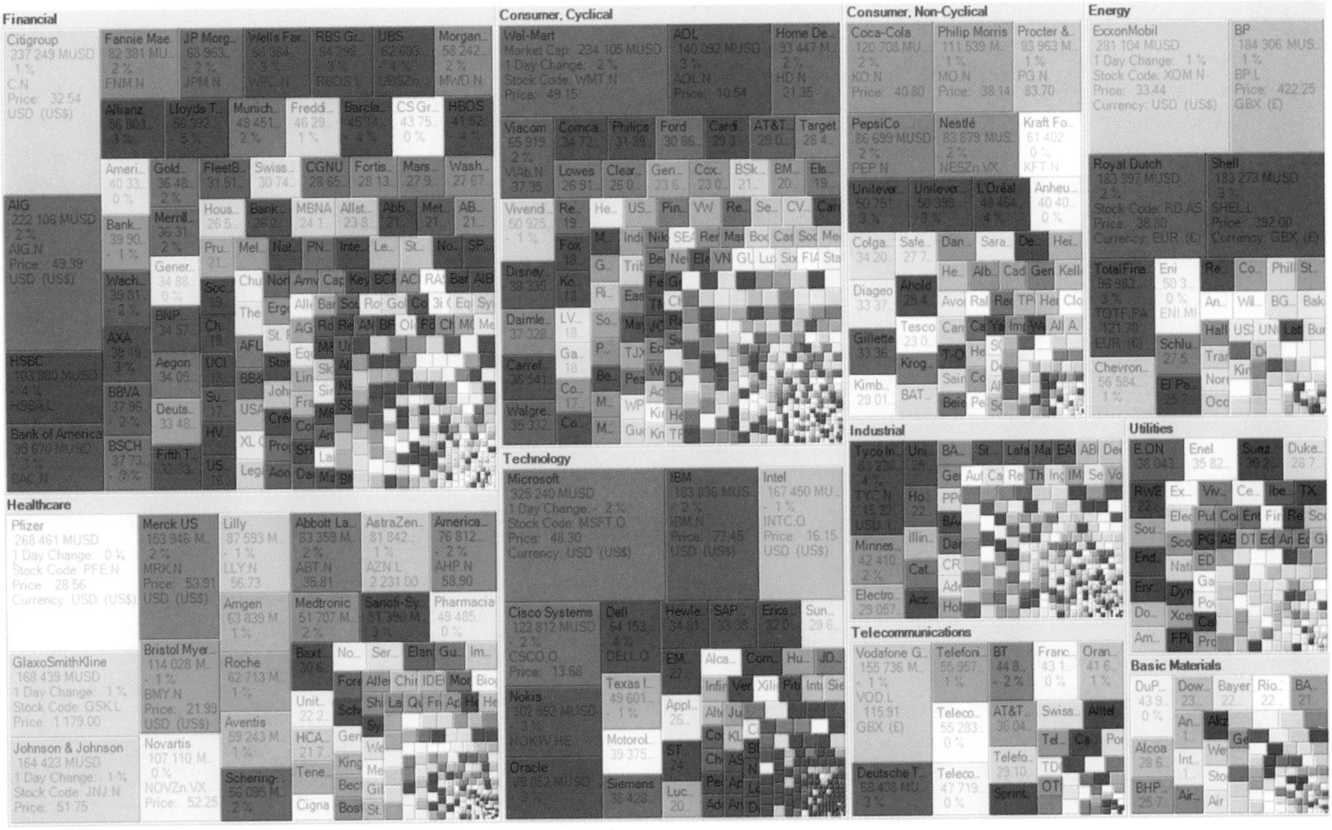

Small Multiples

There are times when the information that we have to display can't be shown in a single graph in an effective way. For example, the information might consist of too many variables for a single graph. Fortunately, we're not limited to a single graph. We can display the information in a series of graphs, which Edward Tufte calls "small multiples." The graphs are arranged in a tabular fashion, consisting either of a single row, a single column, or multiple rows and columns in a matrix. Typically, the same graph appears multiple times, in each instance differing within a single variable.

Let's consider an example. If we need to display revenue data as a bar graph across four sales regions, with bookings and billings shown separately, we could do so in a single graph, as shown below.

FIGURE 8.37. This bar graph displays three variables.

If, however, we must simultaneously display the revenue split among three sales channels (for example, sold directly, through distributors, and through resellers), a single graph won't work. To the rescue comes the small multiples display. As shown below, by arranging three versions of the same graph next to one another—one graph per sales channel—we can show the entire picture within eye span, making comparisons easy. To eliminate unnecessary redundancy, we could avoid repeating the region labels in each graph as well as the legend and the overall title. This not only saves valuable space, which is always important on a dashboard, but also reduces the amount of information that the viewer must read when examining the display.

FIGURE 8.38. This series of horizontally aligned small multiples displays revenue split among three sales channels.

In some cases, we might want the graphs to differ along more than one variable, such as one variable per column and another per row. I call this arrangement a visual crosstab of small multiples. The example below differs by product type across the columns and by region down the rows.

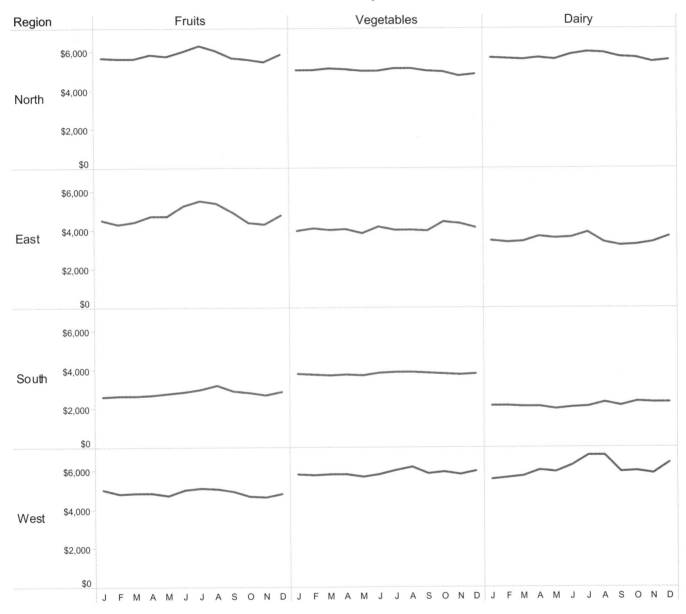

FIGURE 8.39. A matrix of small multiples, created using Tableau Software.

Dysfunctional Graphs that We Should Avoid

You might be wondering why some of the other graphs that are familiar to you are missing from this proposed library. Each is missing for one of the following two reasons:

- It communicates less effectively than an alternative that I've included.
- It is too complex for the typical needs of a dashboard.

The pie chart probably tops the list of often-used graphs that were left out of this library because they communicate less effectively than other means. Pie charts were designed to display part-to-whole information, such as the individual products that make up an entire product line. As we've already discovered, however, part-to-whole information can be communicated more clearly using a bar graph. Another comparison of the two types of graphs used to display the same set of part-to-whole data is shown below.

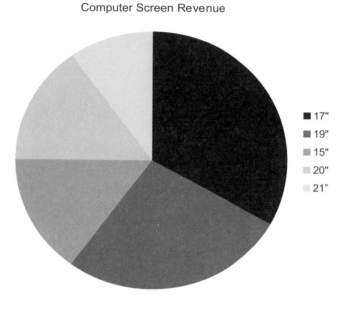

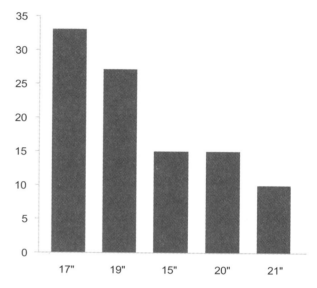

Viewers can process the information in the bar graph on the right much more quickly and easily than the information in the pie chart on the left. Why? Whereas a bar graph uses the preattentive visual attribute of line length (that is, the lengths or heights of the bars) to encode quantitative values, pie charts encode values as the two-dimensional areas of the slices and their angles as the slices extend from the center toward the circumference of the circle. Our visual perception does a poor job of accurately and efficiently comparing 2-D areas and angles. The only thing that a pie chart has going for it is that, when we see one, we automatically know that we are looking at measures that are parts of a whole. Because bar graphs can be used for other types of comparisons, when we use them to display part-to-whole data, we must label them in a manner that makes this clear. As long as this is done, bar graphs are far superior.

A pie chart falls into a larger class of graphs called *area graphs*. Area graphs use 2-D space to encode quantitative values, which is prone to inaccurate interpretation and often to occlusion (a problem that is caused when one object is hidden entirely or in part behind another). The following area graph illustrates the problem of occlusion; revenues for Quarters 2 and 3 in the West and Quarter 4 in the North are completely hidden.

FIGURE 8.40. This pie chart and bar graph both display the same part-to-whole data. The values are much easier to interpret and compare when a bar graph is used.

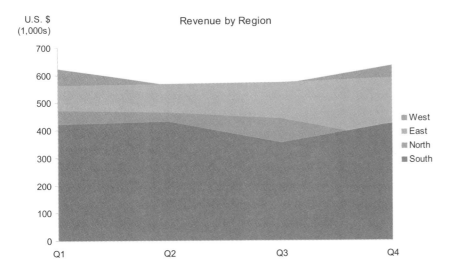

FIGURE 8.41. Area graphs can suffer from the problem of occlusion.

What about stacked area graphs? Occlusion doesn't occur when areas are stacked on one another, but other problems do. The following example displays monthly sales revenues in total and by region.

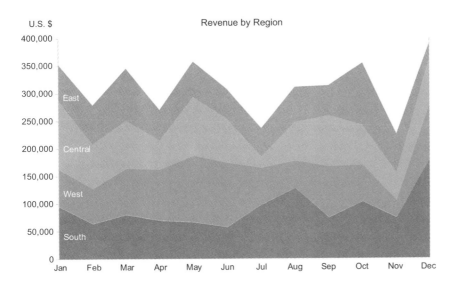

FIGURE 8.42. Stacked area graphs might seem innocent, but they can easily mislead.

They look and function a lot like line graphs, which leads people astray, because not all parts of them can be read like line graphs. We can trace the up and down pattern along the top of the green section to see how total sales changed through time and we can do the same with the top of the blue section to see how sales in the south region changed, but we can't do this to see how sales in the west, central, and east regions changed. The border at the top of each section except the one on the bottom (blue) does not show the pattern of change for it alone, but the pattern of change for it and every section below it combined. The west region's sales through time are represented by the distance between the bottom and the top of the orange section at each position above the individual month names. Unless you're exceptional, you cannot convert this mentally into a meaningful pattern of change. In the following example we can see sales for the west region alone. Imagine trying to get the pattern that we see below by viewing the orange section in the previous stacked area graph.

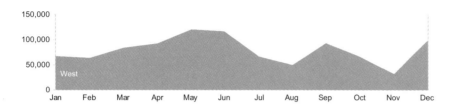

FIGURE 8.43. This graph displays sales for the west region alone based on the same values that appear in *Figure 8.42*.

If we need to display both the total of something (for example, total sales) and its parts (sales by region) as they change through time, we should consider using two regular line graphs, one immediately above the other: one to show the total and the other to show the parts, as illustrated below.

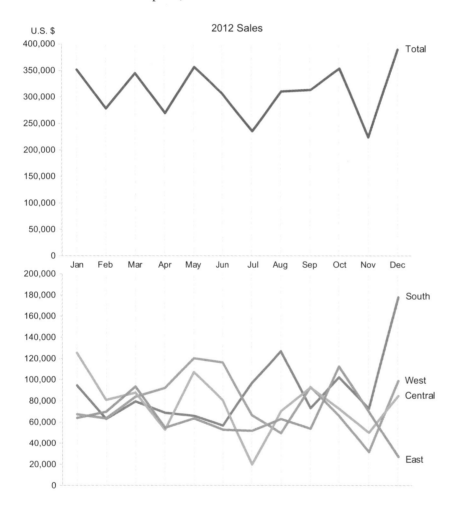

FIGURE 8.44. This pair of graphs displays the patterns of total sales (above) and regional sales (below) through time in a way that makes both easy to see.

If space is an issue, these graphs can be much smaller—especially shorter—and still work quite well.

Another chart that's surfacing more and more often these days on dashboards is the *radar graph*, a circular graph that encodes quantitative values using lines that radiate from the center of the circle to meet the boundary formed by its circumference. A radar graph is nothing but a line graph with the categorical scale arranged in a circle, as seen on the left in the next example. A radar graph is not as effective as a bar graph (shown on the right), in part because it is more difficult to read and compare values that are arranged in a circular fashion. Linear scanning is more efficient.

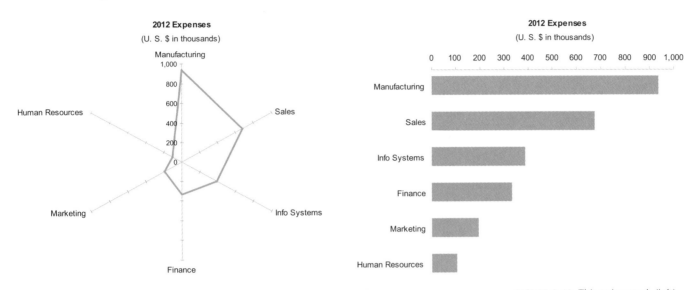

FIGURE 8.45. This radar graph (left) and bar graph (right) display the same expense data. In the radar graph, departments are arranged along the circumference and the quantitative scale for expenses resides along the radial axes that extend from the center. The bar graph is much easier and faster to read.

The *funnel chart* is one of the most absurd graphs that is often used on dashboards. What it intends to do isn't absurd, but the way it's usually designed is. The intention is usually to display a count of items or amounts of revenue that flows through a series of sequential stages and decreases in value with each. More than anything else, funnel charts are used to track sales from initial leads, stage by stage, until those that remain result in actual revenue. The following example tracks visitors to a website, which shows decreasing numbers of those who progress through greater stages of commitment to the site.

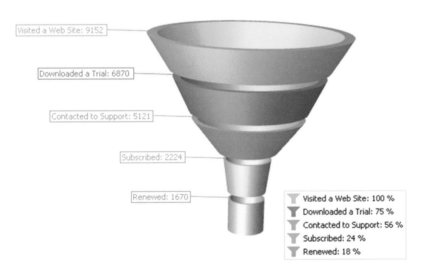

FIGURE 8.46. A funnel chart of website visitors

In this case, the funnel metaphor was definitely taken too literally. As a metaphor, a funnel works well, but depicting the values of each stage as parts of an actual funnel does not. Even if the parts were accurately sized to represent the number of visitors in each stage, it wouldn't support useful comparisons. We must rely on the numbers to see and compare the values as they decrease. This perceptual problem is easily solved, however, by using a simple bar graph, such as the one below.

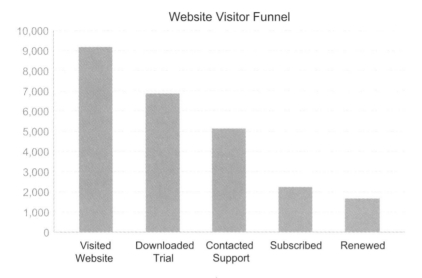

FIGURE 8.47. A funnel process can be represented well as a bar graph.

A funnel process may be enriched in several ways. In the example below, short black lines appear relative to the blue bars to show the previous day's values, and a second graph with red bars directly displays the percentage loss between each stage of the process and the next.

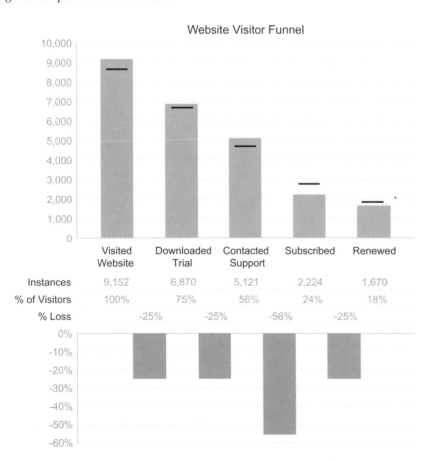

FIGURE 8.48. A funnel process can be represented well as a bar graph.

People who use dashboards to do their jobs need us to display information simply, clearly, and accurately, in a way that they can rapidly assimilate. Colorful 3-D pie charts and shiny funnels are cute and entertaining, but the appeal wears off quickly if they don't deliver the information that's needed. Our goal is to design dashboards that will fully empower people for years.

9   DESIGNING BULLET GRAPHS

As I explained in the previous chapter, a bullet graph functions as a gauge of sorts that is specifically designed to work well on a dashboard. In this chapter we'll look more closely at the characteristics that make bullet graphs effective and at the ways in which they may be designed to suit a myriad of circumstances.

Space-Efficient Design

The linear design of the bullet graph, which can be oriented either horizontally or vertically, allows several of these graphs to be placed next to one another in a relatively small space. The two figures below show how closely bullet graphs can be packed together; imagine how much room would be required to display the same data using circular gauges!

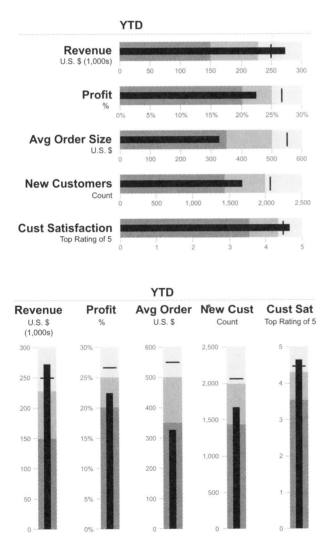

FIGURE 9.1. A collection of horizontally oriented bullet graphs

FIGURE 9.2. A collection of vertically oriented bullet graphs

While scanning a series of bullet graphs, notice how easy it is to detect the measures that have met or exceeded their targets, which are represented by the short lines that intersect the bars. When a measure exceeds this line, a cross shape is formed. This form is easy to see because it can be perceived preattentively and therefore instantly. We can scan the bullet graphs on a dashboard and immediately know which measures are doing well and which are not simply by the presence or absence of these cross shapes where the bars and small lines intersect.

Bullet graphs can be quite small and still work. For example, as illustrated below, even the small screen of a smartphone could display several metrics using bullet graphs. Imagine trying to fit this many radial gauges on a screen this size.

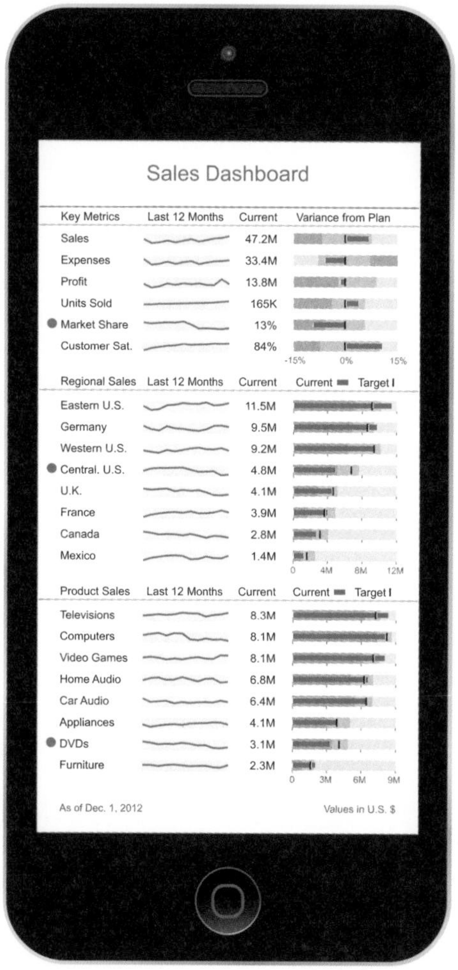

FIGURE 9.3. Several bullet graphs can be displayed in a small space, illustrated by this mock-up of a dashboard on a smartphone.

The Primary Measure

For bullet graphs to communicate information clearly and rapidly, the primary measure that they display must stand out as their most salient component. For this reason, I usually make the bars black or dark gray, but other colors may be used, as illustrated next.

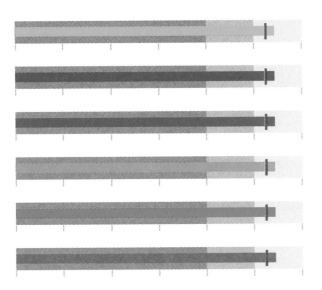

FIGURE 9.4. Colors other than black may be used for the bars in bullet graphs.

I typically avoid the use of green and red, however, because people tend to associate good and bad meanings with those colors. I often use a bright color other than black for all important measures on a dashboard, which nicely highlights everything that's important in a simple, consistent way. When almost everything else is gray, any bright color will pop out.

Ranges of Performance

The background fill colors that encode qualitative ranges (for example, bad, satisfactory, good) in a bullet graph vary by color intensity rather than hue. This ensures that viewers who are colorblind can still see the distinctions. Even though various shades of gray have been used in the examples so far, any hue will work. The following bullet graph uses various intensities of beige.

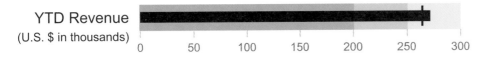

FIGURE 9.5. This bullet graph uses various intensities of beige to encode qualitative states.

We can encode more than three qualitative states with background fill colors, but to avoid a level of complexity that cannot be perceived efficiently and to maintain a clear distinction between the colors, I recommend limiting the number to five. The next example illustrates this practical limit.

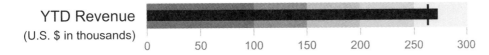

FIGURE 9.6. This bullet graph uses five distinct color intensities to encode qualitative states.

Whenever we're tempted to exceed three qualitative states, we need to ask ourselves whether that level of precision is really needed for performance monitoring. It rarely is.

Multiple Points of Comparison

It is sometimes useful to compare a key measure to more than one other measure. For instance, we might want to compare revenue to the revenue target as well as to the revenue amount on this date last year. The bullet graph easily handles two comparisons by using a distinct marker for each. These distinctions can be displayed using varying attributes of color intensity, line width (that is, stroke weight), or even symbol shapes. The example below uses different symbol shapes to distinguish the two points of comparison.

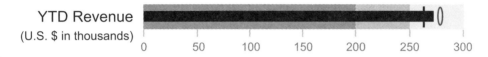

YTD Revenue
(U.S. $ in thousands)

FIGURE 9.7. This bullet graph includes two comparisons.

I recommend limiting the comparative measures to two. More than this will overly complicate and slow perception.

Alternatives to Bars

When I originally developed the design specification for the bullet graph, I called it by a different name: a *performance bar*. I had to change the name, however, because I eventually realized that there were times when the key measure should be encoded using something other than a bar.

Whenever we use a bar to encode a quantitative value, as we've seen in each of the examples of bullet graphs so far, the quantitative scale should start at zero. The value is represented not just by the location of the bar's endpoint, but by the full length of the bar, so a scale that starts anywhere but at zero will produce a bar whose length doesn't correspond to its value. This makes accurate comparisons between graphs very difficult.

It is sometimes useful to narrow the quantitative scale of a bullet graph to display quantitative detail, which means not starting the scale at zero. For instance, suppose that all of the values that need to be included in the bullet graph fall between 90 and 100%, and we want to focus exclusively on this range of values to show subtlety in the difference between the key measure and its comparison (for example, a target). In this case, we should use some means other than a bar to accurately encode the key measure. For example, we can use a mark (a simple symbol shape, such as an oval) to encode the key measure and a mark with a different shape for a comparative measure. Just make sure that the primary measure is the most prominent of the two, as illustrated below with the dark oval.

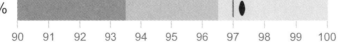

Network Uptime %

FIGURE 9.8. Because the quantitative scale of this bullet graph does not begin at zero, I've used a symbol marker rather than a bar to encode the key measure. In this case, the key measure is encoded as an oval showing that network uptime has slightly exceeded the 97% target measure that is encoded as a short vertical line.

Using a bar to encode the key measure in a bullet graph has the advantage of superior visual weight to highlight the key value, but a small mark, which encodes a value based solely on its position, allows us to narrow the quantitative scale to display greater subtlety in the values and their differences. Using a mark rather than a bar also alerts the viewer that the scale does not start at zero.

A particular mark that I've found to work well is an "X" (see below) because it can be large enough to stand out clearly and yet still display a value precisely at the center where the two lines intersect.

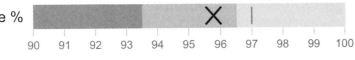

FIGURE 9.9. The shape of an X works well as a marker in a bullet graph.

Even if the primary value and the value to which it is being compared (for example, a target) are the same, a mark shaped as an X will not occlude the point of comparison, as shown below.

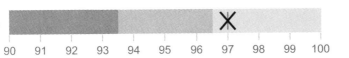

FIGURE 9.10. An X-shaped mark does not occlude a comparative mark that's represented as a short vertical line.

Differentiating Measures that Should Be Read Differently

Performance measures can be favorable when they are high in value (for example, profits and website visitors) or when they are low (for example, expenses and defects). When several measures are displayed together in a set of bullet graphs, it is important that viewers can quickly and easily spot this distinction. One way to design bullet graphs to provide an obvious visual distinction is illustrated below.

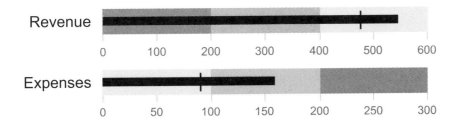

FIGURE 9.11. The visual indicators of the qualitative states of poor, satisfactory, and good performance (dark gray, medium gray, and light gray respectively) run left to right for revenues to indicate that higher is better and in the opposite sequence for expenses to indicate that lower is better.

Notice that in the example above the qualitative states (in this case, poor, satisfactory, and good performance), which are represented by shades of gray in the background, differ in sequence from poor to good, or good to poor, depending on the nature of the measure. To broadcast this distinction even more noticeably, bullet graphs can be designed like the next example.

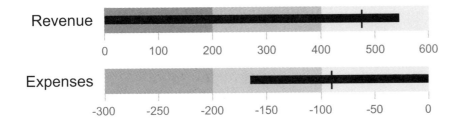

FIGURE 9.12. Running the bar and the quantitative scale from right to left is often an effective way to distinguish measures that are better when lower.

In this case, the direction of the bar and the quantitative scale in the second graph is the opposite of the direction in the first graph. This causes the measure that is better when lower to pop out as different from the norm. Running the scale from right to left using negative values is a sensible way to represent expenses because expenses can be easily understood as negative—money that is subtracted from revenues.

Positive and Negative Values

Because some measures, such as profits, can be positive or negative (profits are negative when costs exceed revenues), bullet graphs must be able to display both positive and negative values for the same measure. A common case is when bullet graphs are used to express the variance between two measures, such as how actual expenses vary from budgeted expenses, as illustrated below.

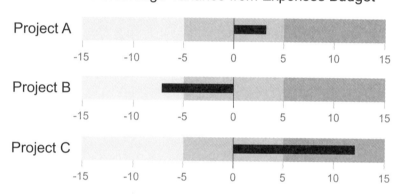

FIGURE 9.13. Bullet graphs must sometimes express a measure that can be either positive or negative in value.

Values Within a Distribution

Sometimes the value that's displayed in a bullet graph needs to be compared to the distribution of an entire set of values. For example, a teacher who uses a dashboard to monitor the performance of her students might need to see how individual students compare to others in the class or how her class performs on average compared to other classes. For this purpose, a bullet graph could be designed as shown below.

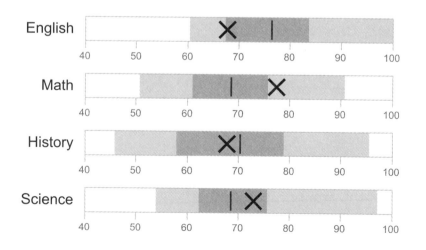

FIGURE 9.14. Bullet graphs may be used to display a value in relation to an entire distribution of values.

In this example, each X mark indicates an individual student's current score, the vertical gray line represents the class median, the dark gray fill color represents the range within which the middle 50% of the students' scores fall, and the lighter gray fill colors represent the ranges within which the bottom 25% and top 25% of the scores fall. At a glance, a teacher could use this series of bullet graphs to see how this particular student is doing compared to his peers. Many measures could be meaningfully compared to a larger distribution of values in this manner.

Multiple Bullet Graphs in a Series

Even though I designed the bullet graph primarily to display a single measure in the context of one or more meaningful comparisons, on some occasions we will find it useful to use an entire series of bullet graphs to display a set of related values so that the values can be compared to one another. In the following example, a series of bullet graphs displays profits for a set of products.

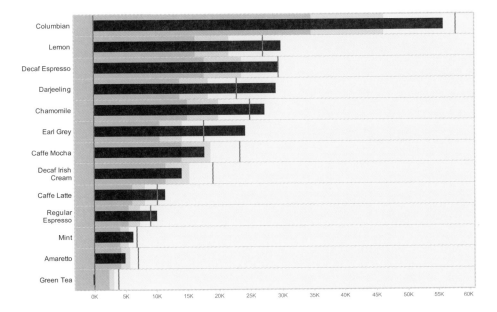

FIGURE 9.15. Bullet graphs may be used to display an entire series of related values for the purpose of comparison.

Notice that the entire series of bullet graphs in this example shares a common quantitative scale, which is necessary to enable comparisons. Using these graphs, we can easily compare profits and see how each product's profits compare to the plan for profits (the short vertical lines) in the context of qualitative ranges of performance (poor, satisfactory, and good, represented by three shades of beige).

Future Projections

Let's look at one more way we can use bullet graphs. Whenever we compare a current measure to a future target, such as revenue as of January 15 compared to a Quarter 1 target, we can easily see how far the measure is from the target, but it's not always so easy to tell whether the measure is on track to meet or surpass the future target, which could still be weeks or even months away. This is true whether we are using a bullet graph or any other graphical means to display this information. This shortcoming in the usefulness of the comparison can be ameliorated by adding a projection of where the measure will be at the end of the period of time that is relevant to the target. The bullet graph below splits the revenue measure into two segments: the actual measure as of today and the projected measure of revenue based on current performance. Combining this information into a single graph provides a rich display that tells us not only how far the measure has progressed along the path to the future target, but also how well the measure is doing today in relation to that target.

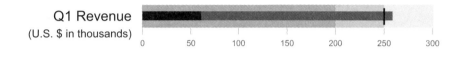

FIGURE 9.16. This bullet graph displays both the actual quarter-to-date revenue (the dark segment) and a projection of expected quarter-end revenue based on current performance (the lighter gray segment). The short vertical line indicates the target revenue for the quarter.

I can state with some confidence that bullet graphs work well because I've conducted informal experiments comparing them to simple radial gauges. In my tests, bullet graphs outperformed radial gauges both in efficiency and accuracy of perception. The number of test subjects was too small to satisfy scientific standards, so I'll refrain from claiming specific degrees of superior performance. These tests were sufficient, however, to enable me to state without reservation that bullet graphs work at least as well on dashboards as radial gauges and are able to convey the same information in much less space. I believe that makes them superior.

Since the introduction of bullet graphs in 2005, most dashboard products now support them. Some products that don't support them directly, such as Excel, can be used to construct them from other graphs. Unfortunately, not all products support them well. As you might imagine, many vendors feel that bullet graphs must be spruced up with visual effects and bright colors, which undermines the effectiveness of a graph that can communicate clearly and directly when designed with eloquent simplicity.

10 DESIGNING SPARKLINES

Sparklines can be designed to feature various aspects of time-series data. Just as for other quantitative graphs, we must first determine the information that a client needs from sparklines before deciding how these displays ought to be designed. We should design graphs to achieve the client's information needs without overcomplicating them and thus slowing perception. When used on dashboards, sparklines should always tell their story at a glance.

Beyond Trend Arrows

People often use simple up or down trend arrows to display the direction in which a measure is moving, but these can be ambiguous on a dashboard. When we watch the stock report on the evening news and see a trend arrow pointing upwards, we know exactly what it means: the price of the stock increased on that day. When we look at the month to date (MTD) revenue measure below, however, it isn't obvious whether the upward trend arrow indicates that revenue is trending upward overall for the year, the quarter, the month, or just since yesterday.

⬆ Revenue $83,298

A sparkline, as shown below, dispels this ambiguity, because it displays the entire period of history across which the trend applies.

Revenue $83,298

Knowing that this sparkline represents the revenues that have come in during the past 30 days, we can see that, even though they went up since yesterday (perhaps this is what the upward pointing trend arrow in *Figure 10.1* was saying), they have trended downward during this period as a whole. Sparklines tell a richer story than trend arrows. They can tell even richer stories than this with a bit of enhancement.

Enriched with Context

Although always small and simple, sparklines can include a bit more information than what I've shown so far. The following sparkline includes a light gray rectangle whose height represents the number of manufacturing defects that are acceptable, which in this case is 12. We can see that during the past thirty days (the full range of the sparkline) the number of defects has exceeded the acceptable upper limit on three days. The optional dot marking the final value in the

FIGURE 10.1. Simple trend arrows are often used on dashboards, but what they mean is sometimes unclear.

FIGURE 10.2. This sparkline provides a clear picture of the historical trend leading up to the present measure.

sparkline ties the end of the sparkline to the current value of five by rendering them in the same color.

 5 Daily Defects

FIGURE 10.3. This sparkline displays 30 days of manufacturing defect history compared to the acceptable range.

In the example below, the dark sparkline represents the immediately preceding 12 months of revenues, and the lighter line provides context by showing revenues during the 12 months prior to the current period. Because the contextual information is much less prominent than the primary sparkline, we can focus on the most recent 12 months' revenues without being distracted by the information about the prior 12 months, but the context is still clearly visible when we wish to focus on it.

FIGURE 10.4. This sparkline compares the immediately preceding 12 months (the dark line) to the prior 12-month period (the light line).

For rapid performance monitoring, it sometimes makes sense for sparklines to display variance from a target rather than raw values. The following sparkline presents variance between actual and budgeted expenses during the most recent 12 months. Values in the white area are below budget, and those in the gray area are above budget. When the information is rendered in this way, we can see at a glance the difference between values that are below budget and those that are above.

FIGURE 10.5. This sparkline displays the variance between the past 12 months' expenses and the expense budget. Over-spending appears in the gray area.

We'll look at even richer examples of context that can be incorporated into sparklines later in this chapter, but first let's consider a fundamental aspect of sparkline design: setting the quantitative scale.

Scaled for Various Purposes

Even though the quantitative scale of a sparkline is not visible, we must determine its range. Because sparklines are small and especially limited in height, we usually scale them to fill the entire plot area from bottom to top so that we can display patterns and trends of change clearly. We do this by scaling the vertical axis of the sparkline to begin with the lowest value in the series at the bottom and to end with the highest value at the top. In the figure below, the sparkline on the left is scaled in this manner, and the one to the right, which represents the same values, is scaled to fill only 10% of the vertical space. This makes the pattern, which is easy to see on the left, almost entirely invisible on the right.

FIGURE 10.6. Scaling a sparkline to fill the vertical space that's available, as shown on the left, makes it as easy as possible to see the pattern of change.

Sparklines are primarily used to display patterns and trends of change through time. For this reason they are usually scaled to fill the vertical space. However, patterns and trends of change are not the only characteristics of time series that are potentially useful on a dashboard. A sparkline can be designed to feature the following characteristics as well:

- Magnitudes of values
- Magnitudes of change
- Rates of change
- Degree of variability

Not all of these features can be displayed simultaneously, however, because they require different design characteristics, especially related to the sparkline's quantitative scale.

How we scale a single sparkline or a set of related sparklines depends on the following factors:

- Whether the sparkline stands alone or is part of a series of sparklines
- Whether a particular range of values other than the range between the lowest and highest values in the sparkline should be featured to support the sparkline's use (for example, the potential range of values, such as 0 through 10 for a 10-point customer satisfaction rating)
- When part of a related set of sparklines, whether each sparkline will be viewed independently or compared to others
- When sparklines in a set are compared to one another, which of the following comparisons are required, if any, in addition to patterns and trends of change: magnitudes of values, magnitudes of change, rates of change, or degrees of variability.

Sparklines may be scaled for various purposes using any of the following methods:

1. Fill the vertical space by beginning with the lowest value of the sparkline at the bottom and ending with the highest value at the top.

Student Name	Assignment Scores	High Low	Avg Score
Frederick Chandler		71% 60%	65%
Roshawn Dawson		78% 64%	72%
James Martin		79% 69%	74%
Jaime Goss		88% 78%	84%
James Snow		99% 89%	94%
Holly Norton		100% 95%	98%

FIGURE 10.7. These sparklines have been independently scaled to fill the vertical space.

Taking full advantage of the vertical space that's available for each sparkline provides the clearest possible view of patterns and trends through time. In their raw form, illustrated above, sparklines provide no information about magnitude (that is, the actual values that are represented and differences between them). Therefore, the only comparisons that can be made among the series of sparklines involve patterns and trends. When we scale a group of sparklines this way, the same pattern or trend seen in two sparklines might represent significantly different values, magnitudes of change, degrees of variability, and rates of change.

2. Consistently display a quantitative range that is especially useful for interpreting the values.

Region	Daily System Uptime	Avg System Uptime
North	∿	98%
South	∿	97%
East	∿	99%
West	∿	94%

FIGURE 10.8. These sparklines share the same scale, which doesn't vary from day to day.

In this case, because system uptime routinely falls within the 90-100% range, using this range provides a useful consistency from day to day rather than scaling from the lowest to highest values in the series, which in the case above would range from 94-99% but would likely change from day to day. This method may be applied to a single sparkline or to a series, as illustrated above. We would use this strategy when day-to-day consistency is potentially useful to the person who will consult these sparklines.

3. Maintain a consistent scale among a series of sparklines by beginning with the lowest value and ending with the highest value of the entire series.

Student Name	Assignment Scores	High Low	Avg Score
Frederick Chandler	∿	71% 60%	65%
Roshawn Dawson	∿	78% 64%	72%
James Martin	∿	79% 69%	74%
Jaime Goss	∿	88% 78%	84%
James Snow	∿	99% 89%	94%
Holly Norton	∿	100% 95%	98%

FIGURE 10.9. These sparklines share the same scale that begins with the lowest value and ends with the highest value of the entire set.

This scale ranges from 60%, the lowest score in the entire set, to 100%, the highest score in the entire set. Using a consistent scale makes it possible to see differences in magnitude although the large spread in values causes several lines to appear relatively flat, which obscures patterns of change.

4. Maintain a consistent scale among a series of sparklines by beginning with zero and ending with the highest value of the entire series.

Student Name	Assignment Scores	High Low	Avg Score
Frederick Chandler		71% 60%	65%
Roshawn Dawson		78% 64%	72%
James Martin		79% 69%	74%
Jaime Goss		88% 78%	84%
James Snow		99% 89%	94%
Holly Norton		100% 95%	98%

FIGURE 10.10. These sparklines share a scale that always begins at zero, regardless of the lowest value.

When we begin the scale at zero, the differences in the distance from the baseline (zero) to each data point along a sparkline accurately represent differences in values. Scaling a series of sparklines in this manner gives the best view for comparing the magnitudes of values among the entire series. Perceptually, this works best when those magnitudes are not only represented by the vertical positions of data points along the sparkline, but also by the height of the region between the baseline and the data points. When we fill the regions with a color that makes it them easy to see, the reader's eyes are assisted in making height comparisons.

5. View all sparklines in relation to a particular sub-range of values that is significant (for example, the midspread or 1 standard deviation from the mean) by always including that sub-range but also independently scaling each sparkline to include its lowest and highest value.

Student Name	Assignment Scores	High Low	Avg Score
Frederick Chandler		71% 60%	65%
Roshawn Dawson		78% 64%	72%
James Martin		79% 69%	74%
Jaime Goss		88% 78%	84%
James Snow		99% 89%	94%
Holly Norton		100% 95%	98%

FIGURE 10.11. These sparklines always include a specified range that is highlighted using a band of fill color.

The shaded band that appears with each sparkline in this case represents the range of scores that equals a "C" letter grade (70-79%). Notice that all but one of James Martin's scores falls within the C grade range; therefore, the gray band spans almost the entire height of the sparkline's plot area. Notice also that James Snow's and Holly Norton's scores are all well above the C range, which can be easily seen by the fact that the gray bands are relatively short and top out well below the sparklines. By including a common range in every sparkline, we add a rough sense of magnitude as well as an approximate means to compare magnitudes. However, including this common range causes some of the lines to appear flatter than we would ideally prefer when examining patterns of change. Still, the effect is less severe than would result if we used the same scale for all sparklines in the series.

6. Maintain a consistent spread (distance between the lowest and highest values) among a series of sparklines.

Student Name	Assignment Scores	High Low	Avg Score
Frederick Chandler		71% 60%	65%
Roshawn Dawson		78% 64%	72%
James Martin		79% 69%	74%
Jaime Goss		88% 78%	84%
James Snow		99% 89%	94%
Holly Norton		100% 95%	98%

FIGURE 10.12. These sparklines are each scaled to span the same distance—14 percentage points—but differ in their starting and ending values.

Because the largest spread from the lowest to the highest value in any one sparkline is 14% in this case (Roshawn Dawson), each sparkline is scaled to span a 14% range. A consistent spread, even though the scales begin and end with different values, makes it possible to compare slopes along different lines and thus provides a means to compare magnitudes of change. Notice that the sparklines for James Martin and James Snow appear to have nearly identical magnitudes of change, each spanning a range of 11%, but one ranged from 69-79% and the other from 89-99%. Scaling in this manner gives the viewer the means to compare magnitudes of change but sacrifices the ability to visually compare the magnitudes of the values themselves.

7. Display sparklines scaled logarithmically rather than linearly.

Student Name	Assignment Scores	High Low	Avg Score
Frederick Chandler		71% 60%	65%
Roshawn Dawson		78% 64%	72%
James Martin		79% 69%	74%
Jaime Goss		88% 78%	84%
James Snow		99% 89%	94%
Holly Norton		100% 95%	98%

FIGURE 10.13. These sparklines share the same logarithmic scale to make it easy to compare their rates of change.

I recommend using a logarithmic scale in a series of sparklines for two purposes only: to compare rates of change and degrees of variability. With a log scale, equal slopes along the lines represent equal rates of change if the sparklines are all scaled to start and end with the same values. A line that exhibits greater variation in the vertical positions of its values than another line represents greater variability. No other characteristics of change through time can be accurately discerned using a log scale.

Based on these examples, the following conditions can be used to determine which method to use when scaling sparklines:

- For a series of sparklines, when only patterns and trends of change must be compared, use method 1.
- For sparklines that function independently or are part of a series but are nevertheless read independently, use method 1 or 2.
- For a series of sparklines, when the magnitudes of values must be compared, use method 3, 4, or 5.
- For a series of sparklines, when only the magnitudes of change and degrees of variability must be compared, use method 6.
- For a series of sparklines, when only rates of change must be compared, use method 7.

We should keep in mind that no one scaling method can support all of the ways that someone might need to view and compare time series values. In a particular dashboard, for a particular sparkline or series of sparklines, we choose the scaling method that best fits their primary uses.

With so many potential scaling methods, it would be useful if a single way of designing sparklines could be used to serve a range of needs. The next section addresses this hope.

Featuring Patterns and Magnitude Together as Bandlines

There are ways to add information about magnitude and variability without overly complicating sparklines that are scaled to fill the vertical space. The most common way is to mark the highest and lowest values in the series with a simple dot and label those values, either in place or off to the side, as illustrated in the two examples below.

FIGURE 10.14. The magnitude of change can be conveyed by labeling the highest and lowest values.

This approach is not ideal on a dashboard, however, because it expresses magnitude textually, which requires reading (that is, verbal processing). Sparklines of this type cannot be perceived using visual processing alone, so comparisons of magnitude among a series of sparklines would slow to a crawl. To support rapid monitoring, we must encode magnitude information using visual elements. For this purpose, I've created a version of sparklines that I call *bandlines*.

Bandlines use horizontal bands of color in the background of the sparkline's plot area to display information about the distribution of values. This information is similar to that found in a box plot. To use bandlines, we must gather information about how values related to the measure featured in the sparkline are distributed during a period of history that usually extends further into the past than the values that will appear in the sparkline itself. For example, for a sparkline that will display thirty time-series values—one for each of the last thirty days—we might gather information about how its values were distributed during the past six months or year.

We need five primary facts about a set of time-series values to construct a bandline: 1) the lowest value, 2) the 25th percentile (the point at and below which the lowest 25th of the values reside), 3) the median (also called the 50th percentile, which is the point at and below which 50% of the values reside), 4) the 75th percentile (that is, the point at and below which 75% of the values reside), and 5) the highest value. With these five values to mark the boundaries, we've divided the full distribution of values into four ranges, called quartiles (quartile 1 at the bottom through 4 at the top), which each contain one-quarter of the values.

The quartiles are represented visually in bandlines using horizontal bands of color in the background. Three shades of a single hue, usually gray, in sequence from light to dark are used to divide the full spread of the distribution into three sections: the lightest for the first quartile, a medium shade for the midrange (also called the interquartile range, consisting of the second and third quartiles), and the darkest for the fourth quartile.

To determine percentiles in a set of values, we begin by arranging the values in order either from high to low or low to high. Once they're in order, we can find the 50% percentile (the median) by counting down from the top until we reach the value that is in the middle of the list. When the list contains an even number of values, the 50th percentile is the average of the middle two values (that is, their sum divided by two). The 25th percentile is determined in a similar manner, but this time we find the value that falls in the middle between the lowest value and the 50th percentile. The 75th percentile falls between the highest value and the 50th percentile, and is calculated in the same manner.

Quartile 4

Midspread (quartiles 2 and 3)

Quartile 1

FIGURE 10.15. Bandlines represent the first quartile, the midspread, and the fourth quartile as three intensities of a single color.

Within the midspread band of color, a horizontal white line is used to mark the median's position, which divides the midspread into the second and third quartiles.

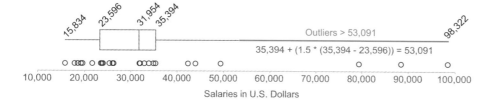

Median

Quartile 4
Quartile 3
Quartile 2
Quartile 1

FIGURE 10.16. Bandlines represent the median as a white line that divides the midspread.

And finally, within the first and fourth quartiles, if any values qualify as outliers, they are individually highlighted.

Outliers > 53,091

35,394 + (1.5 * (35,394 - 23,596)) = 53,091

Salaries in U.S. Dollars

FIGURE 10.17. Outliers are usually determined as values that are greater than a distance of 1.5 times the midspread above the 75th percentile or below the 25th percentile.

Low outliers are identified by solid black data points (dots) along the sparkline, and high outliers are identified by white data points with a thin black border.

FIGURE 10.18. Outliers are represented as black dots on the low end and white dots with a black outline on the high end.

Bandlines reveal the following features of a time series:

Feature	Visual Representation
Trend	Overall direction of change (mostly up, relatively flat, mostly down)
Pattern of Change	Varying slopes along the line
Magnitudes of Values	A combination of vertical position of values along the line and background fill color
Magnitudes of Change	A combination of the slope of a line segment and in some cases the line's migration from one band of background color to another
Degree of Variability	Variation of vertical positions along the line and in some cases the line's migration from one band of background color to another

The following examples illustrate how bandlines appear and are interpreted:

	Values are spread across all quartiles. This time series trends upward and spans an extensive range of values.
	Values all fall within the bottom quartile. This time series trends upward within a narrow range of low values.
	Values all fall within the midspread: some above and some below the median. This time series trends downward and spans the middle two quartiles.
	Values all fall within the top quartile. This time series trends slightly upward within a narrow range of high values.
	Values all fall within the bottom quartile and one is a low outlier. This time series trends upward within a narrow range of extremely low values.
	Values all fall within the top quartile, and the last two are high outliers. This time series trends upward within a narrow range of extremely high values.
	Values fall within the midspread (slightly) and top quartile, and one is a high outlier. This time series trends upward across a larger-than-usual range of mostly high values, one of which is extreme.
	Values fall within the midspread and bottom quartiles in roughly equal proportions. This time series trends slightly upward but remains among the lower half of values.

FIGURE 10.19. A typical set of bandlines, with descriptions

Notice that the bandlines in these examples are all scaled to fill the vertical space; in each, the lowest value is positioned at the bottom and the highest at the top of the plot area. This was done to provide the clearest possible picture of the trend and pattern of change in each bandline. When we require more precise magnitude comparisons across a set of related time series, a set of bandlines may all share the same quantitative scale, just as is often the case with regular sparklines. When a common scale is used, and values vary significantly in magnitude with some items having much greater values than others, lines that represent relatively low values often look flat, which hides information about patterns and trends of change. One of the advantages of bandlines over plain sparklines is that bandlines may be independently scaled to fill the vertical space of the plot area to optimally feature patterns and trends of change, yet they provide information about magnitude that will allow the viewer to differentiate variability within a small range from greater variability.

Basing the bands on quartiles causes the ranges that they represent to vary in the quantitative distances that they span. The full spread of values is not divided into four equal quantitative ranges, but rather into four groups, each consisting of 25% of the values. If the line extends equal distances into two of the quartiles, this does not necessarily mean that its values ventured in equal proportions into those two ranges because the ranges can differ in quantitative distance. For example, the bandline below is fully contained within the midspread and appears to extend roughly as far into the third quartile (above the white median line) as it does into the second quartile (below the median). The lower boundary of the second quartile at the bottom and the upper boundary of the third quartile at the top are not visible, however, so we can't tell whether one covers a greater quantitative distance than the other. If the second quartile extends across a greater distance than the third, then the proportion of the third quartile into which the sparkline ventures is greater.

FIGURE 10.20. All of these values reside within the midspread, some above and some below the median.

Although this might seem like a problem, it provides useful information. A line that appears to extend equally into two ranges does in fact extend equal magnitudes into them, which users will understand intuitively, but, by delineating quartiles rather than equal quantitative distances, we gain information about the values contained in a bandline relative to the norm, which is especially useful when monitoring performance.

Despite the useful information about magnitude that is provided by bandlines, scaling to fill the vertical space sometimes comes at a cost. Restricting information about magnitude to a maximum of six distinct distribution ranges—low outlier, bottom quartile, midspread (divided into second and third quartiles by the median), top quartile, and high outliers—will not provide adequate precision for some uses, especially when a time series resides entirely within a single quartile. For example, when we view the following bandline, we know that all values are in the bottom quartile and that none qualify as outliers, but we can't discern whether the values vary slightly or greatly within the quartile.

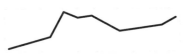

Even when the line spans two quartiles, as it does below, we know that values ventured roughly equal distances into the first and second quartiles but nothing about the degree. It's possible that values varied only to a slight degree near the 25th percentile (that is, the boundary between the first and second quartile).

For most performance-monitoring purposes, knowing the quartiles in which values reside is adequate information about magnitude, but sometimes we must provide greater precision. The trick is to do this in a way that doesn't complicate interpretation or slow down perception. We can achieve this in two ways.

The first method modifies the scale of the bandline by filling the vertical space only when values span a quantitative distance that equals or exceeds the distance of the midspread. When they span a smaller distance, the scale is increased to equal the distance of the midspread. This does not mean that the entire midspread will always appear in the plot area of the bandline but that the scale from bottom to top will equal the same distance that lies between the bottom and top of the midspread. The two bandlines below on the left, if scaled in this manner, could look like either of the two alternatives on the right, depending on the midspreads.

Scaled to fill space   Rescaled to equal midspread distance

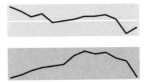
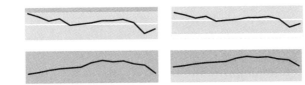

When we use this scaling method, time series that vary little in value avoid the exaggerated appearance of significant variation. Lines that represent little variation will appear more flat and will not fill the vertical space.

The other method of providing additional magnitude information is more informative, but it requires additional space. The information contained in bandlines may be supplemented by displaying range bars alone or a combination of range bars and strip plots next to them to provide distribution information in a way that is easier and faster to perceive and compare. I call these

FIGURE 10.21. All of these values reside within the first quartile, but we can't tell to what degree they span the quartile.

FIGURE 10.22. We can tell that these values venture roughly equal distances into the first and second quartiles but not whether they span equal portions of those quartiles.

FIGURE 10.23. Bandlines may be scaled to cover a minimum distance equal to the midspread.

sparkstrips. Here's a version next to the set of bandlines that we've seen before, which uses range bars alone.

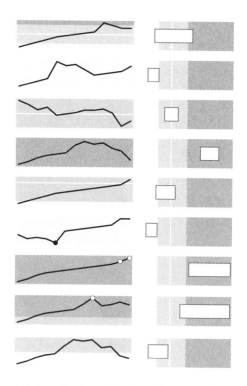
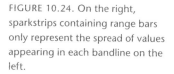

FIGURE 10.24. On the right, sparkstrips containing range bars only represent the spread of values appearing in each bandline on the left.

When we use sparkstrips, the bands in bandlines need not span a distance equal to the midspread because the magnitude information that we aim to reveal by doing this can be provided more effectively in the sparkstrips. In the next example, all of the bandlines that were shown previously have been supplemented with magnitude and variation information through the addition of individual values, each marked as a small circle.

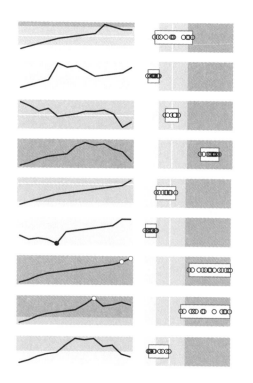

FIGURE 10.25. On the right, sparkstrips containing range bars and strip plots communicate rich information about the distribution of values in the corresponding bandlines.

When a distribution of values is displayed in this way, with a mark such as a dot for each value, it is called a *strip plot*. Sparkstrips are always consistently scaled to display the full range across which the values are historically spread, not just the range represented by a particular bandline. This gives us an efficient way to compare the distributions among bandlines and convey information about magnitude and variability as well. If we display strip plots on top of the range bars, as in the example above, we provide richer information about the distribution's shape without overcomplicating the sparkstrips.

Bandlines may be modified to represent meaningful ranges other than quartile-based distributions. In Chapter 13, *Putting It All Together*, I'll show an example that uses the colored bands to represent student performance in a course based on grades A, B, C, D, and F because grade-based ranges are meaningful to the teacher who uses the dashboard.

Process Behavior Sparklines

In this section I introduce a specialized type of time-series display called an *XmR Chart*. Yes, the name of this chart is one that only a statistician could love. The "X" in XmR stands for the statistical average of a set of time-series values and the "mR" stands for the moving range of those values. The XmR chart comes from the world of *statistical process control*. Most of us have probably heard of control charts. The XmR chart is one of them. It is used to display a set of time-series measures of a process primarily for the purpose of spotting points in time when those measures change behavior. A change in a measure's behavior can signal a change in the performance of the process that it measures.

Measures of a process go up and down in time, but most of the variation is random, routine, and therefore meaningless in that we can't do anything about it. Abnormal variation indicates that something is happening that can be traced to a cause and therefore potentially managed. For example, a marketing campaign could cause sales to increase in a way that indicates an effect of the campaign. We want to discriminate signals in the data (variation that indicates something has changed) from noise (random variation). Statistical process control methods have been developed to do this.

No one understands and explains these methods better than Donald Wheeler, who has written many fine books on the subject, including *Understanding Variation*. In his many years of helping organizations manage performance, he has noticed that, "Unfortunately, most managers are proud of their ability to interpret noise as if it were signal." Statistical naiveté of this sort is common. I won't try to explain process control methodology and statistics in this book, but I do want to draw our attention to their existence and demonstrate how an enhanced version of sparklines can be used on dashboards to monitor measures in this way. My source for this version of a sparkline is Stacey Barr, the Performance Measure Specialist. Stacey helps organizations measure, monitor, and improve performance. Although performance management has been a hot topic for years, few organizations actually know how to measure performance, a skill they need to master before they can manage performance. Stacey relies in part on statistical process control methods and encourages her clients to use dashboards that employ these methods to monitor performance.

Donald Wheeler (2000). *Understanding Variation*, Second Edition. SPC Press, page 111.

To support this practice, Stacey often uses a sparkline version of XmR charts, which she calls a *Smartline*; for our purposes here I'll call it a *performance behavior sparkline*.

Here's an example of a typical XmR Chart with each of its components labeled:

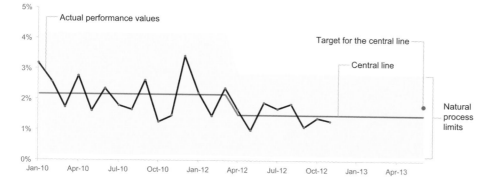

FIGURE 10.26. An XmR Chart

It is common to display targets on time-series graphs as horizontal lines. This encourages the comparison of each newly added measure value to the target line. However, Stacey thinks that this practice "ignores routine variation and wrongly treats every difference as a signal." Consistent with encouraging a focus on the central line as the current performance level rather than on individual points, she prefers to use points to represent targets instead of lines. In this example, a specific improvement target has been established. The blue dot represents a target for higher performance on average as of June 2013. Using this graph, we would want to see the central blue line representing average performance move up to meet or exceed the target on or before June 2013. Independent of the target, we would also use this chart to identify abnormal variation. If the central line and natural process limits have been properly calculated, meaningful variation—an actual signal in the data—could be identified by any of the following three features:

- Any value that falls outside of the natural process limits
- Any eight or more consecutive values that all reside either above or below the central line
- Any three out of four consecutive values that are closer to a natural process limit than they are to the central line

To identify abnormal variation using an XmR chart, we only need to recognize these three patterns; we don't need to know the actual values or the actual dates on which events occurred. For this reason, we can eliminate both axes and scales, leaving only the information that's contained in the plot area of the graph. In other words, we can reduce this chart to the abbreviated the form of a sparkline. Here's the same information, this time displayed as a sparkline:

FIGURE 10.27. A performance behavior sparkline

The formulas for calculating the central line and the range between the upper and lower natural process limits are relatively simple, but, rather than providing them here, I encourage you to take some time to learn about XmR charts from experts such as Stacey Barr or Donald Wheeler.

Learn from Stacey Barr at www.staceybarr.com and read Donald Wheeler's fine books, starting with *Understanding Variation*.

Expressing Degrees of Change

When monitoring performance, we often find that information about relative change is more useful than actual values and magnitudes. For example, a series of sparklines that displays weekly revenues for a set of products might provide more information about changes in performance and make it easier to compare the historical performance of one product to another if the sparklines expressed the degree of change rather actual revenue amounts. Here's an illustration: imagine that each sparkline has a percentage scale that includes zero, with positive percentages above and negative percentages below. The first week's value in every case is 0%, and then each successive weekly value represents either a positive or negative percentage difference relative to the first week. In the example below, sparklines on the left display actual values, and those on the right display percentage variance relative to the first value in the series.

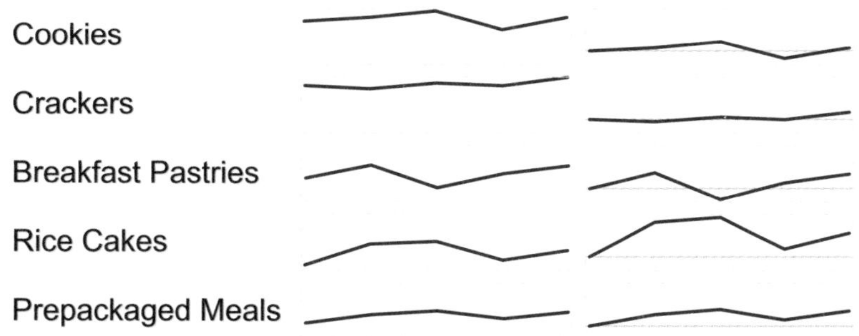

Cookies

Crackers

Breakfast Pastries

Rice Cakes

Prepackaged Meals

FIGURE 10.28. Sparklines expressed as actual values on the left and degrees of change on the right

Expressing relative change rather than actual revenue values emphasizes the degree to which each product has improved or declined in sales over time in relation to itself, not to other products. This approach also displays variability and rates of change in a direct way, making it easier to compare these patterns among products. For someone who manages performance, this is often more useful than magnitude comparisons.

Displaying the Plot Area

A set of sparklines positioned one above the other in a column can look unruly, like a family of glowworms wriggling in space invading one another's territory and fighting for position. This is especially true when the sparklines are scaled to fill the height of the plot area with little space between them. In this arrangement, it can be difficult to focus on one sparkline without being distracted by the others near it.

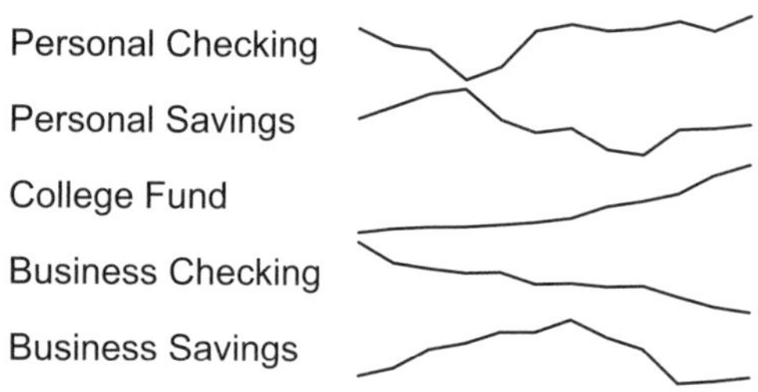

Personal Checking

Personal Savings

College Fund

Business Checking

Business Savings

FIGURE 10.29. Sparklines can appear to intrude on one another when arranged close together.

Even when the sparklines share a common scale to enable magnitude comparisons, it can be difficult to judge the positions of values relative to one another if their plot areas aren't visible. In the example below, which has the highest final value: crackers or rice cakes?

Last 12 months of sales

Cookies

Crackers

Breakfast Pastries

Rice Cakes

Prepackaged Meals

FIGURE 10.30. When sparklines share a common scale, magnitude comparisons can be difficult if their plot areas aren't visible.

The same set of sparklines appears again in the example below, but now the plot area of each has been defined by a light gray rectangle. Notice how this subtle addition makes magnitude comparisons easier and more precise.

Last 12 months of sales

Cookies

Crackers

Breakfast Pastries

Rice Cakes

Prepackaged Meals

FIGURE 10.31. Displaying the plot areas of sparklines makes magnitude comparisons easier.

When the plot areas aren't visible, the slope of one sparkline can influence our perception of another's slope in a misleading way. In the example below, I've highlighted the sparklines for Zinfandel and Chardonnay to illustrate this concern. When viewing the Zinfandel sparkline, our perception of its upward slope is exaggerated by the downward slope of the Chardonnay sparkline below it. With sparklines that are near one another, we can't view one without seeing it in the context of others. The effect on perception is subtle but significant enough in some cases to warrant mitigation.

Product   Past 12 Months

Cabernet

Zinfandel

Chardonnay

Sauvignon Blanc

Merlot

FIGURE 10.32. Our perception of the slope of a sparkline can be influenced by the slope of sparklines above and below it.

Two ways to counteract this effect are illustrated below: light borders and light background fills.

Product	Past 12 Months		Product	Past 12 Months
Cabernet	～～～		Cabernet	～～～
Zinfandel	～～～		Zinfandel	～～～
Chardonnay	～～～		Chardonnay	～～～
Sauvignon Blanc	～～～		Sauvignon Blanc	～～～
Merlot	～～～		Merlot	～～～

FIGURE 10.33. By displaying the plot area of each sparkline, we can somewhat mitigate the perceptual influence of sparklines on each other.

When we do this, it's important keep the border or background fill color just visible enough to clearly delineate the plot area, easily seen but subtle. Two other means can be used to do this, which delineate entire rows rather than the sparklines only. The first involves a technique that is often used in tables, called *zebra striping*: using a light fill color in the background across entire rows of information, illustrated below.

Last 12 Months	Top 10 Referrers this Month	Referral Count	Referral % of Total	Since 1 Yr Ago	Average Rev $
～～～	www.clothingconnection.com	1,103			72
～～～	www.getithere.com	782			61
～～～	www.ellingswear.com	688			90
～～～	www.trimthebill.com	413			32
～～～	www.looknofurther.com	330			52
～～～	www.cheapstuff.com	301			19
～～～	www.bargainbasement.com	297			29
～～～	www.dressforsuccess.com	239			42
～～～	www.relaxwear.com	174			22
～～～	www.nobrainer.com	168			10
			0% 10% 20%	-50% 0% 50%	

FIGURE 10.34. Fill color behind every other row, called zebra striping, can be used to delineate rows and define the heights of plot areas.

The second uses light lines between each row, illustrated below. Notice that in this example, zebra striping could not be used because fill colors were used in the graphs that display the grades, so they couldn't also be used to delineate the rows.

Student		Grade		Scores
		F D C B A		
Frederick Chandler	F	●	53%	＼∕
Bae Kim	F	●	59%	∕∖∕
Fiona Reeves	D	●	65%	∿∖
Brian Francis	D	●	65%	∿∕
Anthony Harper	D	●	69%	∿∕
Christopher Murphy	C	●	70%	∕‾
Kirsten Holmes	C	●	72%	＼∕
Roshawn Dawson	C	●	72%	‾∖∕

FIGURE 10.35. Light lines can be used to delineate rows and define the heights of plot areas.

Sparklines can play a significant role in dashboards, but only if they're properly designed.

11 OTHER DASHBOARD DISPLAY MEDIA

Graphs offer a visual means to display quantitative information, but dashboards may include more than numbers, so our library of display media must include a few other forms of communication as well. In this chapter we'll consider the roles of icons, text, images, and drawing objects.

Icons

Icons are simple images that communicate a clear and simple meaning. Only a few icons are typically needed on a dashboard. Although other icons are useful on occasion, the most useful icons are those that communicate the following three meanings:

- Alert
- Up/down
- On/off

Alert Icons

It is often useful to draw attention to particular information on a dashboard especially when something is wrong and requires attention. An icon that works as an alert shouts at the viewer, "Hey, look here!" For an icon to play this role well, it needs to be exceptionally simple and noticeable. Having 10 variations of an alert icon, each with its own subtly different meaning, is far too complex for a dashboard. Ideally, we limit alert levels to one; at most, we use two. A single alert icon catches the eye much more effectively than multiple alerts with various meanings.

A common alert scheme on dashboards uses the traffic signal metaphor, composed of three colors with different meanings: green for good, yellow for satisfactory, and red for bad. Beware. If we use alert icons to evaluate everything in this way, everything will shout, but nothing will stand out. Adding an icon to create an alert only works if the presence of alert icons is the exception rather than the rule. When too many items vie for attention, viewers learn to ignore them, and, if possible, turn them off.

We should think of alerts not as scoring mechanisms, but as the means to draw attention to information that requires a response. And we shouldn't make the mistake of thinking that something must be wrong for a response to be required. Something might deserve a response because it's incredibly good, such as a great sales opportunity or a department that is managing its expenses so well that others should emulate it.

Simple objects that appear next to information to indicate when attention is needed work well as alert icons because an object that appears only in certain circumstances is perceived preattentively as an "added mark." This particular preattentive attribute is not tapped into when the traffic light alert system is used because, although the color used on the image of the traffic light to represent the data might change, nothing is actually added; the traffic light itself is always there.

If we assign a particular color that isn't used for any other purpose to an icon, that icon can be easily found in a fast, preattentive search. We can spot instances of a particular color much faster than instances of a particular shape. I've found that a simple unvarying shape, such as a circle of a particular color, usually works best as an alert icon. If we must indicate multiple levels of alerts (for example, critical and less critical), then, rather than using distinct shapes, we should stick with one shape and vary the color intensity only. However, as noted above, we should limit the states that generate alerts to two. More than two become too complicated for rapid perception. Better yet, we should stick to a single state: the information either needs attention or it doesn't. Let the information itself, rather than the alert icon, convey the level of criticality.

Traffic signal colors of red, yellow, and green are conventional, but they don't work for the 10% of males and 0.5% of women who are colorblind. The following figure illustrates this point by showing the colors green, yellow, and red on the left and what a person with the predominant form of colorblindness would see on the right.

A solution that works for everyone involves distinct intensities of the same hue, such as light red (in place of yellow) and dark red, as shown below.

Up/Down Icons

Up/down icons convey the simple message that a measure has gone up or down compared to some point in the past or is greater or less than something else, such as a target. Financial information is common on dashboards, so a simple indicator of the up or down movement of stocks, profits, and so on is often useful. Fortunately, a conventional symbol is already in use to communicate these meanings: a triangle or arrow with the tip pointing either up or down. The color of the arrows might vary as well (usually green for good and red for bad) to make them stand out, but, again, this is a problem for those who are colorblind. This problem can be avoided by using colors that vary greatly in intensity as

FIGURE 11.1. Unless we are careful, the use of distinct hues to encode different meanings won't work for viewers who are colorblind. The icons on the right simulate what someone who is colorblind would see when looking at the icons on the left.

FIGURE 11.2. The simple alert icons on the left use varying intensities of a single hue to encode different meanings. The two on the right simulate what a person who is colorblind would see when looking at the two shades of red on the left. Varying intensities of any single hue are distinguishable by everyone who can see.

red for the icon that indicates movement in

figure below illustrates a

ı.

FIGURE 11.3. Simple up and down
icons

ı simple sense of up or
he pattern of change is

. For example, if we display
ʒe want to flag some as
con would do this nicely.
ıuch as products in a list, or
chedule that includes events
ıy simple icons could be used
ʒ, and Xs below are probably
ırdless of which icon we
ick to it. Consistency might

✱ ✓ X

FIGURE 11.4. Sample on/off icons

Text

All dashboards, no matter how graphical, include some information that must
be presented as text. This is both necessary and desirable, for some information
is better communicated textually rather than graphically. Text is always used on
a dashboard to label items, such as "Revenue 2012 YTD" next to the bullet graph
below, but it can serve other purposes as well. In addition to the label in the
example below, the bullet graph's value is expressed textually to the right
because this case requires precision.

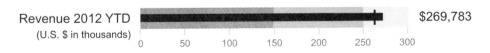

FIGURE 11.5. Numbers must be
presented as text, in addition to
graphics, when precision is required.

When people often need to obtain precise values from the dashboard, we
should express those values as text so that no further action is required to access
them. If people only occasionally need precision, we can make it possible for the
value to appear as text only while hovering with the mouse over an object such
as the bullet graph above.

Text is necessary when information cannot be communicated graphically. Imagine a dashboard that is used by a Chief Information Officer (CIO) to update her awareness every morning, not just of the computer network's performance, but also of the status of the department's most critical projects. Her dashboard might include a section such as the following:

Project	Status	Funding Approved	Sched. Start
Professional services module	Pending available staff	X	05/10/13
Upgrade MS Office	Cost-benefit analysis		02/15/13
Failover for ERP	Preparing proposal		06/02/13
Upgrade data warehouse HW	Evaluating options	X	04/15/13
Executive dashboard	Vendor assessment		07/01/13

FIGURE 11.6. None of this information lends itself to a concise form of graphical display although the X marks function as icons of sorts.

When text is the most effective means of communication, we use text. We should be careful, however, not to include text for information that people will only need to read once or twice. For example, an instruction such as "Click boldfaced items to access related information" would be familiar after a day or two of using the dashboard, so we wouldn't want to clutter and use space on the dashboard for this. Place information that people need only in the beginning or infrequently in a separate "Help" screen that is easy to access whenever needed.

In Chapter 12, *Critical Design Practices*, I'll provide guidelines for selecting fonts that work well on a dashboard, but, for now, we're done with text.

Images

Having the means to display images such as photos, illustrations, or diagrams is sometimes useful on a dashboard but rarely so in my experience. If the Director of Human Resources thinks of each department in terms of the person who heads it, his dashboard might include small photos of those individuals to label each department, as in the following example.

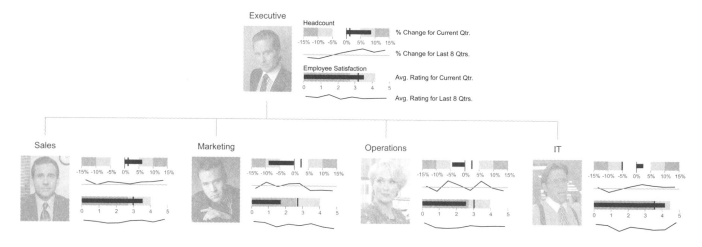

FIGURE 11.7. Photos used to identify department heads in a dashboard.

Images are unnecessary in most dashboards and take up valuable space, so we use them only when we must. I avoid photos in particular unless nothing else will do the job because they add a great deal of visual complexity that slows down perception.

Drawing Objects

It is sometimes useful to arrange and connect pieces of information in relation to one another using simple drawing objects. For instance, when a dashboard displays information about a process, it can be helpful to arrange separate events in the process sequentially and to indicate the path along which the process flows, especially when branching among multiple paths is possible. Another example is when we need to show connections among entities, perhaps including a hierarchical relationship, such as in an organization chart. Entities can easily be displayed as rectangles and circles, and relationships can be displayed using lines and arrows. Rectangles or circles could represent tasks in a project, for example, with arrows connecting them to indicate their relationships and order.

The next two figures illustrate how some drawing objects might be used. These objects can also be used to highlight and group information, which we often need to do in dashboard design. Switching between rectangles and circles is an easy way to distinguish different types of entities. Lines and arrows both show connections between entities, but arrows display the additional element of direction.

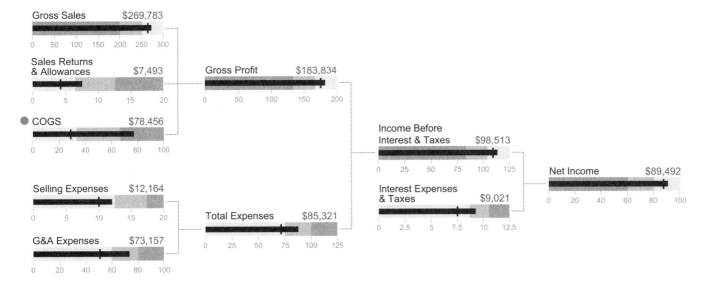

This approach has been used with great success in actual dashboards. The next example was created by Keith Smith using QlikView.

FIGURE 11.8. Simple drawing objects can be used to clarify relationships among the components of net revenue.

Desktop Office/Laser Equipment
Market Shipments & Vendor Share
3Q 2010

Δ ‡(YoY) = year-over-year
Δ ↔(Seq) = sequential

REGION ▾ USA
COUNTRY ▾ USA

Single-function printer 59.4% / 53.2%

Top 7	$ (K)	Share	Ranking	1Q06-3Q10	Δ↔(Seq)	Δ‡(YoY)
HP	$246,768	58.6%			13.7%	36.2%
Lexmark	$42,413	10.1%			-25.0%	-30.5%
Xerox	$38,144	9.1%			29.3%	8.8%
Ricoh	$24,718	5.9%			19.7%	80.4%
OKI	$15,754	3.7%			4.2%	0.4%
Dell	$14,634	3.5%			4.8%	15.4%
Kyocera Mita	$12,583	3.0%			9.3%	-27.3%
All Brands	**$421,166**				8.2%	13.2%

Total Market 100%
Our Mix 100%

Top 7	$ (K)	Share	Ranking	1Q06-3Q10	Δ↔(Seq)	Δ‡(YoY)
HP	$326,873	46.1%			12.7%	40.4%
Lexmark	$84,021	11.9%			-9.1%	-7.1%
Xerox	$71,634	10.1%			7.8%	6.3%
Ricoh	$54,566	7.7%			10.1%	95.3%
Brother	$24,947	3.5%			2.9%	-5.9%
Kyocera Mita	$24,584	3.5%			36.6%	22.3%
Canon	$24,251	3.4%			4.3%	-15.1%
All Brands	**$708,902**				8.3%	17.3%

Multi-function printer 40.6% / 46.8%

Top 7	$ (K)	Share	Ranking	1Q06-3Q10	Δ↔(Seq)	Δ‡(YoY)
HP	$80,105	27.8%			9.8%	54.9%
Lexmark	$41,608	14.5%			16.0%	41.4%
Xerox	$33,491	11.6%			-9.3%	3.6%
Ricoh	$29,848	10.4%			3.2%	109.6%
Canon	$24,086	8.4%			4.5%	-15.2%
Brother	$16,040	5.6%			0.3%	4.8%
Sharp	$13,338	4.6%			26.8%	-22.4%
All Brands	**$287,736**				8.4%	23.7%

Color 19.6% / 33.3%

Top 7	$ (K)	Share	Ranking	1Q06-3Q10	Δ↔(Seq)	Δ‡(YoY)
HP	$65,547	47.2%			21.9%	48.2%
Xerox	$23,858	17.2%			25.0%	3.6%
Ricoh	$19,848	14.3%			26.4%	98.3%
OKI	$6,976	5.0%			8.5%	1.3%
Lexmark	$6,165	4.4%			-1.0%	-42.2%
Dell	$5,282	3.8%			7.3%	19.6%
Konica Min...	$3,463	2.5%			-9.5%	-31.7%
All Brands	**$138,882**				18.6%	17.9%

Mono 39.8% / 19.9%

Top 7	$ (K)	Share	Ranking	1Q06-3Q10	Δ↔(Seq)	Δ‡(YoY)
HP	$181,221	64.2%			11.0%	32.4%
Lexmark	$36,248	12.8%			-28.0%	-28.1%
Xerox	$14,286	5.1%			37.1%	18.6%
Kyocera Mita	$10,024	3.6%			8.5%	-30.7%
Dell	$9,351	3.3%			3.4%	13.2%
OKI	$8,778	3.1%			0.9%	-0.3%
Brother	$7,822	2.8%			5.9%	-16.8%
All Brands	**$282,284**				3.8%	11.0%

Color 10.7% / 12.4%

Top 7	$ (K)	Share	Ranking	1Q06-3Q10	Δ↔(Seq)	Δ‡(YoY)
HP	$26,965	35.5%			-0.1%	18.7%
Xerox	$8,917	11.7%			-10.3%	41.7%
Brother	$7,571	10.0%			1.3%	4.8%
Lexmark	$6,747	8.9%			19.6%	78.5%
Sharp	$5,896	7.8%			30.6%	-23.8%
Konica Min...	$4,795	6.3%			46.9%	7.5%
Canon	$4,122	5.4%			-4.0%	42.7%
All Brands	**$76,052**				5.7%	18.5%

Mono 29.9% / 34.3%

Top 7	$ (K)	Share	Ranking	1Q06-3Q10	Δ↔(Seq)	Δ‡(YoY)
HP	$53,141	25.1%			15.5%	83.3%
Lexmark	$34,861	16.5%			15.3%	36.0%
Ricoh	$28,934	13.7%			4.3%	123.3%
Xerox	$24,574	11.6%			-8.9%	-5.6%
Canon	$19,963	9.4%			6.5%	-21.7%
Kyocera Mita	$10,258	4.8%			66.6%	325.2%
Brother	$8,469	4.0%			-0.6%	4.7%
All Brands	**$211,684**				9.4%	25.7%

Total Market Category Shipments, All Channels & Vendors as reported by US Quarterly Hardcopy Peripherals (HCP) Tracker, 13 Aug 2010

FOR INTERNAL USE ONLY

Even though a lot more information could have been placed on this dashboard by arranging the information differently, this arrangement works best for Keith's clients because it fits their mental model well.

———

FIGURE 11.9. This simple dashboard by Keith Smith uses position to display a hierarchy and lines to show relationships among different types of printers.

The library of dashboard display media that I've described in this and the preceding three chapters is not comprehensive, and it will certainly grow with time, incorporating new graphic inventions that suit the purpose and constraints of dashboards. But I expect it to grow slowly. Just because a vendor introduces a new visualization technique doesn't mean it belongs on a dashboard. Remember the criterion we use to evaluate a technique: does it communicate rapidly and clearly?

Now that we've finished our examination of visual display media, it's time to consider a few design activities that will help us produce effective dashboards.

12 CRITICAL DESIGN PRACTICES

A few important aspects of a dashboard's visual design remain for us to consider. Beyond selecting appropriate display media and reducing non-data pixels to a minimum, we must also pay attention to several other aspects of design to guarantee that our dashboards work effectively. Knowledge of a few more design strategies will help us blend all aspects of a dashboard into a pleasing and functional display.

In this chapter we'll consider ways to accomplish each of the following:

- Organize information to support its meaning and use.
- Maintain consistency to enable quick and accurate interpretation.
- Put supplementary information within reach.
- Make the experience aesthetically pleasing.
- Expose lower-level conditions.
- Prevent excessive alerts.
- Keep viewers in the loop.
- Accommodate real-time monitoring.

Organize Information to Support Its Meaning and Use

We can't just take information and throw it onto the dashboard anywhere we wish. How the pieces are arranged in relation to one another can make the difference between a dashboard that works and one that ends up being ignored even if the information they present is the same. The following guidelines help us determine how to arrange information on the screen:

- Organize groups according to activities, entities, and use.
- Co-locate items that belong to the same group.
- Delineate groups using the least-visible means.
- Support meaningful comparisons.
- Discourage meaningless comparisons.

Organize Groups According to Activities, Entities, and Use

A good first cut at organizing information is to form groups that align with activities within the organization (order entry, shipping, budget planning, etc.), entities (departments, projects, systems, etc.), or the way the dashboard viewer will use the information (for example, the need to compare revenues and expenses to determine profitability). These are natural ways to organize most information.

In an organization, because entities and activities are parts of an interconnected system, someone whose role spans many of these individual units might prefer to see information organized in a way that is more integrated and aligned with the way she uses that information. For instance, a CEO stands above the divisions found in an organization's structure and usually wants to see relationships among data that are holistic, perhaps based on the relative importance of each item to the company's bottom line from greatest to least. In such a case, items that might be separated into distinct groups to serve the needs of others in the company would be grouped together to serve the CEO's needs. Also, if there is a particular sequence in which information should be scanned to understand it as efficiently as possible, grouping and ordering items accordingly would make sense.

When organizing information on a dashboard, we start by learning precisely how the information will be used.

Co-locate Items that Belong Together

Once we've determined the items that belong together to suit the dashboard viewer's task, the best means to connect those items is to place them close to one another and delineate them in a subtle manner from surrounding groups. Using position to group items visually is a strategy that is preattentively and thus rapidly perceived.

Delineate Groups Using the Least-Visible Means

All visible means that we use to delineate groups of information, such as borders and background fill colors, qualify as non-data pixels. Therefore, they should be only as visible as necessary to do the job. What is the least-visible means to delineate groups of information? The answer is white (blank) space. When enough empty space surrounds a group of information to set that group apart from others, the group is delineated without adding any visual content to the dashboard that might distract attention from the information. We use white space to separate groups of information whenever more forceful delineation isn't necessary.

Because dashboards are often high-density displays, they do not always have the room to allow us to use white space alone to delineate groups. When a dashboard is too full for white space to adequately separate groups, subtle borders are usually the best means to use. You might be surprised at how light a line can be and still do the job. Take a look at the figure on the next page for an example of how we can use white space or light borders to delineate the same groups of data.

Product	Units Sold	Actual Revenue
Shirts	938	187,600
Blouses	1,093	114,765
Pants	3,882	62,112
Skirts	873	36,666
Dresses	72	2,088
Total	6,858	$403,231

Region	Units Sold	Actual Revenue
North	2,263	133,066
South	1,920	112,905
East	1,303	76,614
West	754	44,355
Canada	618	36,291
Total	6,858	$403,231

Channel	Units Sold	Actual Revenue
Direct	2,057	120,969
Distributor	1,921	119,903
Reseller	1,783	104,840
OEM	1,097	64,519
Total	6,858	$403,231

Warehouse	Units Sold	Actual Revenue
Virginia	2,537	149,195
California	1,920	112,905
Texas	1,372	80,646
Calgary	1,029	60,485
Total	6,858	$403,231

Product	Units Sold	Actual Revenue
Shirts	938	187,600
Blouses	1,093	114,765
Pants	3,882	62,112
Skirts	873	36,666
Dresses	72	2,088
Total	6,858	$403,231

Region	Units Sold	Actual Revenue
North	2,263	133,066
South	1,920	112,905
East	1,303	76,614
West	754	44,355
Canada	618	36,291
Total	6,858	$403,231

Channel	Units Sold	Actual Revenue
Direct	2,057	120,969
Distributor	1,921	119,903
Reseller	1,783	104,840
OEM	1,097	64,519
Total	6,858	$403,231

Warehouse	Units Sold	Actual Revenue
Virginia	2,537	149,195
California	1,920	112,905
Texas	1,372	80,646
Calgary	1,029	60,485
Total	6,858	$403,231

FIGURE 12.1. The four tables on the left have been separated effectively using white space alone, but the four on the right, because they are closer together, have been separated using light gray borders.

Support Meaningful Comparisons

Measures of performance come alive only when seen in context. Context is provided primarily through comparisons to related measures. For example, knowing that quarter-to-date sales revenue is $92,354 is meaningful only when that figure is compared to one or more other measures that can be used as yardsticks, such as a target or the amount of revenue that was earned by this date in the prior quarter. We can encourage meaningful comparisons by doing the following:

- Combining items in a single table or graph (if appropriate)
- Placing items close to one another
- Linking items in different groups using a common color
- Including comparative values (for example, ratios, percentages, or variances) whenever useful for clarity and efficiency

In the example below, three measures have been combined in a single line graph to simplify comparison of their values and patterns of change. Revenue, expenses, and profit could be easily combined in a single graph because they share a common unit of expression (U.S. dollars) and are within a reasonable distance of one another in magnitude. This would not have worked as well if profits were much lower because the line that represents profits would have appeared too flat for the pattern of change to be easily discerned.

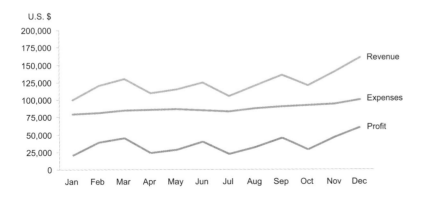

FIGURE 12.2. Sometimes comparisons among different measures can be supported by displaying them in the same graph.

The next example combines two data sets with different units of measure in a single graph by placing one quantitative scale on the left vertical axis and another on the right.

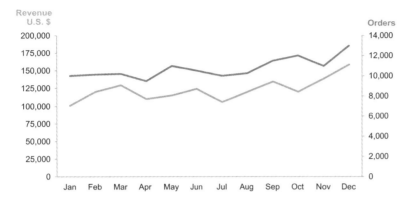

FIGURE 12.3. Measures with different units of expression (U.S. dollars and a count) can be combined in a single graph that has two quantitative scales.

Be careful with this approach, however, because it can lead to confusion. A similar graph appears next, but the values have been slightly altered. When you look at the data, does anything particular catch your eye?

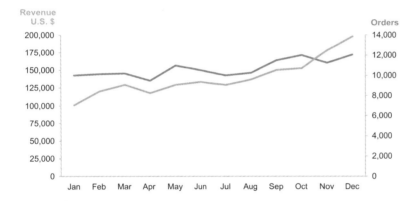

FIGURE 12.4. The values in this graph have been slightly altered from those in *Figure 12.3*.

If you're like most people, your eyes are drawn to the place where the two lines intersect. This is typical, because intersecting lines pop out. Visual perception in humans is highly evolved to notice intersections such as the crossing of these lines because intersections often provide useful information, such as the fact that one object is nearer than another. In this graph, what does the intersection of the two lines mean? Absolutely nothing. In a normal line graph with a single quantitative scale, the intersection of two lines is meaningful: one set of values exceeded the other at that point. When the two lines relate to different quantitative scales, however, their intersection is entirely arbitrary. So in this graph our eyes were powerfully drawn to something that is meaningless. That's a distraction that we should attempt to avoid.

What I just described is only one of several potential problems with dual-scaled graphs. A more fundamental problem is the fact that when people see values in a graph they compare those values, including their magnitudes, but magnitude comparisons among measures that have different quantitative scales are misleading. With awareness and practice, people can learn to avoid inappropriate comparisons and conclusions, but if there's any chance that users of a dashboard might be misled, it's better to avoid dual-scaled graphs.

The one meaningful comparison between monthly revenue and the number of orders is of the pattern of change. If order volume went up when revenue went down, for example, that would tell us something useful. To support this comparison, rather than combining revenue and order volume in a single graph, we can place them in separate graphs, one immediately above the other, as illustrated below.

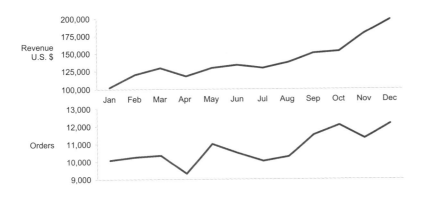

FIGURE 12.5. Patterns of change in measures that use different units of expression—in this case dollars and a count—can be compared by placing one graph above the other.

Although it isn't necessary, in this case because we're only comparing patterns of change and are not interested in magnitudes of change, I've narrowed each quantitative scale to begin a little below the lowest value and end a little above the highest value of each data set. Doing so made it easy to see patterns of change by spreading the values nearly across the full height of the graph. It also allowed me to reduce the heights of the individual graphs to fit both in a space that is no taller than the single graph in *Figure 12.4.*

The table below illustrates how values can be expressed directly as comparative units of measure to facilitate comparisons. Both the "% of Total" and "% of Fcst" columns contain values that are comparative by their very nature. Especially when we want to communicate the degree to which one value differs from another, percentages express this more directly than raw values.

Product	Units Sold	Actual Revenue	% of Total	Forecast Revenue	% of Fcst
Product A	938	187,600	47%	175,000	107%
Product B	1,093	114,765	28%	130,000	88%
Product C	3,882	62,112	15%	50,000	124%
Product D	873	36,666	9%	40,000	92%
Product E	72	2,088	1%	50,000	4%
Total	6,858	$403,231	100%	$445,000	91%

FIGURE 12.6. We can use comparative values to directly support comparisons.

Discourage Meaningless Comparisons

Not all of the information on a dashboard must be compared or linked to everything else. If we're not vigilant, we might inadvertently make design choices that encourage the comparison of unrelated data. For instance, in the following dashboard, some of the color choices produce this unintended effect.

The orange in three of the graphs consistently represents "Americas," but in the final graph on the bottom right, it suddenly means "QTD Q/Q Growth." As a result, our eyes are drawn to connect things that aren't connected.

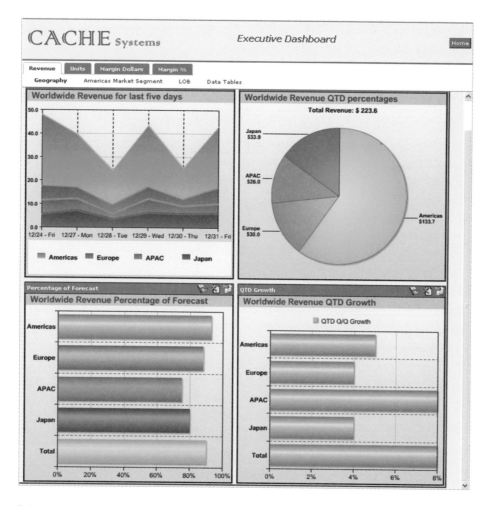

FIGURE 12.7. This dashboard inadvertently encourages meaningless comparison through an inconsistent use of color.

We can discourage meaningless comparisons by doing the opposite of the practices mentioned above:

- Separate items from one another spatially (if appropriate).
- Use different colors.

Maintain Consistency to Enable Quick and Accurate Interpretation

Differences in appearance always prompt us to search, whether consciously or unconsciously, for the significance of those differences. Anything that means the same thing or functions in the same way ought to look the same wherever it appears on a dashboard. Even something as subtle as arbitrarily using dark axis lines on one graph and light axis lines on another could lead viewers to perceive this difference as meaningful.

It's important to maintain consistency not only in the visual appearance of the display media, but in our choice of display media as well. If two sections of data involve the same type of quantitative relationship (such as a time series) and are intended for similar use (for example, to compare a measure to a target measure for the same series of months), we should use the same type of display for both (for example, a line graph). We should never vary the means of display for the sake of variety. Our goal is to always select the medium that best communicates the information and its message even if that means that our dashboard consists of the same type of graph throughout.

Nothing in a dashboard should change from day to day or moment to moment except the information that it displays and alerts that appear to highlight items. The layout shouldn't change. The types of charts used for each piece of information shouldn't change. Information shouldn't change through selections or filters. The only interaction that should be available is a means to get to additional information when something on the dashboard demands attention and that information is needed to determine an appropriate response. Why? Because the dashboard is a means of rapidly updating the viewer's awareness of the current situation. A dashboard that doesn't change becomes familiar through use. With a little practice, every time the user looks at it, he knows how to perceive it without taking time to acquire a fresh orientation. An input channel is immediately established between the dashboard and the mental model in the user's brain that enables a rapid transfer of fresh information to update the mental model. This won't happen if the dashboard's appearance is inconsistent. This won't happen if the user makes changes to the dashboard's structure, means of display, or data selection. When all but the information remains consistent, the part of the user's brain that thinks consciously and reflectively is freed to focus immediately and entirely on the information because everything else is familiar.

Put Supplementary Information Within Reach

As single-screen monitoring displays, dashboards do not provide all the information needed to perform a job or pursue a particular set of objectives. They provide the initial overview that is needed for monitoring at a high level, but they might need to be supplemented with additional information to provide the viewer a more comprehensive understanding and ability to respond.

The information that's needed for high-level monitoring should all reside on the dashboard, if possible. Supplementary information that's often or even occasionally needed should be placed within easy reach. This supplementary information usually consists of a deeper level of detail or broader range of context about the information that appears on the dashboard. To preserve consistency in the dashboard, we provide access to this information without introducing any lasting change in the dashboard. We can do this in three different ways, depending on the nature and amount of the information needed: 1) through pop-up windows invoked by hovering, 2) through temporarily altered states (changes to the way that information is expressed invoked by a sustained click), and 3) through access to a separate screen when more than a little information is needed.

Pop-Up Windows

On the occasions when a little more information is needed about content that appears on the dashboard, this information can be revealed instantly in a pop-up window (a tooltip). The user merely hovers over the item in question with the mouse, and a small window with additional information appears, then immediately disappears when the mouse moves on. Nothing about the dashboard itself changes. For example, if the precise value that's represented by a bullet graph or a point along a sparkline is needed, hovering over that spot would provide easy and instant access. Pop-up windows can be used to provide more than a single piece of information when needed, but they work best when they contain quickly accessible nuggets.

Altered States

I'm not using the term "altered state" to suggest that we dole out hallucinogenic drugs with a dashboard (although that might lead to new and imaginative insights!). Rather, I'm talking about temporary alterations to the way information is expressed or arranged when a different view is occasionally needed. For example, if sales are expressed in a graph as revenue in dollars, but they occasionally need to be seen as percentages of total revenue or as the number of units sold, this alternative view could be temporarily invoked by clicking on the graph and holding down the mouse button, causing the new view to appear in the graph only as long as the button is held down. This supplemental information would then disappear immediately once the mouse button is released. Rather than invoking this change of state through something like radio button controls, which would leave the altered state intact, the method that I'm describing can never cause confusion because it only appears as the result of a deliberate act and does not persist once that act is completed.

This same click-hold-release means of invoking alternative views can also be used for purposes other than changing how information is expressed. For example, if a tabular arrangement of students in a class usually orders them by performance on assignments from worst to best, there might be times when the teacher who uses the dashboard would want to see students ordered by attendance or overall grade point average. These alternative sortings could be invoked using the mouse button as described above so that the dashboard always returns to the state that's familiar after the alternative view has been examined.

Another example might involve alterations to the scales of graphs. Perhaps a series of sparklines that are each independently scaled to fill the vertical space should on occasion be viewed with a common scale to enable better magnitude comparisons among them. Their scales could be temporarily altered using the click-and-hold method for a quick comparison; when the mouse button is released, the sparklines return to their usual form.

It's important that this method of enriching the dashboard with alternative views not be overdone. Providing access to other views complicates the dashboard, so we should reserve this for views that are frequently and critically needed.

Independent Screens

All of the information that a viewer might need to respond to a situation cannot be shown on a dashboard. The dashboard provides an overview of the most important information that must be monitored, but when something demands a response, additional information might be needed so that the viewer can fully understand the situation before determining the appropriate response. There can be quite a bit of additional information needed, which is best delivered on a screen separate from the dashboard, in a way that can be easily accessed and with a convenient return path to the dashboard.

We want to provide access to supplementary screens of information without cluttering the dashboard by adding a bunch of controls. Rather than placing buttons or icons all over the dashboard for navigation, it's best to allow access to be invoked by directly interacting with information already on the dashboard. For instance, if an alert icon appears next to information about something, access to additional information could be invoked by clicking the icon. In a situation when more than one additional screen of information might be needed, and a choice must be made, this could be handled by right-clicking the alert icon, which would cause a pop-up menu to appear, from which the appropriate screen could be selected.

By providing predefined displays of supplementary information on separate screens rather than changing the dashboard itself to provide this information, we keep the dashboard pristine and thus always familiar.

Expose Lower-Level Conditions

Sometimes information that exists at a lower level of detail than what's displayed on the dashboard must be viewed to understand and address circumstances needing attention. For instance, the vice-president of sales in a company might monitor a breakdown of sales activity by major regions, such as the North America, South America, Europe, Asia Pacific, and the Middle East. At that high level, Europe could look fine even though sales in the United Kingdom are doing horribly; this information would remain hidden below the surface unless there is something on the dashboard that informs the vice-president that individual countries need attention. An alert that says "All is fine at this regional level, but something deeper is amiss" could appear on the dashboard next to Europe.

If we use simple alert icons, as I suggested previously, we can use a simple variation of them to convey this type of information. For example, if a solid red dot indicates that something on the dashboard needs attention, a red dot that consists of the border only could be used to indicate that something deeper down needs attention. This dot could be clicked to automatically access the lower level of detail.

FIGURE 12.8. A simple variation of an alert icon can be used to draw attention to something that doesn't appear on the dashboard because it resides at a lower level of detail.

Just don't overdo it. Always keep in mind that the dashboard is a rapid monitoring display, not a detailed management report.

Make the Experience Aesthetically Pleasing

In 1988, Donald Norman, a cognitive scientist, wrote a wonderful book entitled *The Design of Everyday Things*. This book is a classic in the field of design and convincingly argues that the effectiveness of something's design should be judged by how well it works and how easy it is to use. In the years after his book was published, some designers accused Norman of ignoring the value of aesthetics. I suspect that this critique was one of his motives for writing another book entitled *Emotional Design: Why We Love (or Hate) Everyday Things*.

In *Emotional Design*, Norman describes the psychological and physiological benefits of aesthetically pleasing design. If applied to dashboard design, Norman's point would be that aesthetically pleasing dashboards are more enjoyable, which makes them more relaxing, preparing the viewer for greater insight and creative response. This is not a departure from his earlier assertions in *The Design of Everyday Things* but rather an extension asserting that aesthetics, when not in conflict with a product's usability, possess intrinsic qualities that also contribute to usability. Norman convincingly reframes the discussion as a matter not of usability versus aesthetics, but of usability versus anything that flagrantly undermines usability, which good, aesthetically pleasing design manages to avoid.

I love visual art. I appreciate beauty for its own sake. Moments of great beauty exalt me. Information design, however, is about communication: getting an intended message across in a way that results in useful understanding. Aesthetics are an important component of information design but not in the same way that they are in art. If a dashboard is not designed in an aesthetically pleasing way, the resulting unpleasant experience for the viewer undermines the dashboard's ability to communicate. On a dashboard, our aesthetic talent ought to be applied directly to the display of the information itself, not to meaningless and distracting ornamentation. The aesthetics of dashboard design should always express themselves straightforwardly, striving for the eloquence that emerges uniquely from simplicity.

The dashboard shown on the following page, although simple enough, is a glaring example of design that is anything but aesthetically pleasing. How can we avoid creating a similar monstrosity? Let's look at a few guidelines that will help us achieve a simple aesthetic without compromising the data.

Donald Norman (1988). *The Design of Everyday Things*. Basic Books.

Donald Norman (2004). *Emotional Design: Why We Love (or Hate) Everyday Things*. Basic Books.

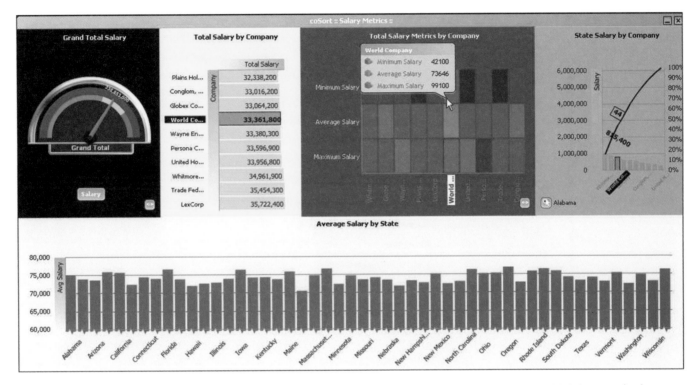

FIGURE 12.9. An example of a downright ugly dashboard

Choose Appropriate and Meaningful Colors

Poor use of color is perhaps the most common offense in a dashboard's appearance. Colors that are bright or dark naturally demand more attention. Too many bright or dark colors can quickly become visually exhausting. Here are two important guidelines for selecting colors:

- Keep bright colors to a minimum, using them only to highlight information that requires attention.
- Except for content that demands attention, use less-saturated colors such as those that are predominant in nature (for example, the colors of the earth and sky).

The figure below illustrates bright, fully saturated colors on the left that should be used sparingly to feature data and softer, semi-saturated colors on the right that are easy on the eyes and should therefore be used for most data.

FIGURE 12.10. Avoid the use of bright colors such as those on the left except to highlight particular data. Stick with the more subdued colors on the right for most of what's displayed.

Information on a dashboard should stand out clearly against the background. Black text against a white background, which is typical in printed books, provides maximum contrast, which makes the text as easy as possible to read. Because computer screens emit light, however, black text against a pure white background that's shining into the viewer's eyes can cause eyestrain. The easiest way to remedy this on a dashboard is to soften the background color by adding just a touch of another color to the white, as illustrated below.

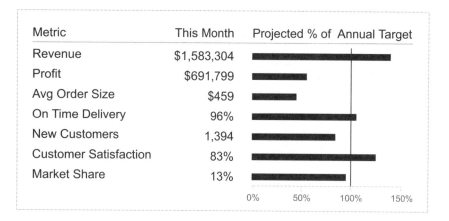

FIGURE 12.11. A slight touch of yellow has been added to the white background to soften the contrast between it and the black information in the foreground.

Those who develop dashboards that will be viewed on a mobile device, such as an iPad, might have been told that the background color should be black. This opinion did not result from actual research. I suspect that someone used a black screen for a mobile application in the early days of the iPhone or iPad, and others thought it looked cool and followed suit. This is a fashion, not a best practice. So far, no one has actually done any research to compare the effectiveness of light vs. dark backgrounds on mobile devices.

FIGURE 12.12. An iPad dashboard with a dark background from RoamBI

Those who have been around as long as I have probably remember when all computer screens had dark backgrounds. The original IBM PC displayed green text on a black background. When multi-color monitors were originally introduced, the resolution was much lower than that of monochrome screens, but, as the resolution improved, the default color for the background of displays switched from dark to light. The light background caused text and images to look clearer and be easier to read. Imagine reading a book with black pages and white text. Why would this approach, which would seem absurd in a book, work differently on a computer screen?

One justification for dark screens that actually seems to have merit is that black is the absence of light, so the use of black on a screen requires less energy. On a mobile device, depending on the type of screen, this might translate into longer battery life. If this is true, then this practical benefit will need to be weighed against the ease of use of light backgrounds vs. dark. Another argument that I've heard is that dark backgrounds are less reflective and thus easier to read in some lighting conditions, such as when a person is using a tablet device outdoors in direct sunlight. I haven't subjected this to rigorous tests, but my informal observation doesn't support this claim. Screens with black backgrounds are highly reflective, so much so that we can use one in a pinch as a mirror to check whether any spinach salad remains in our teeth after lunch.

The same software vendors that seem to believe that black backgrounds are appropriate and indeed required for mobile devices tend to also offer charts with flashy lighting and 3-D effects. It is interesting that these same vendors seem to believe that mobile device screens should use a light background when they display text, such as books, for reading. Why would the presence or absence of graphics change the game? Until some actual research is done that supports the merits of a dark background and develops best practices for its use, I suggest that we stick with a light background.

Use High-Resolution Text and Images

The high density of information that typically appears on a dashboard requires that the graphic images be displayed with exceptional visual clarity. Images with poor resolution are hard to read, which slows down the process of scanning the dashboard for information (and is just plain annoying). Years ago, when the software that handled computer graphics was primitive, and screens had low resolution, nothing but a straight line could be drawn on the screen clearly; everything else looked jagged and pixelated. Notice the fuzziness along the border of the gauge below.

FIGURE 12.13. The poorly resolved edges of this gauge look fuzzy.

Looking at something that appears fuzzy is an uncomfortable experience. Our eyes struggle to bring it into focus, but they can't because the problem resides in the image itself. With the advanced state of today's computer graphics, there is no longer any excuse for poorly resolved images on a dashboard. If software cannot draw a curved line that is crisp and clear, we should throw it out and get a product that can.

Align Content Whenever Appropriate

Take a look at the dashboard below. Does anything about its design bother you?

FIGURE 12.14. This dashboard by LogiXML looks sloppy because the white panels, which look like they should be aligned, are slightly off.

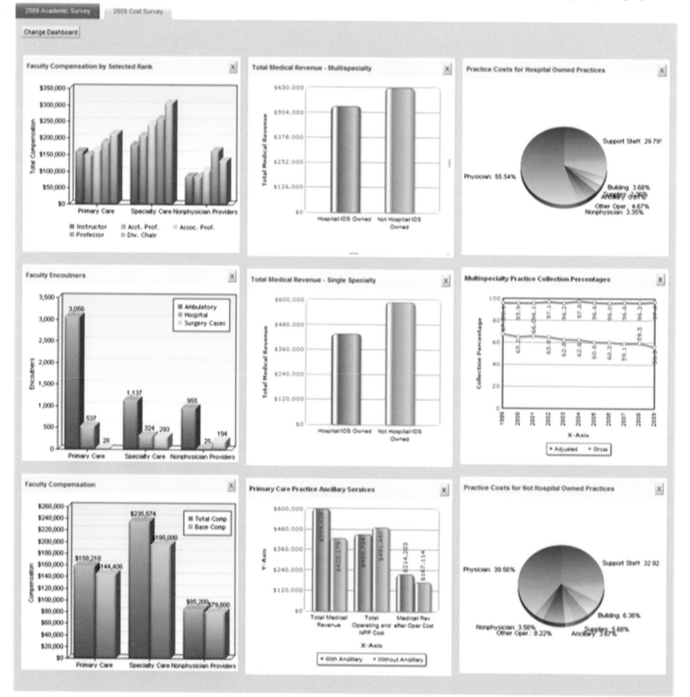

Notice that the white enclosures for the graphs don't look quite right. Their relatively uniform design suggests that they should all be equal in size and perfectly aligned into three rows and three columns, but they're not. They vary ever so slightly, enough to create discomfort even if we're not consciously aware of what the problem is. When items should be aligned because they belong together or look like they should be aligned because of the dashboard's layout as in the previous example, we need to take the time to align them precisely. This only takes a moment. Every good dashboard product makes this easy to do by providing alignment controls. Proper alignment contributes a great deal to the aesthetics of a dashboard's appearance.

Use a Legible Font

My final recommendation regarding dashboard aesthetics involves the display of text. We should use the most legible font we can find. The figure below illustrates two fundamental ways in which fonts (also known as *typefaces*) are distinguished.

Fine Legibility		Poor Legibility	
Serif	Sans-Serif	Serif	Sans-Serif
Times New Roman	Arial	**STENCIL**	**Impact**
Palatino	Verdana	CHARLEMAGNE	SYNCHRO LET
Garamond	Tahoma	Zapfino	Chalkduster

FIGURE 12.15. Examples of some fonts that are easy to read and some that are not.

First, some fonts are designed for legibility, and some are designed for effects, such as to evoke a particular mood, style, or period of time. Ornate text might be appropriate for a poster advertising the circus or a Broadway play but not for a dashboard. For a dashboard, we want the font that can be read the fastest with the least amount of strain on the eyes. Try to imagine reading a book that was printed in Zapfino.

Second, some fonts have serifs and some do not. Serifs are small embellishments at the edges of characters, such as the four pointed perpendicular flourishes that appear at the ends of the letter T below.

FIGURE 12.16. This Times New Roman uppercase letter T includes serifs.

Fonts that are sans-serif (that is, without serifs) are straight and clean, lacking embellishments. So you might be wondering, which is easier to read: serif or sans-serif fonts? Many studies have been conducted to answer this question, and what they've found is that well-designed serif and sans-serif fonts are equally legible when printed at high resolution on paper. Unfortunately, dashboards are presented on computer screens, and, at the time of this writing, even the best screens cannot equal the high resolution of print. When viewed on a screen, serifs, because of their small size, often appear blurry, which reduces their legibility. For this reason, until screens come closer to the resolution of print, I recommend that we stick with sans-serif fonts.

One other consideration should be kept in mind when selecting a font. Text is easier to read when individual letters vary in width depending on their shape. Notice the upper version of the word "Terminal" in the figure below, which is printed in Arial; the letters "i" and "l" are quite compact, designed to occupy only the width needed. Notice also that the letter "e" requires a little more width than the letter "r." Now take a look at the same word at the bottom of the figure, which is printed in Courier font. Notice that every letter has the same width, regardless of shape. Courier was designed for typewriters, which couldn't handle variable-width characters. Compared to variable-width fonts, fixed-width fonts are harder to read and less attractive. I advise avoiding fonts with letters of equal width.

Terminal
Terminal

FIGURE 12.17. Some fonts provide variable-width letters, such as Arial at the top, and a few old fonts use equal-width letters, such as Courier at the bottom.

Before we move on from character width, we must take one more feature of fonts into account. Even though letters should vary in width, numbers should not. A column of numbers will only line up properly if every digit is the same width. Fortunately, most fonts provide variable-width letters but equal-width numbers.

The best strategy is to find a font that works, and stick with it throughout the dashboard. There's no reason to use more than one. If some text must look a little different than other text—perhaps headings for sections of the dashboard should stand out as different from text that is used to label information in graphs—distinguish them by varying their sizes or using different colors.

Prevent Excessive Alerting

If you're more than 40 years old, you no doubt remember how annoying car alarms were when they first became popular. In the early years especially, they were poorly designed, which caused them to split the air with their awful scream at the least provocation. In the city, they sounded so often that we learned to ignore them. As a result, they failed to do their job because an actual car theft would get no more attention than the little boy who cried wolf. There's a lesson in this for us today. Don't allow the dashboard to create too many alerts, or they will be ignored. Make sure that the thresholds of activity (for example, a reduction in sales) that trigger alerts are set such that they draw attention to real problems—real signals that require response—not just routine changes. No one likes to be yelled at all the time. Teach your dashboards to be courteous, even tempered, and smart enough to tell the difference between signals and noise.

Keep Viewers in the Loop

People who build industrial situation awareness monitoring systems, such as those used by pilots who fly commercial passenger jets, have learned an important lesson that we should bear in mind: these systems cease to work if we over-automate. Situation awareness is only maintained when people are kept in the loop. If we automate to the point that things happen without involvement of those using the system, they lose awareness. We can automate to our heart's delight, but we must do it in a way that keeps people engaged enough to maintain awareness.

Later in the book I'll show a dashboard that I designed for the manager of a telesales group, a team of people who take calls throughout the day from customers who are making purchases. Information about all members of the team appears on the dashboard so that the manager can monitor their activities and intervene when needed throughout the day. Members are sorted in order based on current overall performance, from worst to best. When someone's performance drops below a specified threshold, the manager always responds initially in the same way: he sends an instant message that pops up on that person's screen with a few basic statistics about performance. This alerts the telesales representative to correct the problem or request assistance. When building a dashboard for this telesales manager, any well-intentioned developer might think, "Why not fully automate this process so the manager doesn't need to waste his time with this repetitive activity?" Such good intentions will get us in trouble. If this activity was fully automated, the manager would no longer remain in the loop, and situation awareness would be lost. The more effective response would be to automate everything except for a single simple step that the manager must take to initiate the action. I designed the telesales dashboard to require the manager to click the name of the person who fell below the threshold of acceptable performance, which was indicated by a visual alert, and the system did the rest. That simple action, trivial in cost to the manager, was not trivial in its effects. It kept the manager in the loop.

Accommodate Real-Time Monitoring

We just considered a job that requires real-time monitoring. The manager of a telesales group can't wait until tomorrow to find out that at this very moment customers are waiting on hold so long that they're hanging up. He needs to know this and respond right now. The frequency with which a dashboard should be updated with fresh data depends on the nature of the job that it supports. If the dashboard user can respond tomorrow, which is often the case, a daily dashboard will suffice, but if he must respond within five minutes, it must be updated more frequently than that. Dashboards that need to be updated frequently, throughout the day, must be designed a little differently than those that are updated daily.

If a client begins each morning by scanning her dashboard to update her awareness for the day, she might take a minute or two to examine it. If she looks at the dashboard throughout the day—not every second, of course, but frequently—she must quickly spot situations that need attention and respond immediately. By keeping three specific dashboard design practices in mind, we will support the requirements of real-time monitoring more effectively:

- Reduce information to what's essential.
- Provide a means to temporarily halt updates.
- Provide audio alerts.
- Time-stamp alerts.

Reduce Information to What's Essential

When someone is constantly monitoring information on a dashboard—information that is constantly changing—he can't handle as much information as when he monitors the dashboard less frequently. For clients who constantly monitor their dashboards, we reduce the information that appears on the dashboard to the essentials that must be constantly monitored and make it easy to access less essential but nevertheless important information in the moment that it's needed.

How much complexity can someone handle on a real-time dashboard? The answer, of course, is "It all depends." People who are highly expert can handle more complexity that those who are not. We need to get to know those who will use the dashboard, including their limits, and then use our judgment to determine as best we can the optimal level of complexity that the dashboard should display. Then we test for usability. We should not expect people to use the dashboard adeptly without training or practice. Let them work with it for awhile and then determine through testing whether it is possible to increase complexity or whether it's necessary to decrease it.

Provide a Means to Halt Updates

When information on a dashboard is frequently changing, there are times when the user will want to examine it closely, without distraction. This requires a means to temporarily freeze updates. We can do this with a control that can be clicked, but we need to make sure the user remains aware of the fact that the information has become stale. Perhaps after a minute without updates, the freeze button, which now functions as an unfreeze button, will turn bright yellow. Perhaps after a minute more it will turn bright red. Perhaps after five minutes it will start blinking. And finally, not long after that, the dashboard should sound an alarm—quietly at first but increasing in volume until the button is once again clicked, and the updates resume.

Provide Audio Alerts

Even when a dashboard is used throughout the day for real-time monitoring, the user doesn't look at it constantly. For example, the telesales manager takes phone calls, does administrative work, occasionally walks around to interact with the team, and leaves his office to attend meetings or get lunch. When critical alerts that require immediate response appear on the screen without notice (that is, the manager doesn't do what the dashboard requires to acknowledge that he is aware of an alert, such as clicking the alert icon), within a short time it might become necessary to sound an alarm, either audibly or through some other means that cannot be ignored, such as sending him a text message. The alarm relays a simple message from the dashboard: "Look at me."

Time-Stamp Alerts

If an alert appears when the user isn't watching the screen, which will happen often, it's important that he knows the time the alert arrived when he finally does notice it. A simple time stamp that either appears next to an alert indicator or can be quickly accessed by hovering over it will usually suffice.

We've now covered the principles of effective dashboard design, so it's time to bring everything together in the form of a few well-designed examples.

13 PUTTING IT ALL TOGETHER

A great deal of information has been presented in this book so far, step by step, concept by concept, and principle by principle. Now it's time to tie everything together, to see these concepts and principles fully demonstrated in the form of sample dashboards. The proof of the principles is in the efficacy of the result: dashboards that can be monitored and understood at a glance.

The dashboards in this chapter are arranged into three sections. We'll begin by examining dashboards that were submitted to a competition that I judged in 2012. By examining design approaches that worked, and some that didn't, we'll see what happens when the principles taught in this book are implemented, and what happens when they aren't. Next, we'll look at some examples of dashboards that I've designed to support various real-world activities. And, finally, to show that dashboards are improving as people take the lessons that I teach to heart, we'll look at a few good dashboards that were designed by others.

Lessons from a Competition

While preparing to write the second edition of this book, I organized and judged a dashboard design competition. I did this for several reasons. One was to gather a fresh set of dashboards to include in this chapter to show what happens when the principles of this book are put into practice, as well as the opposite—what happens when these principles are unknown or ignored. I wanted examples of many dashboards that were all designed for the same purpose, based on the same information, so that nothing would differ among them other than elements of design.

The competition involved a dashboard that would be used by a teacher. Here's the description that competitors received:

> This competition involves the design of a dashboard that would be used by a high school teacher to monitor student performance (behavior, aptitude, and achievement). The particular person who will use this dashboard—Susan Metcalf—teaches mathematics at the fictitious Silver Oaks High School. She will ordinarily look at the dashboard prior to each class session to update her awareness regarding the students in that particular class in an effort to prevent or resolve problems and to help each student improve as much as possible. Information has been provided for a single Algebra 1 class, along with some summary information regarding the entire school and the school district, which can serve as context for evaluating this class' performance. The current date is Tuesday, May 1, 2012, approximately 80% into the current school term.

Even though a dashboard designed for this purpose would ordinarily provide access to additional information to supplement the overview, which could be viewed by navigating to different screens or through tooltips, this won't be addressed in this competition. Concern yourself only with the design of the initial dashboard that this teacher could use to rapidly monitor what's going on with her students in preparation for the day's class.

This Excel file [the one that I provided to competitors] contains information that may be included in the dashboard in six separate worksheets:

- *Student Data: Contains the bulk of the information about individual students*
- *Student Absences: Contains the dates when individual students were absent during the current term*
- *Student Tardies: Contains the dates when individual students arrived late for class*
- *Class Data: Contains summary information for the entire class*
- *School Data: Contains summary information for the entire school*
- *District Data: Contains summary information for the entire school district*

Information in the class, school, and district worksheets can serve as context that can appear in some form on the dashboard if you believe it would be useful.

In total, 91 dashboards were submitted to the competition. No one participated half-heartedly or on a whim. Considerable work was involved, which narrowed the list of competitors to people who took dashboard design seriously and considered themselves reasonably skilled. I'll begin by showing the winning dashboard and the runner-up, to see what we can learn from the design choices that they exhibit. Next, I'll use other dashboards that were submitted, in whole or in part, to illustrate ways that design flaws affected usability. Finally, I'll present my own version of the dashboard to fully illustrate the design practices presented in this book.

Lessons from the Winners

During the judging process, the competitors' identities remained unknown to me. I began by narrowing the 91 dashboards that were submitted to the best 8. I then used the following criteria to score these as objectively as possible:

Attribute	Percent of Score
Comprehensive information	9
Important information is highlighted	9
Use of graphics whenever appropriate	9
Good choice and design of graphics	9
Aesthetically pleasing visual design	8
Sufficient information to decide if action is necessary	8
Good hierarchy of importance exhibited through salience	7
Good support for comparisons	7
Legibility	7
Organization is clear	6
Good hierarchy of importance exhibited through position	6
Everything is visible without scrolling or paging	5
Clear meanings	4
Good use of space	3
Scalable design	3
Overall	100

The winning dashboard, with a score of 90.4 out of 100, was designed by Jason Lockwood. Jason lives in Switzerland where he currently works as a usability and design consultant for *IMS Health*. Here's his dashboard:

FIGURE 13.1. The winning Student Performance Dashboard, designed by Jason Lockwood

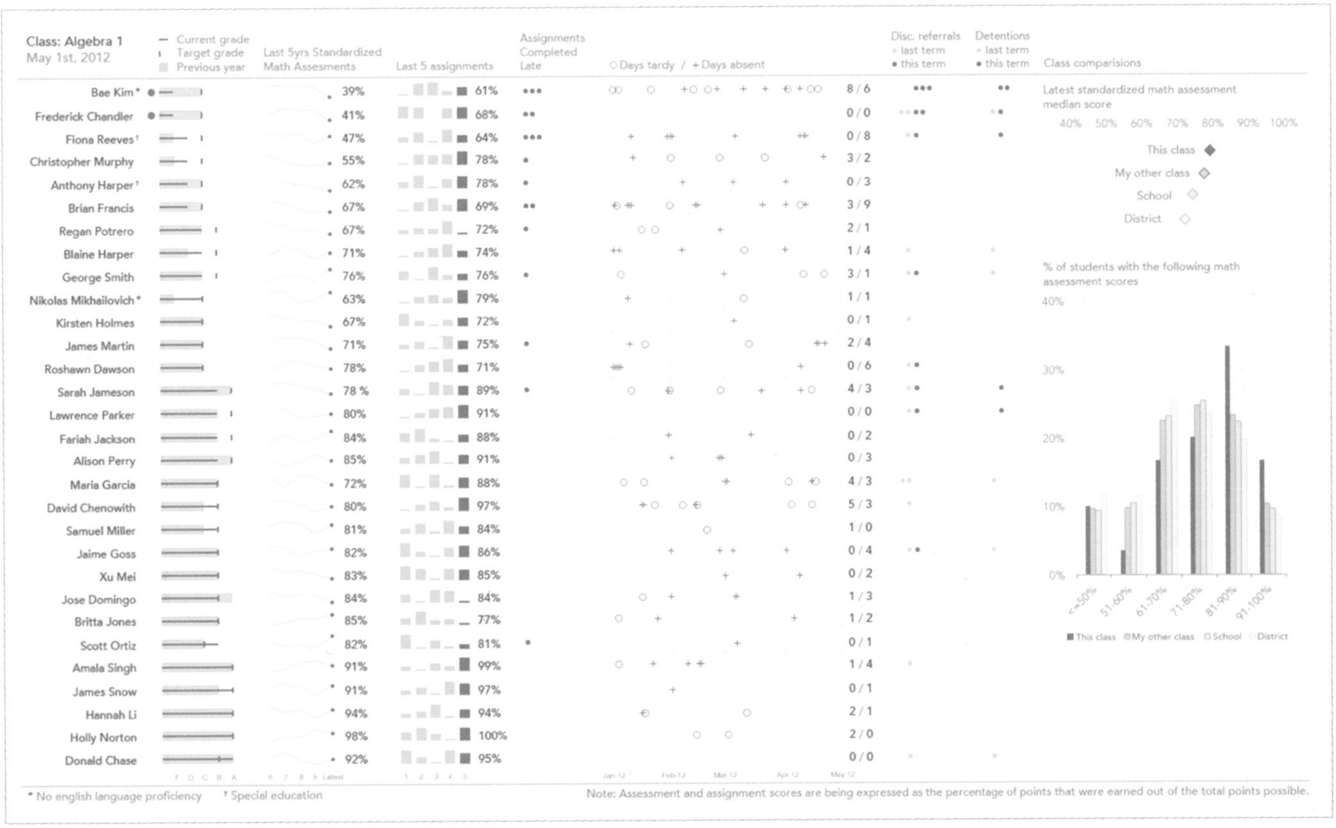

One of the first things you probably notice is the aesthetic quality of this dashboard. Jason's use of color, layout, and reduction of non-data-ink make it pleasing to the eye in a way that enhances usability. Because he used color sparingly, the red alert icons make it easy to spot the students that are most in need of immediate attention (although the icons could be a little bigger to make them pop more). The tabular (rows and columns) arrangement of student information (one student per row) makes it easy to see everything about a particular student with a quick horizontal scan and easy to compare a particular metric across all students with a quick vertical scan. All of the most important metrics are consistently represented using the same dark shade of blue, which clearly features them above other information. This design is scalable; more students could be easily be added. Meaningful patterns in individual student attendance information (days absent and tardy) can be easily seen. Here's how Jason describes his design:

1. Introduction

In the course of my work as a UX engineer, I have the chance to try to bring good data visualization practices to my clients. However, many of the "dashboards" requested by those clients are closer to reporting solutions. Seeing this competition, I was delighted to be able to try my hand at a real dashboard. It was a very challenging and satisfying exercise, during which I learned a lot. I have designed this purely as a visual mock-up in Photoshop. I have the great luck of working with some very talented programmers who are incredibly adept at translating my mock-ups to pixel perfect, working solutions, which provides great freedom for me.

2. Overall design strategy

There is a lot of information contained within the data sheet, so one of the major challenges would be how to be able to display all of it in a clear way, on a single screen. I felt that all the information was pertinent to the goal of the dashboard, so did not want to exclude anything. That led to the compromise of designing to a slightly higher screen resolution of 1400px width than what perhaps may be standard. However, that being said, I have designed it in a way that on a SXGA monitor, the entirety of the student information would be visible, and the less important, class comparison information would be off screen.

I usually base the overall colour palette on the visual identity of the client. As this was not provided, I invented the idea that the school colours were blue and grey. I would therefore use monochromatic shades of blue for data representation, grey for text and labels. For the background, I am using an off-white with a slight orange tint. This creates a subtle complement to the blue, making the data stand out a little bit more.

I chose Avenir as a font as it provides a good contrast between upper and lowercase letters for good legibility, as well as very clear numerals. With only a few exceptions (title and legends), I kept a 12pt font size to provide consistency.

3. Student data

Breaking down all the data in the Excel sheet was an interesting exercise. First step was to prioritize the information. What would the teacher want/ need to see first. I decided that the grades were crucial (that is, after all, the overall measurement of the student's performance). With the grades I grouped together the other pure assessment information: last 5 year assessments, last 5 assignments. The assignments completed late info provides a nice segue (and visual break) from scores to more behavioural information: Absences/tardies, Disciplinary referrals and detentions.

I sorted the students by their current grade, from worst to best, so the teacher can view the problem cases first. Secondary sort is on difference of current grade from target.

Having ordered the information, the next step was to visualize. The grades lent themselves very well to a bullet chart, efficiently portraying the target, current and previous scores. I used sparklines for the last 5 year assessment scores (being an interval axis), and micro-columns for last 5 assignments. For assignment late count (and later detentions and referrals) I used dots to represent the counts, as I find these are clearer to view than straight numbers.

I chose to try to represent not only the amount of the tardies and absences but also their temporal occurrence. Hopefully this can allow the teacher to identify patterns not just for each student, but for the entire class. This ends up almost like a scatter chart.

Last up for the behavioural data are the detentions and referrals, which again I represent as dots, with past term information in a lighter shade and to the left of the implied axis for comparison.

Once all the student information was portrayed, I decided that some sort of aid was needed to help the user view the information in rows. I decided on zebra striping as I believe, while it is technically more non-data ink than row lines, it is clearer and subtler at the same time (a line has two edges, top and bottom, as does a solid box, but only half as many boxes are required).

To compare the overall class performance to other classes/school/district, I combined the information from the summary tabs to create two graphs: a dot graph to show latest median assessment scores and percentage of students' assessment scores in percent groups. I chose a dot graph in order to emphasise the variation between the groups, but also to line up with the percentage groups of the second graph.

On the second graph, I have unfortunately had to rotate the category labels. I would normally not do this, but I did not want to reduce the font any more (even reduced to 10pt, it would still be too crowded) or expand the screen any further.

I finally added indicators on the student name to show English proficiency and special ed status, with the legend in the footer, along with the data qualification note.

4. Conclusion

Overall, I am quite pleased with the outcome of this design exercise. I believe I have managed to represent all the information in a clear and well structured way that would fulfill its user's needs. I have shown this to a couple teachers and received positive feedback (and requests to produce it).

Like Jason, I am quite pleased with this design. It exhibits many of the principles that I teach in this book. It's my job, however, to suggest improvements whenever possible, so here are a few that come to mind:

- Left-aligning the students' names would produce a clear left edge, which would make it slightly easier for the teacher to find a particular student.
- The horizontal dark blue line that appears in the graphic to the right of each student's name represents the key measure: the student's current grade. Because this line is so thin, however, it is not sufficiently salient. Thickening it slightly would solve this problem.
- The sparklines that appear in the "Last 5 Years Standardized Math Assessments" column were designed to fill the vertical space of the plot area. This works fine if only the patterns and overall trends of change are of interest. If, on the other hand, the teacher wants to compare the magnitudes of values and degrees of variability among her students, the sparklines would need to be designed differently.
- Bars are not the best way to display the five assignment scores. A line would make the pattern of change easier to see. The usefulness of the bars is further compromised by the fact that their quantitative scales do not begin at zero, so their heights do not accurately represent their differences.
- The histogram (a bar graph that displays one or more frequency distributions) on the lower right is not the best choice for comparing the four distributions of student assessment scores (this class, my other classes, the school, and the district). A frequency polygon (a line graph that displays one or more frequency distributions) with four lines to show the four distributions, would serve this purpose better.

The runner-up dashboard, shown on the following page, was designed by Shamik Sharma using *Excel 2010*.

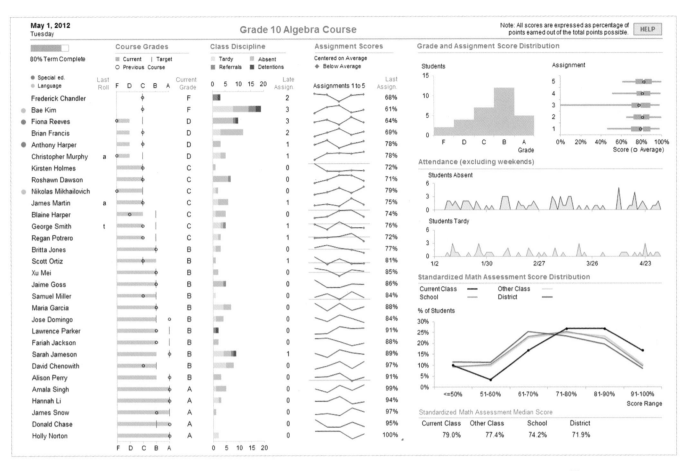

FIGURE 13.2. The runner-up dashboard, designed by Shamik Sharma

Once again, notice the pleasing aesthetics of this design. Also notice the additional displays of class-level information on the right, which don't all appear in the winning dashboard. The two distribution graphs on top, in particular, provide useful overviews of the class as a whole. Notice as well how the distribution graph of assessment scores in the bottom right corner, which uses lines in the form of a frequency polygon, is easier to read than the histogram in the winning solution.

Placing information about individual students on the left and summary information about the class as a whole on the right, though logical, misses an opportunity. In most cases, the summary information is an aggregation of information that also appears on the left per student. Segregating the student and class level versions of this information into two sections has made it difficult to see the relationships between them. Later, when I show my version of this dashboard, we'll see how these relationships can be made obvious. Finally, compared to the winning solution, notice that in this dashboard it isn't as easy to spot the students who need attention, and that student attendance information in the "Class Discipline" section is aggregated in a way that hides the patterns of change through time. Overall, however, this is a well-designed dashboard.

Lessons Learned from Flaws

Every dashboard that was submitted to the competition could be improved—some more, some less. I have no doubt that this is true of my own version of the dashboard as well, which we'll see in the next section. First, however, let's examine the following flaws that showed up in some of the other dashboards prepared for the competition, to reinforce our understanding of what works and what doesn't.

- Too high-level
- Too focused
- Too segregated
- Insufficient context
- Inappropriately sorted
- Overuse of color
- Too complicated
- Haphazard layout

TOO HIGH-LEVEL

Dashboards must be designed with a clear sense of purpose. The dashboard designed for this competition was supposed to help a teacher monitor the performance of her students in an effort to help them achieve their best. An overview of the class as a whole without information about individual students might help the teacher improve her own performance but not that of her individual students. The information presented in the dashboard below is too high-level.

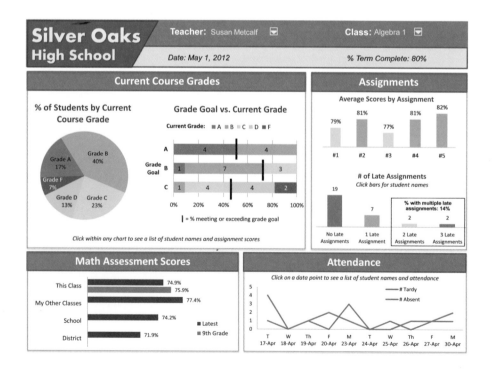

FIGURE 13.3. In this dashboard, critical information about individual students can only be seen by looking elsewhere.

But, you say, charts can be clicked to see related information about individual students. Information about individual students is what's needed to support the primary tasks associated with this dashboard, so the teacher should not have to go elsewhere to see it, and it shouldn't be fragmented across a series of separate screens. All of the important information that the teacher must monitor about each student should be available at a glance.

TOO FOCUSED

This next dashboard errs in the opposite direction from the one above: it focuses too narrowly on one student at a time and lacks an overview of the class as a whole, providing no way to see students compared to one another. This approach could work for looking up information about individual students but not for rapid performance monitoring.

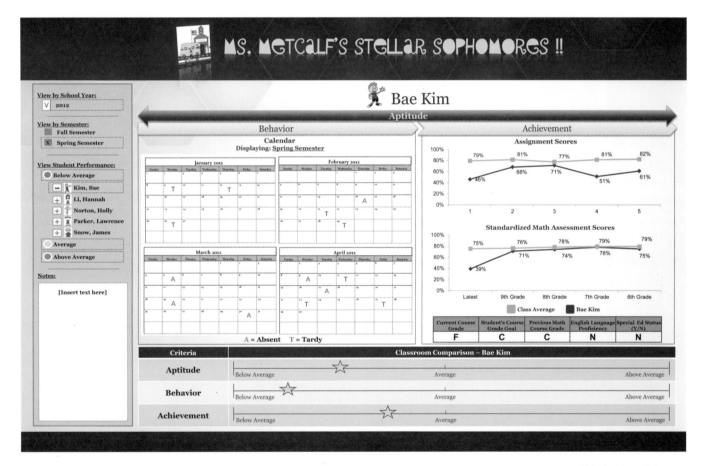

FIGURE 13.4. This dashboard shows information about only one student at a time.

TOO FRAGMENTED

The next dashboard is aesthetically pleasing and clearly organized, but the information is overly segregated. Dashboards err when items that should be seen together are displayed in separate sections. Imagine trying to find all of the information about a particular student, such as Brian Francis. We would need to scan each section individually to see if he's there and then try to combine separate pieces of information about him into a coherent whole.

Similar to the dashboard above, this next example breaks information into chunks that should have been shown together. The one above did so by separating information about students into several topical sections (grades, absences, tardies, referrals, etc.), but the next one fragments the information into smaller chunks, one per student. Try to compare students along a particular measure, such as the number of days tardy. When the information is fragmented in this way, all comparisons are difficult.

FIGURE 13.5. In this dashboard, information about students is overly segregated by topic.

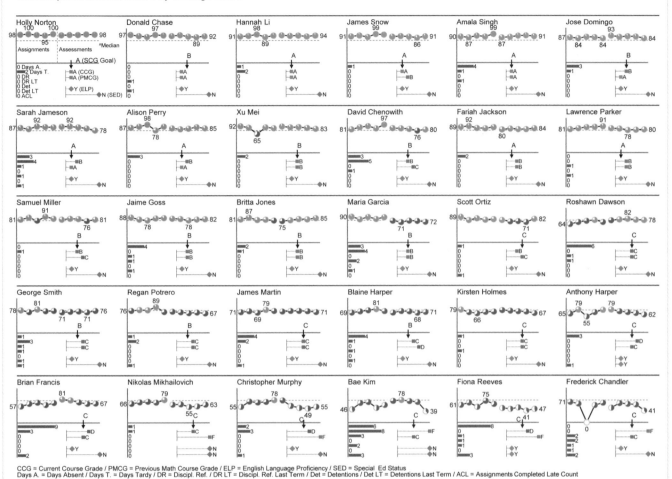

This design also appears cluttered. It's hard to look at. It looms as a massive wall of data that discourages engagement.

INSUFFICIENT CONTEXT

The next example is neat and clean, but this tidy appearance has been accomplished, in part, by leaving out much of the information. Even the categories of information that were addressed lack sufficient context to bring them alive. Consider the students' grades. We can see each student's current overall grade, but the only context to make the grade meaningful is a comparison to the student's goal. What we can't see is how this term's grade compares to last term's or the individual assignments that determine the grade and how the students' scores have changed through time. A student with a B grade could be steadily trending downward from one assignment to the next, ready to drop to a C. We can see how many times a student has been absent or tardy, but we can't see when these events occurred. If all of the absences occurred recently, that would tell a different story—perhaps the student has had the flu—than a uniform distribution of absences across the term.

FIGURE 13.7. This dashboard lacks context that must be seen for some of the measures to be fully understood.

We should take care that, in an effort to simplify a dashboard, we don't oversimplify it by eliminating important context. The goal is to find a way to display essential context without overcomplicating the dashboard and exceeding the cognitive limits of those who will use it.

INAPPROPRIATELY SORTED

This next dashboard has much going for it, but I'll use it to point out a problem that can easily be fixed. Notice the order in which the students have been sorted: alphabetical by first name. If alphabetical order is appropriate, then sorting a list of tenth-grade students by first name rather than last name would be appropriate assuming the teacher knows them primarily by first name. However, alphabetical order is useful for one purpose only; it simplifies the process of finding a particular item in a long list. Reports that are used for looking up individual items benefit from alphabetical order, but dashboards, where we are interested in monitoring performance, do not.

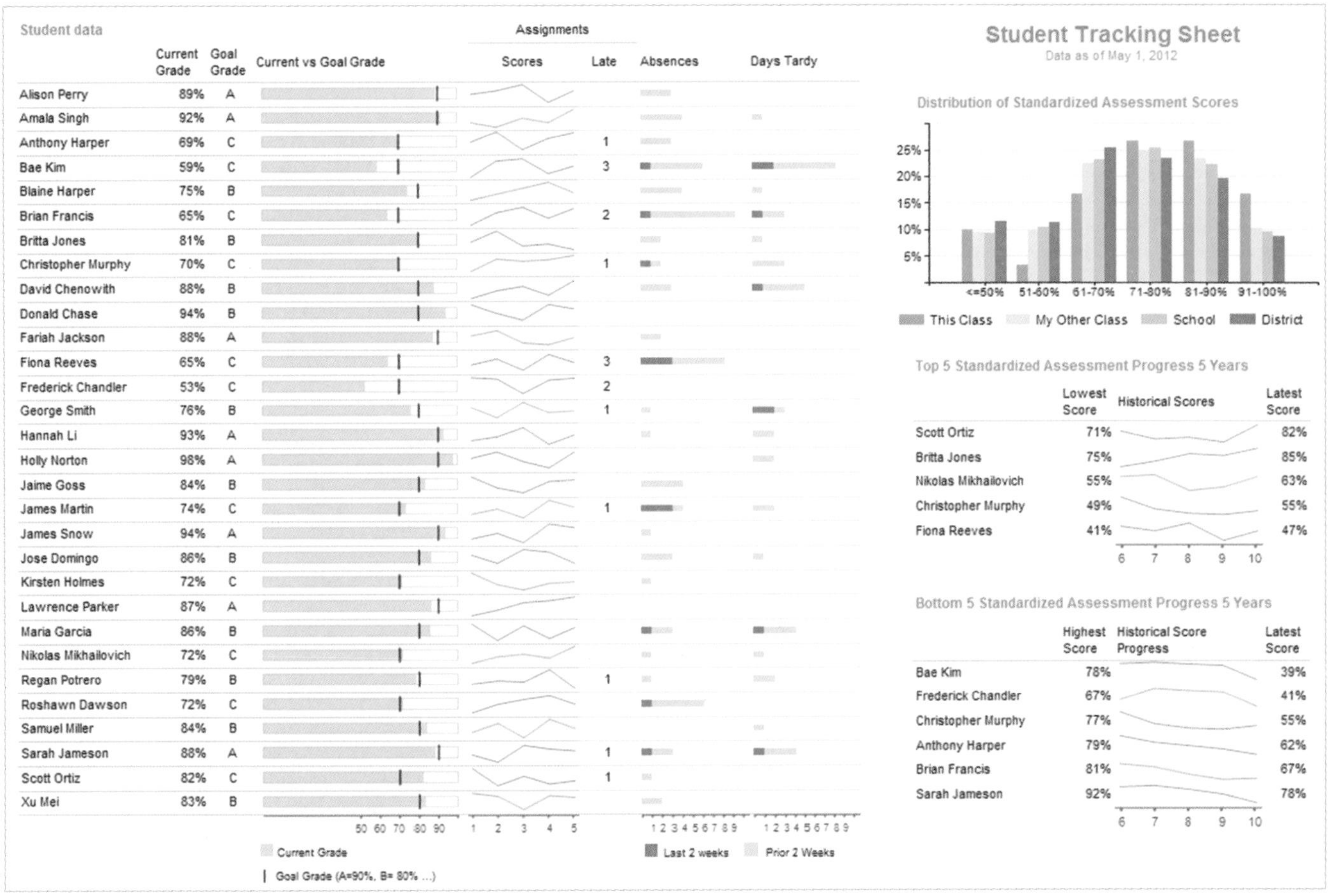

FIGURE 13.8. Sorting the students alphabetically misses an opportunity to show relative performance.

If we sort the students by the primary measure of performance, which in this case is their overall course grade, two benefits emerge immediately: 1) we can see their relative performance, and 2) we can compare their performance to one another more easily because grades that are close in value are located near one another, which makes it possible to see subtle differences. Also, because this dashboard is used by a teacher to spot students in need of help, sorting the list from those most in need of help to those least in need makes the teacher's task easy. You might argue that a student's overall course grade is not the best measure of student need, and you might be right. If there is a different measure that better identifies the degree to which students need help, then sorting by that measure could improve the dashboard's usefulness.

OVERUSE OF COLOR

One of the first things we probably notice about this next example is that we don't know where to look. Colors have been used to qualitiatively score almost every value on the dashboard. The result is an overwhelming amount of color. When everything demands attention, nothing in particular stands out.

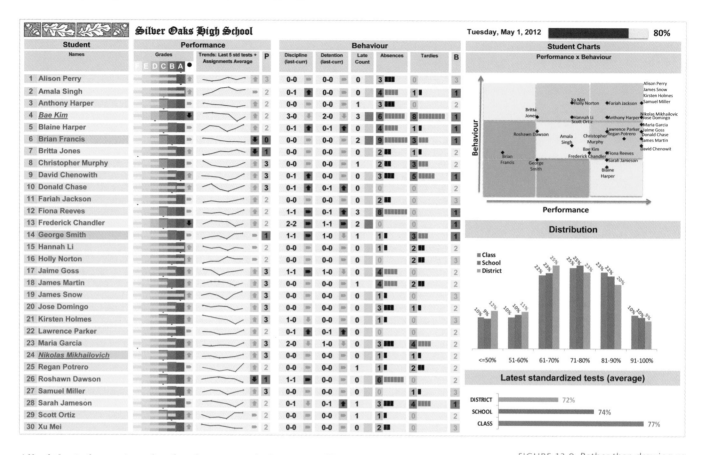

FIGURE 13.9. Rather than drawing us into the information, too many colors can have a confusing or repelling effect.

All of the information that has been encoded using traffic light colors (green, yellow, red) could be shown in visually subtler and more precise ways. I do appreciate the fact that most of the traffic light colors have been softened; otherwise, we wouldn't be able to look at this dashboard at all. The bright reds are the exception; they are far too abundant. This many red items screaming for attention on a dashboard is exhausting.

Another color-related problem that this dashboard illustrates is the use of specific colors to mean multiple things. Notice that red means poor performance in most cases, but in the two graphs in the lower right it means "school"; one color that has multiple meanings is confusing.

TOO COMPLICATED
The creator of this next dashboard had some great ideas, but overall its appearance is intimidating. There are so many symbols to keep track of to comprehend this dashboard (blue circles, blue squares, orange squares, orange diamonds, blue diamonds, blue plus signs, orange plus signs, dark blue bars, light blue bars, gray

bars, vertical orange lines, horizontal orange lines, solid vertical red lines, dotted vertical red lines, "Watch," "Push," and "SpcEd," along with numbers next to some of them at times). It's possible that someone, through a great deal of practice, could learn to perceive this dashboard efficiently, but this much effort shouldn't be necessary.

Metcalf
Algebra I
1 May 2012

Goal / Last Class / Aptitude

Class Scores — F   D   C   B   A

Current Grade
Assignment 1
Assignment 2
Assignment 3
Assignment 4
Assignment 5

Watch A- / B- / C- students	Amala / Britta, Scott / Roshawn, Kristen, Nicholas
Push B+ / C+ / D+F+ students	Alison, Sarah, David / Regan/ Anthony, Christopher, Bae
Absent in last week	Maria, James, Christopher

Disicipline   Tardy (+), Absence (◇)

Grade	Name	Flag
A/A/A+	Holly Norton	
A/A/A	Hannah Li	
	Amala Singh	Watch
A/B/B+	James Snow	
B/A/A	Donald Chase	
A/A/B+	Alison Perry	Push
A/A/B	Sarah Jameson	Push
A/B/B	Fariah Jackson	
A/B/B-	Lawrence Parker	
B/A/A-	Jose Domingo	
B/B/B	Jaime Goss	
	Xu Mei	
	Britta Jones	Watch
B/B/C+	Maria Garcia	
B/C/C+	David Chenowith	Push
	Samuel Miller	
C/C/C	Scott Ortiz	Watch
B/C/C	George Smith	
B/C/C-	Regan Potrero	Push
B/D/D+	Blaine Harper	
C/C/C+	Roshawn Dawson	Watch
C/C/C	James Martin	
C/C/C-	Kirsten Holmes	Watch
C/F/F+	Nikolas Mikhailovi..	Watch
C/C/C-	Anthony Harper	SpcEd Push
	Brian Francis	
C/F/F	Christopher Murphy	Push
	Fiona Reeves	SpcEd
C/C/D	Bae Kim	Push
C/C/D-	Frederick Chandler	

A
B
C
D
F

50%   60%   70%   80%   90%   100%   1   2   3   Feb 1 Mar 1 Apr 1

50% of scores | Current grade : Min. required avg. to improve grade
O3 Assig. 3   □ Last assig.   ■ Low score

■ Referral   ◇ Absence
▬ Detention   + Tardy
☐ Last year   + Last week

FIGURE 13.10. This dashboard contains so many symbols whose meanings must be memorized that it can't be used efficiently for monitoring.

HAPHAZARD LAYOUT

Once again, in this next example, we see a high degree of fragmentation, which undermines our ability to get a clear picture of individual student performance. What should be noticed in particular, however, is the way that information has been laid out on the screen. Positioning and sizing of sections looks haphazard, as if they were created independently by different members of a committee without coordination, and then somewhat randomly placed on the screen wherever they could fit. We definitely shouldn't stretch charts to get them to line up or fit into a predetermined grid, but a little extra effort to coordinate the whole could have eliminated some of the disjointed appearance of this dashboard.

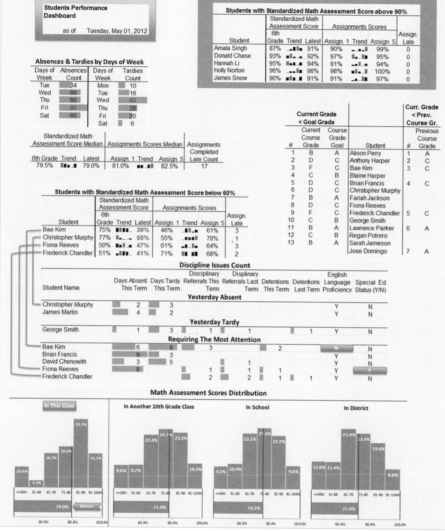

FIGURE 13.11. The layout and some of the visual elements of this dashboard give it a haphazard appearance.

Visual elements have been applied in a haphazard way as well. Notice the blue backgrounds that encase the title in the upper left and the "Students with Standardized Math Assessment Score above 90%" section to the right. These appear as bold borders to highlight sections of the dashboard that don't deserve to be featured. Even if they did, their position at the top the the screen would be sufficient. Notice also the red highlighting with gradient effects to make certain items pop out. Our eyes are strongly drawn to these items, but for what reason? Are the facts that Bae Kim lacks English language proficiency and Fiona Reeves is a Special Ed student something that the teacher is likely to forget without being reminded in this heavy-handed way? Does the arrow that points to the median in the bottom row of graphs need to shout "Look at me, look at me"? And finally, notice the black lines that were used to divide tables into sections when much lighter lines would suffice. These elements of design make the dashboard look a bit sloppy.

Lessons from an Evolving Example

I'm now ready to show you my version of the Student Performance Dashboard. Notice that I'm referring to this dashboard as an "evolving example." I have never designed anything that I couldn't improve later. As new ideas come to mind—and they often come from students in my courses—I'll continue to improve this dashboard with each new printing of the book. Despite the evolutionary nature of design (time is a great teacher), I'm confident that the dashboard below does the job well.

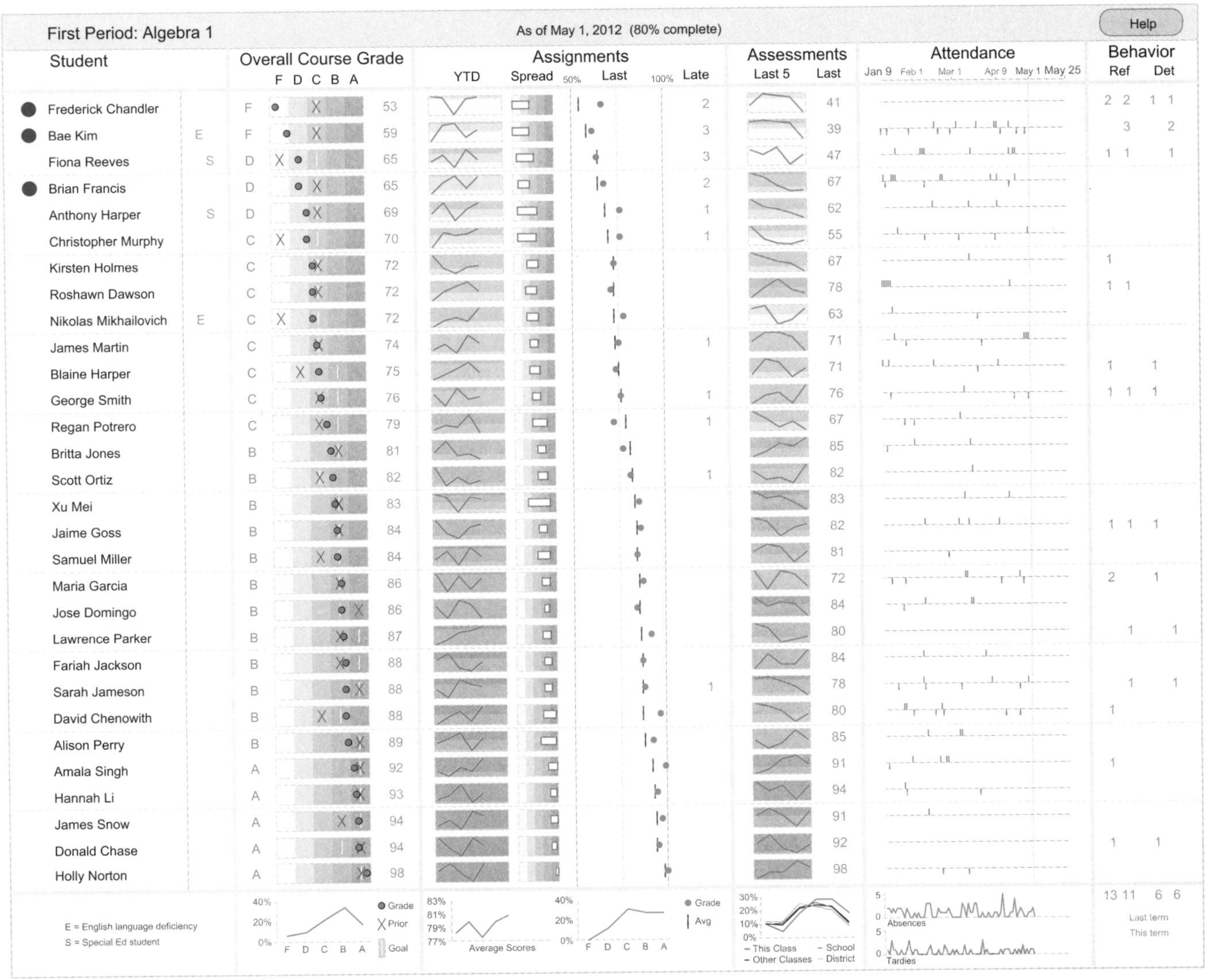

FIGURE 13.12. My own version of the Student Performance Dashboard

Examine this dashboard on your own for a few minutes, through eyes that can now recognize what works and what doesn't. Examine each measure and the way that it's expressed, including the context. Look at each component, both on its own and in relation to the whole. Consider the overall visual design: how it draws us into the information and draws our eyes to what's important.

I hope the reasons for each of my design choices became clear as you examined it closely. You might have noticed that I incorporated several of the ideas that were exhibited by dashboards that were submitted to the competition, especially the two winning solutions. Yes, I adopted others' good ideas, and for this reason I didn't give myself an award! Here are a few of the good qualities of this dashboard that were present in others as well:

- All of the information is present.
- It is easy to spot the students who are most in need of attention.
- The organization is clear.
- The students that most need attention are clearly featured, using simple blue icons.
- Graphics have been used to support efficient scanning of the information.
- Everything about a student can be seen by scanning across a single row.
- Students can be compared easily by scanning down the columns.
- Even though there is a great deal of information, little training would be required to learn how to interpret this dashboard.
- The information has been displayed in an aesthetically pleasing manner.
- It is scalable in that more or fewer students could be accommodated by simply adding or removing rows.

Now let's consider a few ways that this design succeeds where others fell short.

- Student-level and class-level information has been well integrated.
- The sparklines are more informative.
- It is easier to see time-based attendance patterns (absences and tardies).

Placing class-level summaries below related student-level information clearly shows the relationship between the two and makes comparisons between them easy. By using the bandline version of sparklines that I described earlier in the book, I was able to provide a quick glimpse of history that revealed not only patterns and trends, but also information about the magnitudes and variability of values. In this case, however, rather than using bands of fill color to show ranges of distribution based on percentiles, I used them to show grade ranges (F, D, C, B, and A), which better serves the teacher's needs. To show historical attendance information, I designed a display that was similar to that in the winning solution by Jason Lockwood but is a little easier to comprehend at a glance.

After reading the preceding chapters of this book, you can, I hope, appreciate the design choices that were made to produce this dashboard and understand why they support performance monitoring far better than many real-world dashboard examples.

Additional Illustrative Examples

The dashboards in this section will continue to put flesh on the bones of the design principles that I've taught in this book and will also suggest ideas for designing dashboards that serve various purposes under different circumstances.

Sales Dashboard

Apart from executive dashboards, no one type of dashboard is used more often than a sales dashboard. Those in charge of sales need to keep their fingers on the pulse at all times, even when all is well. Sales strategies might need to change quickly when new opportunities, problems, or competitive pressures arise. A well-designed dashboard can be a powerful tool for a sales manager.

I began designing the sample dashboard that we'll look at next by selecting the information that seemed most important for a sales manager to monitor. Each item in this list is a measure of what's currently going on in sales.

- Sales revenue
- Sales revenue in the pipeline (expected revenue divided into categories of probability)
- Profit
- Customer satisfaction rating
- Top 10 customers
- Top 10 potential deals
- Market share

Most sales divisions focus primarily on revenue, slicing it in various ways. In this dashboard, total revenue for the quarter and year is further divided into regions and products.

FIGURE 13.13. A sample sales dashboard, originally designed in 2005

Notice the use of stacked bars in both the "Top 8 Customers this Quarter" and "Revenue QTD" sections. In both cases the bars combine actual sales with the sales pipeline to anticipate total sales by quarter end. Sales divisions typically track expected sales for the current sales period and call it the pipeline. Because some orders are more likely to come in than others, they often weight the pipeline based on specfic levels of probability. In this case four levels of probability exist—25%, 50%, 75%, and 90%—but I've included only the two highest levels in the dashboard. Showing the pipeline as an extension of actual sales for the quarter allows us to predict performance.

This dashboard has been featured in other books and many presentations since it appeared in the first edition of this book. Also, because I have data for it in an Excel spreadsheet, which I created for a competition, several software vendors have created their own versions of this dashboard to demonstrate the capabilities of their products and how they can be used to build dashboards that exhibit the best practices that I teach. Back in 2008, I was asked to design a variation of this dashboard by the software company *CURL, Inc.*, based on a set of requirements that they provided. The company then used *CURL* to create their own working version of the dashboard below.

Similar in purpose to the original sales dashboard, this version focuses on a smaller list of key metrics and monitors sales leads more closely.

FIGURE 13.14. A sales dashboard that I designed for CURL, Inc.

CIO Dashboard

A Chief Information Officer (CIO) must monitor many aspects of an organization's information systems, including projects to implement new systems and update those that exist. My sample CIO dashboard includes information in the following categories:

- System availability (uptime)
- Expenses
- Customer satisfaction
- Severe problem count
- CPU usage relative to capacity
- Storage usage relative to capacity
- Network traffic
- Application response time
- Major project milestones
- Top projects in the queue
- Other critical events

This is a mixture of strategic and frequently updated operational information. Try to imagine how a CIO might use it.

FIGURE 13.15. A sample CIO dashboard

CIO Dashboard (As of December 19, 2012)

Help

Network   ERP   Data Warehouse   Web Site   Email

System Availability (last 30 days)   (I Actual; Acceptable)

Last 12 Months	System	Availability %
	Network	98.5%
	ERP	97.9%
	Data Warehouse	93.2%
	Web Site	98.5%
	Email	100.0%
	HR	96.7%
	Problem Tracking	94.7%

85% 90% 95% 100%

Hardware % of Capacity   (■Actual; Good; Excessive; Critical)

CPU	Today	Overall	79%
Storage	Last 12 Mo.	Today	63%
Bandwidth	Last 12 Mo.	Today	53%

0% 50% 100%

Daily Network Traffic (kilobytes)

— Daily mean for last 6 months — Daily mean for last 7 days — Yesterday

200K
150K
100K
50K
0K

12 1 2 3 4 5 6 7 8 9 10 11 12 1 2 3 4 5 6 7 8 9 10 11 12
AM   PM

Response Time (distribution in seconds)   (Acceptable)

0 1 2 3 4 5 6 7 8 9 10 11 12

DW
ERP
Web
HR

Key Non-System Metrics   (■Actual; Good; Excessive; Critical)

Year-to-Date	Metric	% of Target	Actual
	Expenses YTD		$2,456.5K
	Customer Satisfaction		3.25 of 4
	Level 1 Problems		87

0% 50% 100% 150%

Major Project Milestones (by priority)

Project	Milestone	Days Until/ Past Due	Due Date
ERP Upgrade	Full system test		01/08/13
Add services data to DW	ETL coding		12/15/12
Upgrade mainframe OS	Prepare plan		12/23/12
Disaster recovery site	Install hardware		01/06/13
Budgeting system	Hire team		12/06/12
Web site face-lift	Move into production		01/05/13

-20 -10 0 10 20

5 Top Projects in the Queue

	Project	Status	Funding Approved	Sched. Start
1	Professional services module	Pending available staff	X	02/10/13
2	Upgrade MS Office	Cost-benefit analysis		02/18/13
3	Failover for ERP	Preparing proposal		03/02/13
4	Upgrade data warehouse HW	Evaluating options	X	04/15/13
5	Executive dashboard	Vendor assessment		05/01/13

5 Top Critical Events (next 14 Days)

Event	Group Responsible	Date
Full system maintenance outage from 9-11 PM	G. Jones	12/21/12
Present hardware upgrade proposal to CEO	Self/M. Smith	12/22/12
Tom visiting from Asia office	Self	12/23/12
Prepare quarterly financial for public announcement	Self	01/04/13
Present revised information strategy to steering comm.	J. Kane	01/06/13

Only one section of this dashboard—the upper-left corner—displays near-real-time data. This section includes five alerts: one for each of the major systems to which the CIO might need to respond immediately when a problem arises. If no red icons appear in this section, nothing critical is currently wrong with any of these systems. To better grab the CIO's attention, red icons could blink until clicked or even emit a sound that gradually increases in volume. The alert icons could also link to other screens that describe precisely what is wrong.

The rest of this dashboard provides the CIO with information that is more strategic in nature. Notice that a great deal of contextual information has been provided to complement the measures—especially comparisons to measures of acceptable performance. This is the kind of context that could help the CIO easily make sense of these measures.

There is a great deal of information on this dashboard, yet it doesn't look cluttered. This is largely because non-data pixels have been reduced to a minimum. For instance, white space alone has been used to separate the various sections of the display. A judicious use of color has also contributed to this effect. Besides gray-scale colors, the only other hues we see are a muted green for the name of each section and two intensities of red, for alerts. It is easy to scan the dashboard and quickly find everything that needs attention because the alert icons are unique, visually unlike anything else.

Notice that there is a great deal of text on this dashboard. The "5 Top Projects in the Queue" and "5 Top Critical Events" sections consist entirely of text. This is because this information doesn't lend itself to graphical display. In this case, even though the text must be read rather than being scanned efficiently, it is appropriate. Including information about project milestones, pending projects, and other critical events on this dashboard locates all the most important information the CIO needs in one place. It also supports useful comparisons. Being reminded about coming events that might affect existing systems and being able to look immediately at the current performance of those systems could raise useful questions about their readiness.

Telesales Dashboard

The next sample dashboard was designed to monitor real-time operations so that a telesales supervisor can take necessary actions without delay. Because this dashboard is used to monitor real-time operations that require quick responses, it doesn't display as many measures as the examples we've seen so far in this chapter. Too many measures can be overwhelming when the dashboard is examined throughout the day. Only the following six measures are included:

- Call wait time
- Call duration
- Abandoned calls (that is, callers who got tired of waiting and hung up)
- Call volume
- Order volume
- Sales representative utilization (representatives online compared to the number available)

That's it—and that's plenty for a dashboard of this type.

Imagine that you're responsible for a team of around 25 telesales representatives and are using the following dashboard to stay aware of their activities throughout the day.

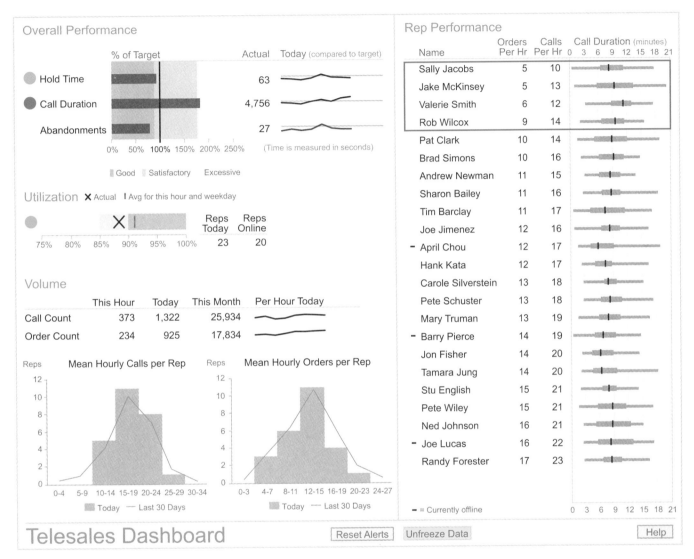

FIGURE 13.16. A sample telesales dashboard

The primary metrics that the manager must vigilantly monitor are the length of time customers are waiting to connect with a sales representative, the length of time sales representatives are spending on calls, and the number of customers who are getting discouraged and hanging up while waiting to get through. Because of their importance, these three metrics are located in the upper-left corner of the dashboard and are extremely easy to read.

When problems arise, such as the lengthy hold times and excessively lengthy calls shown in this example, the manager must quickly determine the cause before taking action. This is when she would switch her focus to the performance of the individual sales representatives, which are visible on the right side of the dashboard. Individuals are ranked by performance, with those performing poorly at the top and a red rectangle highlighting those who are performing outside the acceptable range.

Because this dashboard is for monitoring real-time operations, the data would probably change with updates every few seconds. This can be distracting when the viewer is trying to focus on a problem, however, so a "Freeze Data/Unfreeze Data" button has been provided to allow her to temporarily halt updates. When updates are frozen, the button shines yellow to remind her of this fact. If the display remains frozen for too long, the button begins to blink with a brighter yellow until clicked to once again allow updates. When alerts first appear (the red circles), they blink to attract attention and perhaps even emit an audio signal to alert the manager if she isn't watching the screen. To stop these signals, she would click the red alert. To remind her that she's blocked the alerts from providing urgent signals, the "Reset Alerts" button turns yellow and after a while begins to blink. Once it is clicked, all alerts can once again signal urgent conditions if necessary.

Marketing Analysis Dashboard

Now we'll look at a dashboard that supports a marketing analyst. Like all dashboards, it is used to monitor the information needed to do a job, but in this case that job happens to primarily involve analysis. Dashboards can effectively give analysts the information they need to watch over their domains and spot conditions that warrant investigation. Ideally, dashboards can also be direct launch pads to the additional data and tools necessary to perform comprehensive analyses.

This particular scenario involves an analyst whose work supports the company's website marketing efforts. He monitors customer behavior on the website to identify both problems that prevent customers from finding and purchasing what they want and opportunities to interest customers in additional products. To expose activities on the website that could lead to insight if studied and understood, the dashboard contains the following information:

- Number of visitors (daily, monthly, and yearly)
- Number of orders
- Number of registered visitors
- Number of times individual products were viewed on the site
- Occasions when products that were displayed on the same page were rarely purchased together
- Occasions when products that were not displayed on the same page were purchased together
- Referrals from other websites that have resulted in the most visits

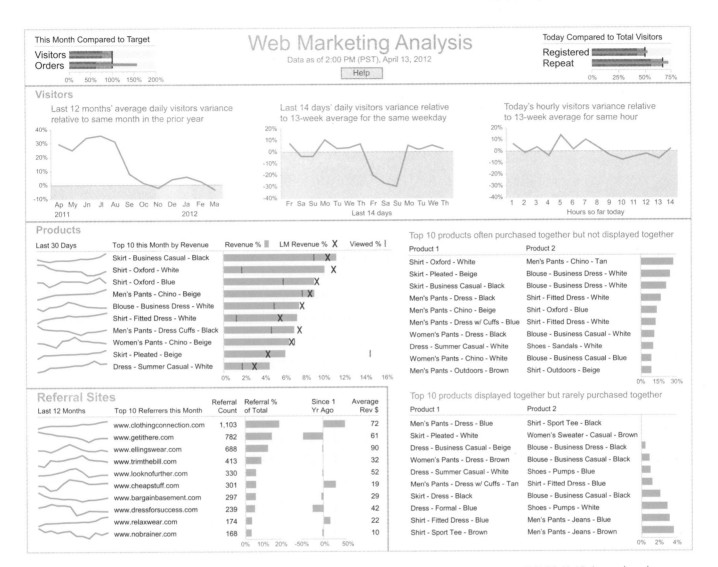

FIGURE 13.17. A sample web marketing analysis dashboard

The information that appears at the top of this dashboard gives an overview of the website's performance through time and lists missed opportunities and ineffective marketing efforts. Notice that the time-series information regarding visitors to the site is segmented into three sections, each featuring a different time interval. The intervals have been tailored to reveal greater detail for the recent past and decreasing detail for information from further back in time.

Much of the information on this dashboard has been selected and arranged to display ranking relationships. Focus on this type of relationship is common when a dashboard is used to feature exceptional conditions, both good and bad. Much of this ranked information is communicated in the form of text, with little graphical content. Given the purpose—to inform the analyst of potential areas of interest—text does the job nicely.

FIGURE 13.17. A sample web marketing analysis dashboard

Service Installation Dashboard

The final dashboard is similar to one that I created for a large telecommunications company to monitor the installation (connects) and de-installation (disconnects) of its services. Information is tracked at the level of major services (phone, internet, etc.) and major categories of installation or de-installation activity (initial installation, upgrade, move, etc.).

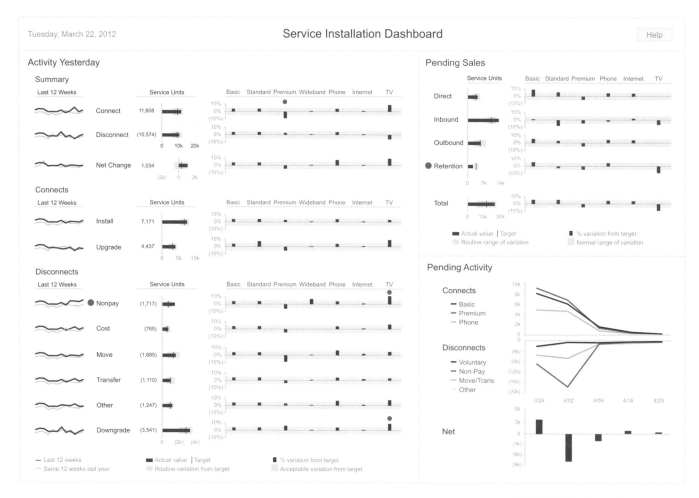

This dashboard was designed to make abnormal circumstances easy to spot. Notice that gray bands of background color are often used to mark normal vs. abnormal ranges or acceptable vs. unacceptable circumstances. Ordinarily, vertical bars as short as those that appear in this dashboard would not provide adequate precision or ease of comparison, but in this case the client wasn't interested in precision, but instead in seeing if a bar fell within or exceeded the normal range.

This dashboard was designed not only to monitor current activity but also to anticipate and plan for future activity as well. Monitoring displays are most effective when they help us peer into the future in ways that allow us to shape the best outcomes.

FIGURE 13.18. A sample service installation dashboard

Good Examples by Others

When I wrote the first edition of this book in 2006, I couldn't find any examples of well-designed dashboards, so I had no choice but to create a few from scratch to illustrate best practices. Now, seven years later, even though poor dashboard design is still prevalent, a growing number of people are demonstrating good design skills. I'd like to showcase three dashboards that were designed by people who are helping organizations discover the true potential of these monitoring displays.

The first is a dashboard for monitoring personal finances, created by Gary Crawford using *XL Cubed for Excel*. This was created for a competition, using information that was provided.

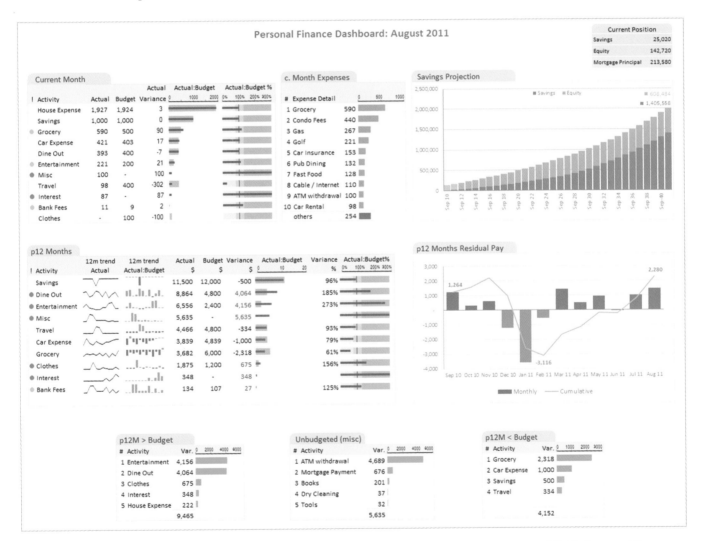

This dashboard displays eight separate sections of information about personal finances. A great deal of information is shown but always in ways that are easy to see and understand at a glance.

FIGURE 13.19. A personal finance dashboard, created by Gary Crawford of XL Cubed

Gary describes his design as follows:

This dashboard provides an overview of Sheila's expenditures and how well she is sticking to budget, along with a high-level forecast of her savings. The colour red is consistently used to signify a problem.

The "Current Position" section in the upper right corner provides a quick general overview.

The "Current Month" section displays recent expenses from greatest to least. The "!" column displays a solid red warning for expenses that are 20% or more over budget and a mid-red warning if over budget by less than 20%. We can see very quickly that "Misc" is an unbudgeted expense item and also that Sheila also has some unanticipated interest payments, possibly because of poor management in previous months. The "Annual:Budget" comparison provides a good sense of the relative impact of individual activities on expenditures overall. This section is supplemented by the "Month Expenses" section, which lists the top ten detail-level expenses for the current month.

The "Savings Projection" section forecasts savings over a 30-year period in relation to Sheila's retirement goals. Completed years are in grey and future years are in blue. We can see that Sheila should exceed her $2,000,000 retirement savings target in 2041, based on the following assumptions:

- *Her house's value rises annually by 1.8%*
- *When her mortgage completes, she will start investing the mortgage amount into savings*
- *She will increase her bi-monthly savings contribution by $25 every 3 years, based on projected increased earnings*

By increasing savings earlier or paying off the mortgage more quickly, Sheila could reach her goal sooner.

The "P12 Months" section displays expenditures during the previous 12 months, from high to low. We can immediately spot serious problems with "Dine Out" and "Entertainment" expenses, which are significantly over target for the year and "in the red" for the vast majority of months. We can also see that "Misc" is unbudgeted, but over the year is the fifth largest activity.

The "P12 Months Residual Pay" section displays the relationship between incomings (pay) and outgoings (expenditures). The red bars going up represent overspending and the blue bars going down represent funds remaining. The line represents the cumulative position. Overages should be investigated for inappropriate spend patterns in those specific months.

The three sections at the bottom display the following expenditure information for the last 12 months: the five with the greatest budget overages, unbudgeted items, and those that Sheila is managing best in relation to her budget.

The next dashboard was created by Katherine Rowell of *Katherine S. Rowell & Associates*, a consultancy that specializes in the data visualization needs of healthcare organizations. As a longtime expert in healthcare information, Katherine designed this example with a keen awareness of the information that a hospital's chief administrator might need to monitor.

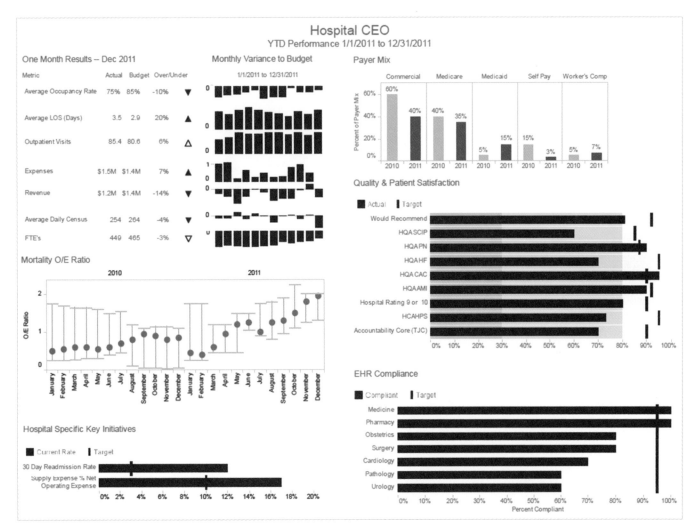

Here's Katherine's description of her design:

FIGURE 13.20. A hospital CEO dashboard, created by Katherine Rowell of Katherine S. Rowell & Associates using Tableau

This dashboard was designed to address the current environment in which a hospital CEO has to navigate—an environment that is shaped by Value Based Purchasing (VBP) and public reporting, where financial, clinical, information technology and patient satisfaction results are all inextricably linked. The concept of VBP and the underlying driver of the information that hospital CEO's require to be successful, is that healthcare buyers (payers, patients) should hold healthcare providers (hospital, doctors, etc.) accountable for both the cost and quality of care they deliver.

In the "One Month Results" section of the dashboard are industry-standard metrics about the hospital's occupancy rate and average daily census

along with high-level financial results—revenue and expenses—all compared to budget. Up and down icons are used to alert the CEO to specific areas that may require further inquiry, along with graphs that feature direct variances of actual performance compared to the budget for the past 12 months.

The "Payer Mix" section allows the CEO to easily monitor any changes to payer mix from the previous to the current year. This information, which helps to inform many of the financial management decisions made by a hospital, makes it easy to see any significant changes.

The "Quality and Patient Satisfaction" section displays results for mandated performance measures (the horizontal black bars) compared to targets (the vertical black lines). This information is important not only as a measure of the hospital's quality of care, but also because a hospital must achieve specific targets to receive full reimbursement from third-party payers. Displaying the information in this manner allows a CEO to understand how well the staff is performing and where they may need to focus their improvement efforts.

All of this information along with hospital mortality rates is now being reported on public websites in an effort to help consumers make informed decisions about where to receive their care. Hospital CEOs cannot afford any surprises about their hospital's performance. Displaying risk-adjusted mortality rates with accompanying confidence intervals over time in the "Mortality O/E Ratio" section allows a CEO to discuss these measures with clinicians in a meaningful way.

Hospital CEO's must also monitor electronic health record (EHR) compliance, not only because they hold the promise of improved patient care but because there are significant financial incentives from the federal government to hospitals that demonstrate their Meaningful Use (MU). In the "EHR Compliance" section, by displaying compliance at the subspecialty level compared to a target rate, the dashboard makes it possible for a CEO to easily and quickly see who is or isn't using the EHR. This makes it clear where attention and resources should be focused.

The next and final dashboard was created by Jorge Camoes of *ExcelCharts.com*. In addition to a great deal of data visualization experience, Jorge is one of the world's great experts in Excel; he's one of those guys who can make Excel do things that were never intended or imagined and certainly never directly supported by its creators. This is not a true performance monitoring dashboard—one that someone would use to track what's going regularly—but is a variation that is designed for the general public to access and view on the web. As such, it is appropriately simple.

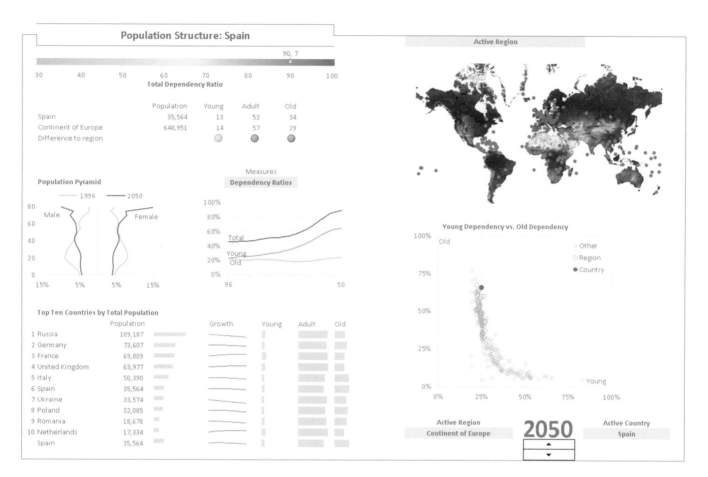

Jorge created this primarily to demonstrate dashboard development techniques that can be used in Excel. Even though Excel was not created for the development of dashboards and lacks some of the functionality that is common in other products, we can, if we know a few tricks, use it to create dashboards that exhibit exceptional visual design.

Our journey is almost complete. All that remains is Chapter 14, which describes steps in the dashboard design process *From Imagining to Unveiling*.

FIGURE 13.21. A world population dashboard, created by Jorge Camoes of ExcelCharts.com

For instruction in the use of Excel for dashboard development, in addition to Jorge Camoes' website www.ExcelCharts.com, you can also find good advice at www.ExcelUser.com and in the book *Excel Dashboards and Reports* by Michael Alexander and John Walkenbach.

The process of designing a dashboard—the phase that occurs once the requirements have been understood but before the actual development of the dashboard begins—is often overlooked or underappreciated. Design is usually done in stages. In this chapter I'll suggest a few practices that we should keep in mind to produce a design that works.

Begin by Sketching

We start by reviewing the client's requirements. With a fresh understanding of the objectives, the relationships among various items of information, the order in which information should be scanned, and the relative importance of various sections of information, we can begin to arrange the information on paper. Must we do it on paper? No, but at this point we want to play with ideas in a manner that is fluid and easy to revise. At this stage, I find it easiest to sketch my ideas, allowing them to take shape and change quickly. I use pencil and paper, but if you can sketch using an electronic medium as freely as you could on paper, go for it.

The goal at this point is to roughly define the sections of information and how they should be arranged on the screen. In other words, we're focusing on the layout. Begin by defining the dimensions of the space. Ideally, everyone who will use the dashboard will do so on a screen with a particular aspect ratio (for example, 16:9, 16:10, 4:3, etc.) and resolution. Draw boundaries on the paper or screen to define those dimensions.

For each section of information, determine the display media that should be used. Perhaps one section will consists of a series of sparklines and bullet graphs, accompanied by labels and text values for each, arranged in a tabular fashion with a row for each measure and a column for each component (for example, sparkline, label, bullet graph, and value arranged in columns from left to right). Perhaps another section should be displayed as a horizontal bar graph with the values ranked from high to low.

If the situation involves many measures that are all associated with a particular set of categorical items, such as the student performance dashboard in the last chapter that consisted primarily of measures associated with individual students, we might want to reserve much of the space for a tabular arrangement of information with a separate column for each measure. If some information is key—always most important to the viewer—or is the logical starting point for the dashboard user, we'll probably want to locate this information in the upper-left corner. If a title and other standard elements such as the date or a

Help button should appear at the top, we reserve a small band for those. If multiple sections of data will consist of line graphs that all span the same period of time (for example, the past 12 months), we might want to arrange them one above the other so that time is aligned, and patterns of change can be easily compared among them. Based on a rough sense of the space that will be needed for various sections of information and their relationships to one another, we can sketch borders for each with an area reserved for every item. Then, we roughly sketch what each section will look like with the appropriate display media (bullet graphs, line graphs, bar graphs, etc.).

Once we have a tentative layout, we put it to the test. We imagine that we are the person who will use the dashboard, and we run through typical scanning scenarios using the layout and revising it as needed to better support meaningful and efficient information gathering.

Refine the Design into a Wireframe

Think of a wireframe as a neater, better looking, and more detailed mock-up of the design. We could do this by hand, but at this point I usually use drawing software such as *Adobe Illustrator*. The wireframe is a document that we can give to the developer to illustrate the design. It doesn't need to be based on real data, but we should definitely think through a variety of real-data scenarios to anticipate their effects on the design, which might require revisions.

In the orginal sketches, we don't want to take the time to get the details right, but here in the wireframe we do. For example, sparklines should show the actual number of values that they will include. Headings, labels, and colors should be exact. The thicknesses of lines should be exact. Don't leave any of these choices up to the developer. As the designers, we determine what the dashboard should look like and do; it is up to the developer to figure out how to make this happen using a given software product.

Along with the wireframe, write a document to explain everything that the developer must know to convert the design into a working dashboard. Be clear that the details matter and that anything that cannot be done to specification should be discussed. If compromises must be made because of software limitations, it will be up to us as the designers to suggest the most effective alternatives possible.

Beware of Focus Groups

We humans engage in two fundamental modes of thinking, sometimes called *System 1* and *System 2* thinking. No one explains this better than Daniel Kahneman, who won a Nobel Prize in 2002 for his work in the psychology of decision making. "System 1 is fast, intuitive, and emotional; System 2 is slower, more deliberative, and more logical."

So what do these two types of thinking have to do with focus groups? Imagine a typical focus group that is being conducted to get people's reactions

Daniel Kahneman (2012). *Thinking, Fast and Slow*. Farrar, Straus and Giroux, inside the dust cover.

to a new television pilot. As people watch the show, they typically engage in System 1 thinking—immediate and emotional reaction from the gut. Focus groups conducted in this way are often appropriate because television viewing is typically processed by our brains in this manner. We usually watch for enjoyment. We're relaxed and aren't thinking deeply or deliberately. Some of the best new television shows have been scored poorly by focus groups, however, because another characteristic of System 1 thinking is a preference for the familiar. For instance, focus groups responded negatively to *Seinfeld*, which went on to become one of the most successful shows of all time.

Unlike focus groups watching new television shows, people facing information that they must understand usually engage in System 2 thinking. This means that when we attempt to get people's reactions to a dashboard's design, we want them to become engaged with it by wearing their System 2 thinking caps. The last thing that we should do is introduce our proposed dashboard design to those who will use it by projecting our wireframe on the screen and asking, "What do you think? Do you like it?" Because their expectations have probably been shaped by horribly ineffective but cute and flashy dashboards, their initial reaction to a well-designed dashboard might not be immediate enthusiasm.

When we present a design, it's a good idea to begin by reviewing the requirements, so they are fresh in everyone's minds. We mention that we thought long and hard about the requirements and took the time to study the best practices of dashboard design based on the science of human perception and cognition. Before revealing our design, we explain that what we've prepared will probably look a lot different from most of the dashboards that they've seen before because most of those are designed to look attractive at first glance but not to perform well during actual use. Finally, we prepare them for what happens next by saying that when we show the design, we'll ask them a series of questions to help them imagine how it will work in actual use. Then, we show them the wireframe.

Without allowing too much time to pass, we ask the first question to guide the group's attention. I often begin with a question such as "Are the groupings of information obvious?" or "Are your key metrics being featured adequately?" What I am trying to do is force them to assess the dashboard's merits using System 2 thinking, to evaluate the design in light of actual use. They must search for meaning, which involves deliberative, conscious thinking. They shouldn't react from their guts, which are attracted to pretty colors, movement, familiar objects such as fuel gauges, and flashy lighting effects. Another great question early on is "Can you easily spot the items that need attention?" In time we might want to ask, "Is enough information being displayed about the items that need attention to decide whether you must respond by taking action?"

It's important to lead clients through several real-world scenarios. Show examples of the dashboard populated with information that represents a real situation that they might face. Walk them through the process that they might follow when using the dashboard to spot the situation, gather the information that's necessary to understand it, and then respond. These engaging simulations will help these future users of the dashboard see for themselves how the dashboard could help them do their jobs.

If we've created a good design and introduce it in this manner, anyone who cares about using it to do real work more effectively will appreciate its merits.

Test the Design for Usability

Our first opportunity for usability testing occurs when we initially introduce our designs. While running through an actual-use scenario, we should expect that someone will spot something that doesn't work ideally or perhaps at all. We will never get everything right on the first try, no matter how skilled we are. It's important that we not respond defensively. Discovering problems at this point is normal and useful. We respond with enthusiasm, grateful that we're getting the kind of feedback that will help us produce an effective solution.

Before passing the design specifications on to the developer, meet with those who will use the dashboard to test the design by running through scenarios, identifying problems, revising the design, and then running through the scenarios again until the design seems right. Once the real working dashboard is developed, more usability testing will be needed, but much less than there would be if we don't test our designs in advance. Most of the expensive, time-consuming post-development corrections can be avoided by doing preliminary usability testing using the wireframe populated with different real-world examples.

Prove the Concept on the Cheap

If this is your first dashboard project, you might not have already purchased a dashboard product to use for developing it. That's fine. In fact, it's a whole lot better than purchasing an expensive tool and discovering that it doesn't work. Consider starting out by using a tool that you already have. What might that be? Almost every organization uses Microsoft Excel. But Excel, you might argue, is not a dashboard product. This is true. Excel probably wasn't designed to do many of the things that you already use it for, but that hasn't stopped you, has it? Even though Excel is not an ideal platform for dashboards—for instance, it isn't set up to pull data from external sources and transform it as needed in an automated manner—it's a viable place to start, especially if funds are tight, and you need some experience before spending a lot of money on a fully functional dashboard product. If you know a few tricks, you can actually use Excel produce a well-designed dashboard (such as the one featured in the previous chapter).

Excel gurus such as Michael Alexander and Charley Kyd have both written good books that reveal useful tricks for developing excellent dashboards in Excel.

Find a Tool that Makes Good Design Easy

I am still waiting for a great dashboard development product to become available. Many of the products that exist today can be used to build effective dashboards, but none make it easy. Most force us to wade through reams of nonsense to get to the few features that actually work.

Useful Display Media

When I wrote the original edition of this book in 2006, some of the display media that I promoted as useful—sparklines and bullet graphs in particular—were not available in any products. This has changed since then. Now most dashboard products support these features. The problem, however, is that most also support huge galleries of silly charts that are never useful. I recommend avoiding any software vendor that tries to win our business with a claim such as "We have a library of over 100 chart types, with many versions of each." Imagine trying to find what you want in the chart gallery below, which includes only the charts related to sales, which is one of 14 categories.

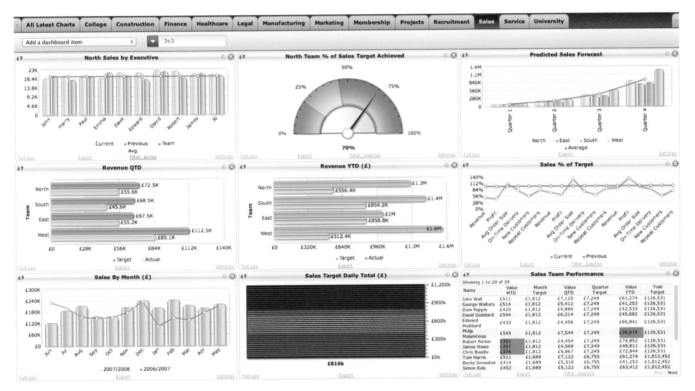

When developing dashboards, we don't want to be faced with an endless list of choices. We don't need more choices, we need a few good choices. When shopping for a dashboard development product, we want to make sure that it supports the few display media that are especially useful on dashboards.

FIGURE 14.1. One category's worth of a particular product's charts from a gallery that includes 14 categories

Well-Designed Display Media

Another problem closely related to the excess of useless charts in most products is that the charts that are provided are poorly designed. Rather than setting the defaults of a chart's appearance and behavior to make those elements effective as vehicles of information, most vendors have spent their time making them as flashy as possible. Consider the familiar bar graph. It is elegant in its simplicity and superbly effective for comparing discrete values. This effectiveness can be easily undermined, however, by adding silly effects, such as those in the examples below:

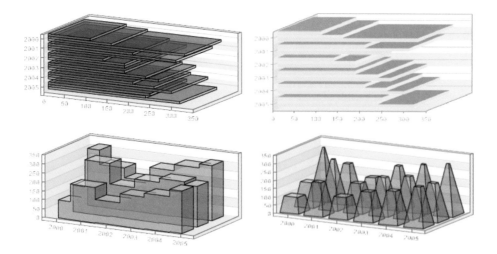

FIGURE 14.2. Unreadable bar graphs from GreenPoint, Inc.

I recommend that we ignore product vendors that care so little about their customers that they're willing to waste their money and time with nonsense like this. There is no room on a dashboard for content that isn't essential to the monitoring task. Software that makes it difficult to design a display that is clean—elegantly simple—will lead us wrong. Any of the following problems will get in our way:

- Charts with borders or sections reserved for titles that can't be turned off when not needed
- Charts with controls (expand, print, drill, etc.) that can't be easily eliminated
- Charts with grid lines that can't be turned off
- Panels or borders that divide the screen into display regions that can't be turned off
- Sections of the screen reserved for specific items (title, controls, etc.) that can't be eliminated

The list goes on, but I hope the general idea is clear.

Layout Flexibility

Another feature that is essential for building effective dashboards is layout flexibility. Most dashboard products lock the designer into a rigid layout structure that prevents flexible placement and sizing of items (charts, text, icons, etc.). Flexible layout is necessary to produce a dense information display that a viewer can easily and rapidly monitor. One of the greatest challenges of dashboard design is displaying a large amount of information in a small amount of space without creating a cluttered mess. To be effective, dashboard content must be organized in a way that reflects the nature of the information and supports efficient and meaningful monitoring. Information cannot be placed just anywhere on the dashboard, nor can sections of the display be sized simply to fit the available space. Items that relate to one another should usually be positioned close to one another. Important items should often appear larger, thus more visually prominent, than less important items. Items that ought to be scanned in a particular order ought to be arranged in a manner that supports that sequence of visual attention. In other words, designing an effective dashboard demands a great deal of flexibility in where items are placed and how they are sized.

Unfortunately, I've found that most dashboard products restrict layout to a grid arrangement. Some are extremely restrictive, requiring a symmetrical arrangement of panels, such as the four-panel design below.

FIGURE 14.3. A symmetrical grid of four panels into which charts must be placed.

Even when grids support more than four panels, they often do not allow us the flexibility to avoid design compromises that undermine the dashboard's effectiveness.

Many dashboard vendors promote a self-service approach to dashboard design, advertising the ease with which anyone can throw together a dashboard. Using a rigid grid system of layout does make it easier for people who lack design skills to place a few charts on the screen. This approach might be appropriate for a portal through which users can access information and tasks, but a dashboard, which is used to monitor what's going on, requires greater design expertise to work effectively. I suspect the reason that most dashboard products use a rigid grid layout has less to do with the self-service idea and more to do with the fact that it is easier to provide grid layout functionality than the flexible layout functionality that is actually needed.

A Final Word

To design dashboards that really work, we must focus on the fundamental goal: communication. More than anything else, we must care that those who use our dashboards can look at them and understand them, easily, clearly, and quickly. Dashboards designed for any other purpose, no matter how impressive or entertaining they are, will become tiresome in a few days and will be discarded in a few weeks. Few things are more discouraging than having our hard work tossed aside as useless.

When I design something that makes people's lives better, helps them work smarter, or gives them what they need to succeed in something that's important to them, I am reminded that one of the great cornerstones of a life worth living is the joy of doing good work. This doesn't just happen; it is the result of effort that we invest because we care. Our dashboards might not change the world in any big way, but anything we do well will change us to some degree for the better. Even if the goals of the organization that we're supporting through a well-designed dashboard don't ultimately matter to us or even seem intrinsically worthy of great effort, *we're* worth the effort, and that's enough. In fact, that's plenty.

INDEX

About the Author . . .

STEPHEN FEW has been working for 30 years as a teacher, consultant, and innovator in the fields of business intelligence and information design. Since 2003, when he founded the consultancy Perceptual Edge, he has focused exclusively on data visualization. He teaches, speaks, and consults internationally with organizations of all types. More than anyone else working in data visualization today, Stephen is respected and sought the world over for his ability to make data visualization accessible in simple and practical ways to anyone who wants to effectively understand and communicate the important stories that reside in quantitative information.

In addition to this book, Stephen has written two other popular books: *Show Me the Numbers: Designing Tables and Graphs to Enlighten*, Second Edition (2012) and *Now You See It: Simple Visualization Techniques for Quantitative Analysis* (2009). He also writes the quarterly *Visual Business Intelligence Newsletter* and teaches his *Visual Business Intelligence Workshop* publicly in several countries each year.

When he isn't working, he can usually be found—in or around his home in Berkeley, California—lost in a good book, savoring a fine wine, hiking in the hills, or instigating an animated discussion about the meaning of life with good friends.

For current information about Stephen and his work, go to www.PerceptualEdge.com.